Literary Landscapes of Time

Latin American Literatures in the World

Literaturas Latinoamericanas en el Mundo

Edited by / Editado por
Gesine Müller

Editorial Board

Ana Gallego (Granada)
Gustavo Guerrero (Paris)
Héctor Hoyos (Stanford)
Ignacio Sánchez Prado (St. Louis)
Mariano Siskind (Harvard)
Patricia Trujillo (Bogotá)

Volume 15 / Volumen 15

Literary Landscapes of Time

—

Multiple Temporalities and Spaces in Latin American and Caribbean Literatures

Edited by
Jobst Welge and Juliane Tauchnitz

DE GRUYTER

ISBN 978-3-11-153080-2
e-ISBN (PDF) 978-3-11-076227-3
e-ISBN (EPUB) 978-3-11-076229-7
ISSN 2513-0757

Library of Congress Control Number: 2022941842

Bibliographic information published by the Deutsche Nationalbibliothek
The Deutsche Nationalbibliothek lists this publication in the Deutsche Nationalbibliografie;
detailed bibliographic data are available on the internet at http://dnb.dnb.de.

© 2024 Walter de Gruyter GmbH, Berlin/Boston Typesetting: Integra Software Services Pvt.

This volume is text- and page-identical with the hardback published in 2023.

www.degruyter.com

Contents

"Children, Butterflies, and Latin American Literary Landscapes."
Introductional Essay by María del Pilar Blanco —— VII

Jobst Welge and Juliane Tauchnitz
Introduction —— 1

I Locations and Spatiotemporal Constellations: Lives, Literary Fields

Gesine Müller
Spatial Dynamics and Colonial Positioning in Nineteenth-Century Spanish- and French-Language Caribbean Literatures —— 19

Sarah Burnautzki
Dissolution of Time and Space in *Memórias postumas de Brás Cubas* —— 35

Anne Brüske
Recreating the World of the Cuban Revolution: Geopolitical Imagination and Entangled Spaces in the Graphic Memoir *Adiós mi Habana* (2017) —— 49

II Literary Landscapes and Temporalities: Regions and World(s)

Miriam Lay Brander
Timescapes of the Desert: Multiple Temporalities in Guimarães Rosa's *Grande Sertão* —— 79

Jobst Welge
Tropical Temporalities: Literary Landscape and Multiple Times in Alejo Carpentier's *Los Pasos Perdidos* —— 99

Jörg Dünne
The Whims of the Climate: Landscapes of Deep Time in Juan José Saer's *Las Nubes* —— 115

III Specters, Ruins, Catastrophes

Carlos Fonseca
The Landscape in Ruins —— 131

Anna Jörngården
Presencing Absence: Ruin as Counter-Monument in Caribbean Literature —— 143

Juliane Tauchnitz
Prisons, Ruins, Bodies, and the Extension of Space and Time in Patrick Chamoiseau's *Un dimanche au cachot* **—— 163**

Christina Kullberg
Whirlwinds of Sounds: Rethinking Hurricane Temporalities through Contemporary Poetry from the Lesser Antilles —— 173

Sara Brandellero
Night-time Mobilities in Contemporary Brazilian Cinema: Spectralities in the 24-hour City and the Case of *Burning Night* **(2019) —— 189**

María del Pilar Blanco
"Children, Butterflies, and Latin American Literary Landscapes." Introductional Essay

The figure of the child, much like the figure of the ghost or spectre, holds a peculiar place across literary landscapes from the nineteenth century to the present. The Latin American literary sphere is no exception. Lurking and moving through the spaces and edges of adult existence, the child is at once the figure that is often seen but not heard and the cipher on which whole societies pin their hopes of progress. In this sense, we could say that children represent two forms of spectrality, one literal and another figurative: like the ghosts of lore, they haunt and witness the events of adult life, which, in turn, is repeatedly read as the focal point of a story. On a second level, and especially since the nineteenth century, the child becomes a repository of anxieties about the future and an embodiment for that complex, strained, and elusive term "progress." Put differently, the nineteenth-century Western world consumed and relished the idea of progress as possible and proximate. Within this grand narrative, which moves across time into the present day, the child appears as the ever-changing figure onto whom all dreams of genealogical and educational success, as well as fears of failure, are pinned. Their expected, future health and virtuous development expected, but not givens, children are the spectres of other temporalities that the adult imagination wishes to, but cannot, divine. What does it mean to read children and spectres together, or children as spectres, as we navigate the literary landscapes of the Americas?

In *La Edad de Oro* (1889), his short-lived magazine for children, José Martí reflects the nineteenth-century mentality I describe above when he writes:

> La juventud es la edad del crecimiento y del desarrollo, de la actividad y la viveza, de la imaginación y el ímpetu. . . Cada ser humano lleva en sí un hombre ideal, lo mismo que cada trozo de mármol contiene en bruto una estatua tan bella como la que el griego Praxiteles hizo del dios Apolo. La educación empieza con la vida, y no acaba sino con la muerte. El cuerpo es siempre el mismo, y decae con la edad; la mente cambia sin cesar, y se enriquece y perfecciona con los años. Pero las cualidades esenciales del carácter, lo original y enérgico de cada hombre, se deja ver desde la infancia en un acto, en una idea, en una mirada.[1]
>
> [Youth is the time of growth and development, of activity and vivacity, of imagination and vigour. . . Each human being holds within him an ideal man, just as each block of marble contains within it a statue as beautiful as the one that the Greek sculptor Praxiteles made

---

[1] José Martí, "Músicos, poetas y pintores," *La Edad de Oro* 1.2 (August 1889), 57–64; 57.

https://doi.org/10.1515/9783110762273-203

of Apollo. Education starts with life, and concludes at the time of death. The body is always the same and decays with age; the mind is always changing, enriching and perfecting itself across time. But the essential qualities of a person's character, that which is original and energetic in each man is perceptible from childhood in an act, an idea, a look.]

Martí emphasizes, in masculine overtones, the metaphoric potential of children: they are moulds, or vessels for the "hombre[s] ideal[es]" of a future time. At the same time, however, he completes (and complicates) this thought with a reflection about the way in which a child may reveal, in a flash or *Augenblick*, a vision of the future. We could think of the "acto," "idea," and "mirada" that in Martí foretells the future in conversation with the Benjaminian notion of the "true picture of the past" that "can be seized only as an image which flashes up at the instant when it can be recognized and is never seen again."[2] The child's future relevance, their messianism is, in Martí's figuration, a momentarily uncoded secret that is uncannily hidden within the folds of their otherwise unknown existence, if we recall Rousseau's reflection in *Émile* on the matter of childhood.[3]

Across Latin American nineteenth- and early twentieth-century literary landscapes, the child is an overflowing symbol of desires for future advancement and, conversely, a repository for anxieties of genealogical and genetic breakdown. We may consider, for instance, the character of young Andrea in Eugenio Cambaceres's *Sin rumbo* (1885), the daughter whose innocence and humanity manages to purify the nihilistic existence of a father (Andrés), and who in the narrative symbolizes a momentary reconciliation of the division between country and city, the barbaric and the civilized. Largely undeveloped as a character in herself, the child as *deus ex machina* remains a powerful motif in this and other narratives of the nineteenth century. In the case of Cambaceres's novel, the male protagonist's salvation comes, again, in a flash before darkness and death settle permanently in the narrative until it reaches its gruesome end (Andrés eviscerates himself). Throughout *Sin rumbo*, readers suspect that Andrea's survival is somehow imperilled by her father's wayward past. A more extreme story of genetic paranoia, or an "aterradora descendencia," is Horacio Quiroga's "La gallina degollada" from *Cuentos de amor de locura y de muerte* (1917), in which the first four children in the Mazzini household are all born healthy until the same illness befalls them, leaving them incapacitated and,

---

[2] Walter Benjamin, "Theses on the Philosophy of History," *Illuminations*, trans. Harry Zohn (New York: Schocken Books, 1968), 253–64; 255.
[3] It is worth remembering Martí's indebtedness to Rousseau's theorization of the natural man in the Cuban's own formulation of the "hombre natural" in "Nuestra América" (1891), an essay that was in the works while the Cuban writer edited and wrote *La Edad de Oro*.

following the degenerationist theories in vogue at the time, exemplary of an incurable atavism.[4] Read together as signs of thwarted progress, the children in these narratives survive in our imagination as static, though excessive vessels for a period's collective disquiet around ideas of science, nation, and modernity.

If for Cambaceres, the child is a powerful, though quiet, symbol of potential national redemption, when we look at the work of another Argentine writer, this time Silvina Ocampo, we recognize a dramatic change of tack in the representation of children. In Ocampo's dazzlingly disturbing stories, children are willing holders of secrets; they are inscrutable and often reflect what Sarah Thomas, writing about Spanish film during the transition period, calls the "mutually adversarial relationship" between children and adults.[5] In Ocampo's "Los funámbulos" from *Viaje olvidado* (1937), for instance, two young brothers, Cipriano and Valerio, thrive on the imaginary world of circus spectacles they have concocted for themselves, despite and in spite of their deaf mother Clodomira, a domestic worker in an urban home. We are told that their lives transpired in the darkness of "cold corridors" ("Vivían en la obscuridad de corredores fríos,") through which the mother's calls to her children flow with the wind currents.[6] These calls, however, are not reciprocated with a response:

> La planchadora Clodomira rociaba la ropa blanca con su mano en flor de regadera y de vez en cuando se asomaba sobre el patio para ver jugar a los muchachos que ostentaban posturas extraordinarias en los marcos de las ventanas. Nunca sabía de qué estaban hablando y cuando interrogaba los labios una inmovilidad de cera se implantaba en las bocas movibles de sus hijos. (22)

> [Clodomira, the ironing woman, sprayed the white clothing, her hand like a watering can, and from time to time she would look over at the patio to see the boys playing and assuming extraordinary poses on the window frames. She never knew what they were talking about, and when she tried to read their lips a wax-like stiffness covered her children's moving mouths.]

Moving acrobatically along the edges of domestic spaces, Ocampo's children are reminiscent of Miles and Flora in Henry James's *The Turn of the Screw* (1898) and, back to twentiethcentury urban Argentina, the murderous young siblings in Leopoldo Torre Nilsson's film *La caída* (1959), based on the novel by

---

[4] Horacio Quiroga, "La gallina degollada," *Cuentos de amor de locura y de muerte* (Buenos Aires: Losada, 1954), 46–54; 49.
[5] Sarah Thomas, *Inhabiting the In-Between: Childhood and Cinema in Spain's Long Transition* (Toronto: University of Toronto Press, 2019), 7.
[6] Silvina Ocampo, "Los funámbulos," *Cuentos completos I* (Buenos Aires: Emecé, 1999), 21–22; 22. These are my own translations.

Beatriz Guido, who co-wrote the screenplay with Torre Nilsson. These young figures warn us of universes, conversations, and schemes that are out of bounds for older intruders. In turn, the adult looks on, baffled, finding intransigence where they imagined they could find innocence, resistance where they figured they would be able to enforce control. Here again, children assume roles akin to those of spectres in a narrative, as they embody an unspoken present, not to mention of an undisclosed future. The secrecy of Ocampo's *funámbulos* also lends these characters an unsettling air of being outside of normative time, their reticence being somehow too knowing, and certainly well beyond their years.

Outlining this disjointed temporality, the children-as-future trope aligns with another reading of the ghostly, this time Abraham and Torok's theorization in *L'Écorce et le noyau* (1978) of the phantom as a "liar" whose "effects," as Colin Davis explains, "are designed to mislead the haunted subject and to ensure that its secret remains shrouded in mystery."[7] The children across the different narratives mentioned here impede any recurrence to coaxing, let alone antidotes of tenderness, care, and gentle indoctrination. This affective dimension succeeds in heightening readers' frustrations about figures we imagined to be under narrative, generational and sociocultural control. In this sense, they thwart the stories that we have repeatedly told ourselves about progress, development, and the value of sentimental educations. Existing outside of the normative times of discipline, they are haunting aporias that mark the otherwise recognizable, private spaces within urban landscapes.

While the children in Ocampo's and Guido's/Torre Nilsson's narratives inhabit distinct domestic spheres, skirting thus any form of formalized education, the contemporary writer Samanta Schweblin transports the inscrutable silence and mystery of children to the institutionalized space of the school. In the micro-story "Mariposas," published in *Pájaros en la boca* (2009), two parents, Gorriti and Calderón, converse about their children (their small feet, the shedding of baby teeth) outside a school while they "esperan ansiosos la salidad de sus hijos" (waiting anxiously for their children to be let out).[8] The reader begins to be put on alert when we're told that "En cualquier momento se abren las puertas y los chicos salen disparados, riendo a gritos en un tumulto de colores, a veces manchados de témpera, o de chocolate. Pero por alguna razón, el timbre se retrasa" (27) [The doors will open any second now and the children will

---

[7] Colin Davis, "Hauntology, Spectres and Phantoms," *French Studies* 59, 3 (2005), 373–79; 374.

[8] Samanta Schweblin, "Mariposas," *Pájaros en la boca y otros cuentos* (New York: Literatura Random House, 2008), 27–28; 27. English version from Schweblin, "Butterflies," *Mouthful of Birds*, trans. Megan McDowell (London: OneWorld, 2019), 25–27; 25.

burst out, laughing and shouting in a tumult of colors, some spotted with paint or chocolate. But for some reason the bell is delayed (26)]. The next part of the story focuses on a butterfly that lands on chatty Calderón's arm, which he proceeds to trap and, in so doing, fatally harms it. As he steps on the moribund butterfly,

> . . . advierte que algo extraño sucede. Mira hacia las puertas y entonces, como si un viento repentino hubiese violado las cerraduras, las puertas se abren, y cientos de mariposas de todos los colores y tamaños se abalanzan sobre los padres que esperan. (28)

> [. . . he realizes something strange is happening. He looks towards the doors and then, as if a sudden wind had breached the locks, the doors open and hundreds of butterflies of every color and size rush out toward the waiting parents.] (27)

This image of butterflies bursting out of school doors is at once beautiful as it is disturbing, for we have been forewarned that "algo raro," out of the ordinary, is indeed happening. While we witness Calderón's anxiety – "[p]iensa si irán a atacarlo, tal vez piensa que va a morir" (28) [He thinks they might attack him; maybe he thinks he's going to die (27) – the other parents are slower to panic as the butterflies stream outside of the school until the last one comes out.

To my mind, Schweblin's micro-story would remain in the realms of fantastical, metaphoric beauty – a tale of children transmogrified into butterflies – if it weren't for the events recounted in the final lines. It is here (at the very end of the narrative, to be exact) that we encounter Calderón's realization that the butterfly he crushed in his fingers could be his own child. For me, the more disturbing lines are those that precede this inevitable realization:

> Calderón se queda mirando las puertas abiertas, y tras los vidrios del hall central, las salas silenciosas. Algunos padres todavía se amontonan frente a las puertas y gritan los nombres de sus hijos. Entonces las mariposas, todas ellas en pocos segundos, se alejan volando en distintas direcciones. Los padres intentan atraparlas. (28)

> [Calderón stands looking at the open doors and through the windows of the main hall, at the silent classrooms. Some parents are still crowding in front of the doors and shouting the names of their children. Then the butterflies, all of them in just a few seconds, fly off in different directions. The parents try to catch them.] (27)[9]

---

9 Schweblin's translator, Megan McDowell, opted to separate the narrative in "Butterflies" using paragraphs and caesuras, whereas Schweblin's story in Spanish is one uninterrupted paragraph. The paragraph cited here stands alone in the English version.

If the runaway butterflies signal the colonization of the story by the fantastic genre, the scene of parents crowding around the doors of a school waiting for children that will never emerge places readers within a scene of horror that is both familiar and universal: the move of expected arrival turned into emptiness, the all-too-sudden shift from presence to absence. In other words, a tale of metamorphosis sits uncomfortably, and unbearably, with one about disappearance. This shift is dramatized powerfully by Schweblin's depiction of the empty and silent school building that, in the end, is inhabited only by the parents' shouting of their children's names.

The eerily silent hall and corridors of the school in "Mariposas" bears an uncanny resemblance to the cold corridors in Ocampo's story. In this sense, both narratives share interesting sonic and spatial configurations that, also similarly, signal breakdowns in reciprocal communication and the haunting silences that absence leaves in its wake. The difference between the two stories lies in the way that Ocampo particularizes the contained, and ultimately tragic silence that separates Clodomira from Cipriano and Valerio, while Schweblin transforms that silence into a mass event. The institutional setting of Schweblin's story forces us to think afresh about spaces of education and their supposed safety, and of the indoctrinations and often-irreversible transformations that can take place within them (who delayed the opening of the school doors, and who opened them at last?, we ask). Set within such a location, the spectral transformation of the children and the chilling absence of those in charge right at the moment when questions begin to flood in, opens into a critique of institutions as bearers of ideological and biopolitical power, with the ability to make humans disappear.

The ending of Schweblin's story leaves us with the irreconcilability between a reading that admits and accepts the fantastic and another that is disturbing and of our world. The beginning of the story, in which Calderón gushes about his child while noting details about baby teeth and foot size, seemingly settles us into a narration of the normal stages of child development – the kind of tale about children that comforts because it details a form of predictable progress. Schweblin thwarts our readerly expectations by leaving us with the possibility of bodies that have followed another species' stages of development, or of an altogether different form of transformation that lies outside the organic core of those young bodies. Regardless of the way we choose to read Schweblin's story, the figure of the child as interrupted promise, unanswered question, and haunted silence lingers indefinitely.

Writing about the Vietnam War in her reflections on precarious lives, Judith Butler explains that it was the pictures of the children burning and dying from napalm that brought the US public to a sense of shock, outrage, remorse, and grief. These were precisely pictures we were not supposed to see, and they disrupted the visual field and the entire sense of public identity that was built upon that field. . . Despite their graphic effectivity, the images pointed somewhere else, beyond themselves, to a life and to a precariousness that they could not show.[10]

As Butler intimates, the image of the child – and especially the suffering child – harbours an immense amount of power, not only in terms of the immediate reactions it beckons, but of that "somewhere else" to which it points, a "beyond" that puts a mirror directly in front of ourselves. The different literary situations pictured in the narratives I discuss here – Martí's universalizing metaphors about the paths from childhood to old age; the innocence that opens itself up to symbolic potentials in Cambaceres; the inscrutable, waxen faces in "Los funámbulos"; and Schweblin's disappeared pupils – are an incomplete inventory of the different ways in which writers have used the figure of the child to comment on human temporality and its potential interruption. They also dwell on the representation of the child as a figure that hinges on an edge between innocence and knowingness, silence and answerability. This is a delicate edge that can ultimately signal the failure of humans and the institutions that they build to secure their continuity as a species. Like the presence of a ghost, then, the child's appearance across our literary and artistic landscapes offers an invitation to pause and reflect on our definitions of human life, and the steps we can take to relate to all generations and forms of that collective life.

Works Cited

Benjamin, Walter. *Illuminations*. Trans. Harry Zohn. New York: Schocken Books, 1968.
Butler, Judith. *Precarious Life: The Powers of Mourning and Violence*. London and New York: Verso, 2004.
Davis, Colin. "Hauntology, Spectres and Phantoms." *French Studies* 59, 3 (2005): 373–79.
Martí, José. "Músicos, poetas y pintores." *La Edad de Oro* 1.2 (August 1889), 57–64.
Ocampo, Silvina. *Cuentos completos I*. Buenos Aires: Emecé, 1999.
Quiroga, Horacio Quiroga. *Cuentos de amor de locura y de muerte*. Buenos Aires: Losada, 1954.
Schweblin, Samanta. *Pájaros en la boca*. New York: Random House, 2008.
Schweblin, Samanta. *Mouthful of Birds*. Trans. Megan McDowell. London: OneWorld, 2019.
Thomas, Sarah. *Inhabiting the In-Between: Childhood and Cinema in Spain's Long Transition*. Toronto: University of Toronto Press, 2019.

---

10 Judith Butler, *Precarious Life: The Powers of Mourning and Violence* (London and New York: Verso, 2004), 150.

Jobst Welge and Juliane Tauchnitz
Introduction

Based in large part on the contributions to an international (and, due to the pandemic, digital) conference at Leipzig University (April 2021) this collection of essays is intended to explore the relevance of different or layered temporalities for the literatures of Latin America and the Caribbean. The central starting point is that the literature of these cultural spaces explores connections between landscape, geography and historical or temporal sedimentation, which in turn are reflected at the level of individual and collective experiences as well as global forces and movements. Landscapes and places in the broadest sense often function in Latin American and Caribbean literatures as spaces that reveal traces of violent, traumatic experiences and historical or temporal layers. Based on these observations, the present volume wants to bring a comparative perspective into play and asks about the specific means employed by literary texts to realize the temporal palimpsest and/or the spatial entanglements on the level of the literary form itself.

Interrelating Spaces and Temporalities

A recent, highly self-reflexive (and transnational) example for such intersections in contemporary literature is the novel *Lost Children Archive* (2019) by the Mexican-US-American author Valeria Luiselli, about the Mexican-North American border region. The novel is structured along the lines of a family road trip (and the model of the American road novel). The family's use of a polaroid camera leads the narrator to reflect about Man Ray's "rayographs" as traces of absent objects. Those photographs/rayographs are said to be "like the ghostly traces of objects no longer there, like visual echoes, or like footprints left in the mud by someone who'd passed by long ago" (Luiselli 2019: 56). Aside from this sense of the past haunting the present, the narrator also reflects on the "visual echoes" of American cultural and photographic history as they underlie her own perception of the landscape:

> I know, as we drive through the long, lonely roads of this country – a landscape that I am seeing for the first time – that what I see is not quite what I see. What I see is what others

Jobst Welge, University of Leipzig
Juliane Tauchnitz, Institut Français Leipzig

https://doi.org/10.1515/9783110762273-001

> have already documented: Ilf and Petrov, Robert Frank, Robert Adams, Walker Evans, Stephen Shore – the first road photographers and their pictures of road signs, stretches of vacant land, cars, motels, diners, industrial repetition, all the ruins of early capitalism now engulfed by future ruins of later capitalism. (Luiselli 2019: 102)

Luiselli's novel, then, envisions landscape as historically layered, haunted, marked by material ruins, and filtered through previous cultural representations or literary models (Welge 2021).

The need to critically approach literature from a spatiotemporal perspective is not in itself surprising, since literary works are arguably always situated in relationship to temporal and spatial frameworks. However, as Adam Barrows has pointed out, the onset of the so-called spatial turn in the humanities since the 1990s, and its concomitant tendency to largely bracket questions of temporality, can only be explained as a reaction to a situation that had for a long time been dominated by a temporal paradigm, exemplified by the significance of Henri Bergson's theory for the interpretation of canonical modernist literature (Barrows 2016: 3). In her pioneering work, the geographer Doreen Massey has noted that often the categories of space and time had been artificially kept apart and even seen as oppositional: "With Time are aligned History, Progress, Civilization, Science, Politics, and Reason, portentous things with gravitas and capital letters. With space, on the other hand, are aligned the other poles of these concepts: stasis, (simple) reproduction, nostalgia, emotion, aesthetics, the body" (Massey 1993: 148).

Recent critical approaches, however, have increasingly taken on the challenge to interrelate spatial and temporal paradigms. Thus, literary criticism after the spatial turn has recognized that the category of place needs to be further elaborated and amplified in a relational and multi-directional sense, including dimensions of temporality, migration, global circulation, and so forth (Prieto 2012; cf. Dünne/Günzel 2006). As the subtitle of our volume makes clear, we propose that not only is there a need to interrelate space and time, but also to pay due attention to the presence of *multiple* temporalities in works of fiction. For instance, in a recent volume on travel writing Paula Henrikson and Christina Kullberg have invoked François Hartog's notion of "regimes of historicity" to highlight the plurality of times, as well as the fact that conceptualizations of time are not given but culturally produced, and they have pointed to broader implications and consequences: "Temporalities can be distinguished as certain articulations of time; they refer to larger concepts of pasts, presents, and futures" (Henrikson/Kullberg 2021: 3).

For us, a central, inspirational point for this focus on multiple spaces and temporalities was the work of María del Pilar Blanco, especially her book *Ghost-Watching American Modernity* (2012), which has fastened on the characteristic obsession with supernatural or Gothic themes in the literature of the Americas (both North and South America). These various phenomena are theorized by Blanco with recourse to the concept of *haunting*, a phenomenon she defines as a "disquieting experience of sensing a collision of temporalities or spaces" in both urban and desert regions of the Americas (Blanco 2012: 182). For instance, Blanco has credited the Mexican Juan Rulfo's landmark novel *Pedro Páramo* (1955) – significantly also invoked by Luiselli's novel – with emblematizing a central trait of the modern Latin American novel, namely its "increasing awareness of simultaneous landscapes and simultaneous others living within unseen, diverse spaces in the progressively complicated political and cultural networks of hemispheric modernization" (Blanco 2012: 7). In her book, Blanco understands the phenomenon of haunting as a subjective disposition or experience of doubt, a crisis of perception that fastens on landscapes marked by different temporal experiences, where certain things are felt but not actually seen. This idea shows itself to be highly productive when dealing with the different kinds of reality that impact on specifically "American landscapes affected by ongoing modernization" (Blanco 2012: 25). To approach the cultural study of landscape via the phenomenon of haunting is particularly suggestive because it helps us to understand how diverging perspectives may envision and condition the relationship between different temporalities and/or places: "We often think of simultaneity in temporal terms, but we should also look at it as an event in which two spatialities are confronted with each other" (Blanco 2012: 26). María del Pilar Blanco has participated in the conference with many acute and inspiring observations and comments, and we are most grateful that she has agreed to contribute to this volume with a special, introductory essay that reconsiders the themes and conceptual discussions from a new perspective, namely the figure of the child as it symbolically dramatizes human temporality as well as literary landscapes in Latin America, from the nineteenth century until today.

Another scholar who has recently emphasized the interrelation of multiple temporalities is Kaisa Kaakinen. As a comparativist she has shown that works of modernist and contemporary literature interrelate the time of the present with various dimensions of an historical imaginary. These procedures are analyzed by Kaakinen in light of the contemporary skepticism vis-à-vis the temporal regime of modernity and the concomitant self-awareness of the contemporary as being inherently plural and diversified:

> If in the modern temporal regime the present could be conceived as a mere transition, a part of a single posited narrative, the more heightened sense of a heterogeneous contemporaneity demands a different conception of the present as a site in which historical narratives and orientations are constructed, debated, and contested. Instead of a site of transition, the present is increasingly experienced as a site of disjunctions. (Kaakinen 2017: 12)

Arguably, this contemporary concern with asynchronous temporalities as well as "social and cultural multiplicities" (Kaakinen 2017: 12), the coming together of different temporalities, of untimeliness and "posttraumatic temporality," of "haunting and the uncanny," not to mention the "copresence of heterogeneous global reading contexts" (Kaakinen 2017: 19), are all elements that apply, *a fortiori*, we might say, to the areas of modern and contemporary "global" Latin American and Caribbean literatures (Welge 2021: 194).

Landscapes in Latin America and the Caribbean, Present Simultaneities

The literary figuration of landscape has always been central to the formation of Latin American and Caribbean literatures, especially since the time of Romanticism. Notably, the thinker and author Édouard Glissant has insisted on the complex interrelations of space and time in the Caribbean. Space has been theorized by Édouard Glissant as a cultural poetics of *relation*, where multiple histories are shared by a common, archipelagic geography. Caribbean literature is intent on appropriating the multiple fragments of the past, and for Glissant landscape is conceived as the container of this temporal simultaneity; he speaks of "the patience of landscape [. . .] not saturated with a single History but effervescent with intermingled histories, spread around, rushing to fuse without destroying or reducing each other" (Glissant 1997: 154). Painting a broad canvas of Caribbean poetics, Timothy Reiss finds here a "geographical remaking of history," "remnants retrieved from history through spirit of place, topographical presence, to compose a future" (Reiss 2002: 356; 357). Drawing on the work of Massey, Mary Gallagher writes that "French Caribbean writing involves a uniquely intense confrontation with the intersection of space and time" (Gallagher 2002: 4). We would maintain that this characteristic applies not only to the French area of the Caribbean and is equally true for much of modern and contemporary Latin American writing.

In Latin America, colonial histories and their aftermath, cultural encounters, and civilizational strata have left their traces in regional landscapes and the (imagined) space of the nation, which has encouraged writers to highlight this continued presence of the past (Alcocer 2011; Lazarra/Unruh 2009). Recently, Victoria Saramago, in her book *Fictional Environments* (2021), has reinvigorated the study of literary landscapes in Latin America, precisely by not only asking how certain regional spaces in Latin America are represented in literature, but also how literature's portrayal has brought about these landscapes in the imagination of readers and how this has in turn impacted, or predetermined our understanding of the real, external landscape. The iconic, regional landscapes of Latin America bear witness to a long history of colonial violence and economic exploitation, yet by being *preserved* in literature, they may also, as a consequence of their "progressive" development (and increasingly with historical distance), be tinged by feelings of nostalgia. In any event, Saramago maintains, these landscapes "reveal the presence of the past in the form of a palimpsest – but a palimpsest that mixes idealized and catastrophic narratives perceived through collective imaginaries" (Saramago 2021: 35).

When speaking about the question of time with regard to the culture of Latin America and other countries of the Global South, many ideology-producing discourses of the nineteenth century (for instance by Euclides da Cunha, as the chapters by Fonseca, Lay Brander, and Welge will discuss in detail) rested on the more or less explicit equation between geographical remoteness and temporal distance. As Stefan Helgesson has pointed out (with da Cunha as one of his prime examples) such an alignment of cultural with temporal difference has also underwritten well-meaning theorizations of post-colonial critics whose formulations of cultural relativism are still undergirded by a binary logic of "different" temporalities, or even by an essentially linear, and hence monolithic conception of the time of modernity. Instead, Helgesson urges us to move toward a much broader understanding of the multiplicity and simultaneity of times:

> Time, then, needs to be conceived of as radically multiple in ways that far exceed the evolutionist, colonial, and culturalist paradigms. Radical polytemporality would go further than Braudel's *durées* and acknowledge all the different modes of time – domestic, national, personal, political, spiritual, geological, technological, agricultural, and so on – that continuously give shape and meaning to human life, and that are impossible to reduce wholesale to concepts such as "culture" or "capitalism". (Helgesson 2014: 557)

Conversely, if such spatiotemporal compressions and constellations are especially characteristic for the geographical areas discussed in this volume, they also resonate with recent theories and debates about the "deep time" of the Anthropocene as well as cultural criticism about our present historical moment. In fact, it has been argued that the temporal regime of modernity – associated with continuous progress, acceleration and the receding of the past – has come to an end, as it were. Instead, it has been proposed that our time's experience of temporality can be understood as an unlimited contemporaneity, the limitless availability of the past in a "broad present" (Assmann 2013; Gumbrecht 2014). Arguably, within this undifferentiated realm of the present, novels, literature, or other media and cultural artifacts may take on the function to make visible its heterogeneity, as sedimented and layered in seemingly "empty" landscapes.

This volume, drawing on recent cultural approaches to temporality and spatiality, also aims to contribute to current discussions of World Literature, which have been modified and diversified in terms of paying closer attention to the interrelation between specific locations and questions of global, universal, or trans-national reach (Ekelund 2021). The modern literatures of Latin America and the Caribbean, we maintain, provide an especially fertile ground for the triangulation of (multiple) spaces, temporalities, and nations.

Specifically, the volume provides a panorama of perspectives and approaches that collectively demonstrate how the literatures of these cultural spaces explore the connection between landscape or geographies and historical or temporal palimpsests, as embodied by the specificities and techniques of literary form. The following contributions are dedicated to individual, yet conceptually interconnected studies of multiple, staggered, or non-simultaneous temporalities in modern and contemporary literature. The volume adopts a comparative perspective and intends to provide common perspectives on, and new approaches to, the fields of Latin American and Caribbean literatures, engaging their linguistic variety with literary works written in Spanish, Portuguese, French, and English. Therefore, the following overview briefly situates the individual essays with regard to the three different, yet overlapping sections of this book.

I Locations and Spatiotemporal Constellations: Lives, Literary Fields

This section focuses on the question of how literary texts, their production and reception are (dis-)located with regard to national, transnational, or global spaces, and how these spaces are linked to specific regimes of temporality, such as, for instance, the experience of non-contemporaneity, a-synchronized, negated temporalities, or alternative realizations and conceptions of modernity. How does literature propose alternative or conflicting models of temporality and space? How are subjects and literary works moved through, conditioned, or traversed by multiple spaces and times? While the first essay (by Müller) considers a broad panorama of literary texts, the two following essays (by Burnautzki and Brüske) are focused on the analysis of single literary texts. Yet all three essays address broader questions about how the literary works are to be located within the geographical and social field in which the works emerge, and how they position themselves within it. Moreover, these essays are concerned with subjects or individual biographies that are located in, or dislocated from certain places or positions. Bo G. Ekelund has usefully specified this notion of location as the (momentary) convergence of spatial and temporal coordinates: "A location [. . .] is not a point in space that somehow exists in itself. Rather, the term designates the way that an individual, a group or a cultural object, such as a text, inhabits or claims a place or position at a given time" (Ekelund 2021: 10).

In Chapter 1, Gesine Müller introduces us to the literary field occupied by (early) nineteenth century novels and narratives of the Caribbean, written both in Spanish and in French. Invoking Glissant's notion of modern Caribbean literature's ubiquitous *relationalité* as well as its dislocated condition, Müller asks the question what sort of spatiotemporal parameters might apply to the Caribbean novels of the nineteenth century, that is, during a time when the colonial situation conditioned any sense of directionality. In order to address this question in a differentiated way, Müller offers an exceptionally broad, yet succinct panorama of four Caribbean texts. Émeric Bergaud's *Stella* (1859), the first novel from Haiti, describes the landscape of the colony of Saint-Domingue as spatialized time, as an aestheticized nature that still awaits the nation-building, civilizational work, which appeals to a European value system in a rather unidirectional way. The novel *Outre-mer* (1835) by the Martinican writer Louis de Maynard de Queilhe negotiates between different geographical settings and aims to preserve the old order, also via a mimetic orientation towards literary models from European Romanticism. The Condesa de Merlín's travelogue from Cuba, *La Havane* (1844), suggests multiple temporal layers in the natural landscape, resulting from a perspective both Cuban and European. The novel *La peregrinación de Bayoán* (1863), by the Puerto Rican writer Eugenio María de Hostos, presents several spatiotemporal thresholds that Müller sees as anticipatory of Glissant's notion of *Antillanité*, comprising a dense network of historical layers, and which she finally illustrates with an emblematic work of the twentieth century, Maryse Condé's novel *Traversée de la Mangrove* (1989), distinguished by a synchronic compression of entanglements and interrelated stories.

Chapter 2 explores the idea of location from two interrelated questions. First, what location is claimed by a narrator who speaks from the afterlife, and how does this radically dislocated narrating subject relate to points in time and space? Secondly, how is the literary text itself (dis)located with regard to the trajectory of literary history in a global, spatially differentiated context? In this chapter Sarah Burnautzki presents a pertinent reading of a classic of late nineteenth-century Brazilian literature, Machado de Assis' *Memórias postumas de Brás Cubas* (The Posthumous Memoirs of Brás Cubas, 1881). Taking up Roberto Schwarz' well-known formula of "misplaced ideas," Burnautzki pushes this concept to radically interrogate and problematize our very habit to conceive of literary history in terms of time and space, teleological narratives, center and periphery, of being ahead or being belated. Machado's novel presents a fascinating limit case within the context of our volume: while virtually devoid of any concrete descriptions of landscape, the eccentric "posthumous" perspective and premise of the *Memoirs* essentially propose the idea of travelling through the protagonist's own past life – and thus making it present again, in defiance of realist conventions of chronology. In fact, the dead otherworldly narrator is dislocated from the ordinary contexts of both space and time, while his hypertrophic and self-reflexive narration trumps and supersedes the "realist" representation of exterior reality. Burnautzki shows how these peculiar procedures foreground the temporality of the narrative performance itself and distort causal and linear relations within the interior diegesis. The essay argues that these seemingly outlandish devices ultimately problematize the critical rhetoric of "belatedness" and "periphery," since the categories of space and time are themselves narratively produced and subject to different (spatially bound) perspectives.

Jumping to the contemporary period, Chapter 3, by Anne Brüske, investigates geopolitical imaginaries and social space and time in the Comic Memoir *Adiós mi Habana* (2017) by German-born, US-based artist Anna Veltfort, who lived during her youth for a decade in Cuba. Brüske is interested in the spatial triangulation that existed when the island of Cuba was variously positioned with regard to the Caribbean, the United States, and the Soviet Union. Veltfort's work, situated by Brüske in a broader context of Cuban-diasporic graphic narratives, is concerned with multiplied spatiotemporal locations and orientations as they emerge from a look back to the time of the beginning of the Cuban Revolution. The book is centered on the life of Connie, a German-American who lived in Havana from 1962 to 1972, a figure who stands in as the former self of the author Veltfort. Following French sociologist Henri Lefebvre, Brüske sets out to discuss the "spatial practices" that occur in a palimpsest-like, multi-temporal social space in conjunction with the media-specific realizations of spatiotemporal relations in the material images of graphic narratives. This specific form of the graphic narrative, enriched by intertextual references and intermedial devices (such as the incorporation of historical photographs, elements of journalism), Brüske argues, is especially suited to express Cuban-centered global imaginaries, whereby the past events and political frameworks (internationalism, socialism, Cold War) are relocated and reframed with respect to the present of the author's diaspora and her readership. The essay shows first how the autobiographical (lesbian) protagonist had been subject to the Revolution's spatial ordering of the capital city, including its perpetuation of a heteronormative spatial order. Secondly, the essay demonstrates how the intertextual composition of the work produces multi-scalar entanglements and imaginary entryways to the Cuban social space during the 1960s and 70s, as well as to a geopolitical imaginary, for a 21st

century readership. According to Brüske, Veltfort's critical and differentiated portrayal of the Cuban Revolution exemplifies a transnational imagination in the form of a spatiotemporal palimpsest.

II Literary Landscapes and Temporalities: Regions and World(s)

This section investigates the inscriptions of time in natural or geographic landscapes as well as the (literary) "history" of those landscapes. The contributions to this section present case studies on the literary modeling of specific landscapes and their (temporally conditioned) relation to regional, national, and global spaces. How do specific regional spaces or natural landscapes represent interactions of nature, history, and culture? How are these landscapes conceived as temporal and/or literary palimpsests? This section offers three readings that explore the cultural significance of paradigmatic "national" landscapes within Latin America. All three chapters fasten on works that may be understood as revisiting Latin American regionalism from a decidedly "modernist" perspective. It is helpful to conceive of these paradigmatic landscapes – the Brazilian *sertão*, the transnational Amazon region, the Argentine *pampa* – in terms of the concept of fictional environments, as recently proposed by Victoria Saramago: "[. . .] it refers simultaneously to the fictionality of novels as they create their environments and to the fact that, as many of these environments disappear in real life, the way they are collectively perceived may remain tied to their depiction in fictional works" (Saramago 2021: 7–8). Moreover, what these works have in common is a double strategy of using the space of the region both in terms of a referential realism and in terms of a self-conscious fictionality, as Saramago aptly remarks with respect to two of the texts discussed in the following: "Guimarães Rosa's *sertão* or Carpentier's jungle is perceived as conveying valuable information about these real places to readers, in spite of the fact that their novels entail so many fantastic, supernatural, or even inaccurate elements" (Saramago 2012: 12).

In this sense, Chapter 4, by Miriam Lay Brander, provides a nuanced analysis of João Guimarães Rosa's great Brazilian novel *Grande Sertão: Veredas* (1956) and its programmatic relation to the backcountry of the *sertão* in the Brazilian region of north-Western Minas Gerais. Lay Brander first establishes a connection with Euclides da Cunha's earlier, equally classic work of *Os sertões* (1902), which is set in the geographically somewhat distant *sertão* of the Northeast, yet which is generally comparable in so far as it also builds on this region's association with underdevelopment, "primitivism" and resistance to progress. If da Cunha's work, then, exemplifies the ideological connection between geographical remoteness and a "backward" temporality, Guimarães Rosa's novel is centered in the narrated report of the "insider" Riobaldo, a landowner and former *jagunço* (gunman). By closely analyzing and categorizing the novel's different strata of temporality, Lay Brander argues that the novel does not simply oppose the *sertão*'s archaic primitivism to technological modernity. Instead, the novel's characteristic amalgamation of local und universal significations represents the landscape of the *sertão* partly under the sign of pre-historic timelessness, partly as subject to the passage of time, and gradually marked by processes of modernization. Drawing on the concept of *timescape* (B. Adam), the essay studies various examples for the inscription of time into a distinct geographical space, tensions between individual and collective, local and universal time. By subjecting the landscape of the *sertão* to movement and by "worlding" a regionalist space, Guimarães Rosa's novel may be understood as a counter-model to the linear and progressivist implications of da Cunha's text.

In Chapter 5, Jobst Welge contextualizes the Cuban writer's Alejo Carpentier's novel *Los pasos perdidos* (The Lost Steps, 1953) within the larger framework of travel narratives and modern literary representations of the Amazon region, thus stressing the extent to which Carpentier is aware of and builds upon the tradition of the Amazon as a *literary* landscape. By developing the idea of how the Amazon has been fashioned as a "land without history," in the writings of the Brazilian writer and engineer Euclides da Cunha, Welge goes on to show (in a argument that echoes Lay Brander's evaluation of *Grande Sertão* vis-à-vis *Os sertões*) that Carpentier's novel, despite its stark oppositions of nature and culture, ultimately shows an "original" landscape *through* the eyes of modernity and as a corollary of modernity's impasses. The chapter is interested in the ways in which Carpentier's novel is conceived as both literary and historical palimpsest. While the notion of time travel is an obvious conceit of the novel, the essay shows how the work enacts not only a retrocession in time, but suggests indeed the co-presence of different temporalities within the space of the jungle. The novel does not simply equate the Amazon space with primeval time and legendary myth (as notably in the myth of El Dorado), but it essentially represents the yearning for authentic, original nature as a corollary of the modern condition. As a literary landscape, the Amazon becomes a palimpsest and universal mirror, indelibly marked not by the absence, but by the presence of modernity. Carpentier's novel enacts a spatiotemporal voyage but also a synchronicity of different temporalities.

In Chapter 6, Jörg Dünne, situating his discussion within recent debates on the "deep time" of the Anthropocene and the meteorologically conditioned space-time of the "terrestrial" (B. Latour), presents a new approach to the 1997 novel *Las nubes* (*The Clouds*) by the Argentinian writer Juan José Saer, which rewrites the history of the pampa as a foundational landscape of the Argentinian nation. This work, taken by Dünne as representative for a "fluvial" current of modern Argentine literature, appears at a turning point in landscape history, where the long-lasting narrative of a horizontal, frontier extension in a desert landscape driven by human heroes is starting to be questioned, since other, more complex types of interaction between humans and their environment appear. The specificity of the literary configuration of landscapes of time in *Las nubes* is the particular experience of spatio-temporality that goes beyond visual control "at one glance," and is in search of an experience of temporality that unfolds at different scales simultaneously, a human and more-than human meteorological or geological scale. Thus, Saer's novel suggests a poetic combination of geopolitics and geohistory, which, Dünne argues, provides us with a particular literary genealogy of what has recently been described as the "critical zone" of the terrestrial in cultural theory.

III Specters, Ruins, Catastrophes

This section considers haunted spaces and temporalities, afterlives of the human past in material remains, buildings, or places, sedimented memories of human (or natural) catastrophes, traumas, historical experiences and their spatial traces as well as temporal repercussions. How do literary texts evoke spectral or catastrophic pasts through their narrative or poetic form? How do literary texts represent material, spatialized, or embodied memories? The particular pertinence of the after-live of the past in Caribbean literature is frequently caused by experiences of colonial violence, the history of slavery, or displacement, which are often of a traumatic nature and have thus left not only material traces on the landscape but also in the body of individuals – as here explored by Jörngården and Tauchnitz. In his study *The Literature of Catastrophe* (2020) Carlos Fonseca has explored different ways in which natural catastrophes have assumed political connotations in works of modern Latin American literature. Going back to the nineteenth century and Alexander von Humboldt's fascination with volcanic eruptions, Fonseca details how the formerly static, tableau-like conception of Natural History becomes mobilized and temporalized: "Catastrophe presents itself as the event that disrupts the continuity of the catalogue, the harmony of its taxonomy, leaving in its place a pure multiplicity" (Fonseca 2020: 51). In short, Fonseca argues, the catastrophic experience of historicity lies at the heart of the *chronotope* of modernity.

In his contribution for this volume (Chapter 7), Fonseca argues how the notion of catastrophe constitutes a nodal point for the political significance of Euclides da Cunha's work *Os sertões* (1902), one of the most significant and influential Latin American texts on "landscape" ever to be written (and which Lay Brander's essay has already discussed in its relation to the discourse of "backwardness"). This account of the infamous War of Canudos (1896–1897) has often been read as a treatise on environmental determinism and the progressive march of civilization upon the barbaric backlands of Brazil. Reading the book against the grain of such canonical interpretations this chapter proposes that a second undercurrent lies below such positivist pretensions: the attempt to think of nature as a critical space of eventfulness, and therefore of historicity, one which escapes the landscaping frames through which the modern nation-state wished to tame it. Paying particular attention to the geo-historical imaginary that da Cunha deploys in his portrayal of the Counsellor's outlaw army and his reading of the Counsellor himself as a *sociological fossil*, Fonseca explores how the figure of the ruin and rubble emerges within the text as a way of thinking through the "critical remnants" that refused to be subsumed within the representational apparatus of the state. Following the catastrophic imaginary at play in *Os sertões*, in particular the cyclical interplay between droughts and floods, and linking it to the geo-historical discourse that saw catastrophes as a way of thinking through the deep historicity of nature, the chapter ends by proposing the concept of *land-archive* as a way of countering the a-historicity of the State's landscaping project.

In Chapter 8, Anna Jörngården takes her cue from the recent political debates on monuments, and draws on influential cultural theories of ruins and material memory (A. Riegl, James E. Young) to discuss ruins as media of counter-memory in a series of representative writings from the Caribbean, in which the fragmented and half-buried colonial past comes to the fore and thereby challenges the monumental history of the colonizer, by turning absence into presence. Thus, in Patrick Chamoiseau's *Guyane: Traces-mémoires du bagne* (1993), an essay on the French penal colony in Guiana, Jörngården discusses how, in the context of the author's notion of *trace-mémoires* ("memory traces") ruins are mobilized to communicate the traumas of history. In this interpretation, the physical remains of the prison structure signify the preservation of past human suffering, ruins as receptacles of emotion. *After the Dance* (2002) by Edwidge Danticat is an essayistic travelogue about Haiti's history, in which the author talks about her visit to the city of Jacmel, where she comes upon an abandoned steam engine of a former sugar plantation. The ruination of this object signifies a multilayered condensation of Haiti's and the Caribbean's relation to the history of modernity. Finally, Jörngården identifies in Paule Marshall's novel *The Chosen Place, The Timeless*

People (1969) about the fictive Bourne Island, a former British colony in the Caribbean archipelago, a ruined and deeply haunted landscape that forces the characters to confront traumatic events in their own past, and which transmits the unfinished history of colonialism to subsequent generations.

In Chapter 9, dealing with Patrick Chamoiseau's novel *Un dimanche au cachot* (A Sunday in the Dungeon, 2007), Juliane Tauchnitz develops a concise reading of this work concerned with the problem of colonial violence in the sugar plantation and slave economy of Martinique as well as its possible repercussions in the present. The novel superimposes the situation of a frame narrative by an auto-fictional narrator, centered on a girl imprisoned in a dungeon, with the narrator's report of a supposedly historical event about a forgotten slave, named *L'Oubliée*, and similarly locked up in this same dungeon. Tauchnitz emphasizes how this duplicated narrative situation, subject to a differentiated pacing, achieves the effect of an immediate making present of the past, and hence an abolition of chronological clock time. The essay emphasizes the importance of the human body as, literally, the embodiment of a dialectic of remembrance and forgetting. The place of the *cachot* embodies in turn a temporal palimpsest, while the forgotten slave's body points to the totality of all forgotten slaves. The essay briefly invokes Glissant's notion of *space-time* (*espace-temps*) to emphasize how Chamoiseau's narrative brings forth the notion of a concrete space while simultaneously undoing the notions of solid time and space.

Turning to recent poetic production from the Lesser Antilles, Christina Kullberg asks in Chapter 10, how hurricanes as natural catastrophes, often associated with political upheavals (as Fonseca has detailed), have impacted the figuration of landscape and temporality in a Caribbean context. Kullberg analyzes contemporary poetry (by Georges, Sekou, Sorhaindo) that engages directly with the 2017 hurricanes with the help of Glissant's notion of the *tourbillon* ("whirlwind"), which refers to an intermingling of natural and cultural times, with respect to landscapes or spaces that have been submitted to historical forces. Referring also to the semantics of *trou* ("rift"), Glissant explores phenomena of temporal superimposition that defy linearity, thereby also suggesting a spatial metaphoric notion of time itself. In Kullberg's reading, also drawing on Kamau Brathwaite's anti-linear concept of *tidalectics*, the poems embody such notions of space-time as they are characteristic for the Caribbean diaspora. The essay analyzes concretely how the poetic artifacts realize notions of the co-presence of calendric time and distorted or abolished temporality; the contraction or expansion of space and time; cyclical time and deep time; "chaotic" forms of simultaneity, silenced pasts, ruined landscapes. While mirroring the recent hurricanes in their idiosyncratic form and language, these contemporary poems also exemplify the multilayered temporalities that distinguish a Caribbean poetics.

Chapter 11, by Sara Brandellero, discusses the recent Brazilian fiction film *Burning Night* (*Breve miragem de sol*, 2019), directed by Eryk Rocha. Brandellero considers the film in the light of theoretical conceptualizations of night-time and with respect to debates of the burgeoning field of "night studies." This transdisciplinary field of study addresses aspects of human experience often neglected by a focus dominated by a daytime perspective. The chapter's starting points are the concept of night as "frontier," which problematizes the commercialization and colonization of the night space-time, and the concept of haunting or spectrality in the everyday (Blanco & Peeren 2013), through which the chapter discusses the representation of the figure of the night-time taxi driver who, while the city 'sleeps,' unveils to us the invisible side of the 24-hour-city. Brandellero's essay complements this volume's focus on literature with a case study of contemporary cinema. It extends the analysis of spectral spaces to the urban settings of Latin America (as programmatically argued by Blanco 2012), drawing, like Brüske in her essay on Havana, on Henri Lefebvre's notion of spatial practices.

As this example suggests, the division of the essays in the three sections of this volume seeks to identify common points of intersection between different cultural areas and periods, yet it is also pragmatic. Just as the essays develop common points of inquiry within each of the three sections, they also dialogue and overlap with conceptual and thematic issues of essays within other sections. The re-occurrence of the figure of Euclides da Cunha in three of the essays (Lay Brander; Welge; Fonseca) is a case in point. We hope that readers of this collection will encounter many more of such echoes and connections. We also hope that the readings of Latin American and Caribbean literature (and cultural artifacts) presented here will promote further inquiries into the crossing of boundaries, between cultures, spaces, and times.

Bibliography

Alcocer, Rudyard J. (2011). *Time Travel in the Latin American and Caribbean Imagination: Rereading History*. London: Palgrave Macmillan.

Assmann, Aleida (2013). *Ist die Zeit aus den Fugen? Aufstieg und Fall des Zeitregimes der Moderne*. Munich: Hanser.

Barrows, Adam (2016): *Time, Literature, and Cartography after the Spatial Turn. The Chronometric Imaginary*. London: Palgrave Macmillan.

Blanco, María del Pilar (2012): *Ghost-Watching American Modernity: Haunting, Landscape, and the Hemispheric Imagination*. New York: Fordham University Press.

Blanco, María del Pilar/Peeren, Esther (eds.) (2013): *The Spectralities Reader: Ghosts and Haunting in Contemporary Cultural Theory*. New York: Bloomsbury Academic.

Dünne, Jörg/Günzel, Stephan (eds.) (2006): *Raumtheorie. Grundlagentexte aus Philosophie und Kulturwissenschaften*. Frankfurt am Main: Suhrkamp.

Ekelund, Bo G. (2021): "Land, language, literature: Cosmopolitan and vernacular claims to place." Introduction to: Ekelund, Bo G./Mahmutović, Adnan/ Wulff, Helena (eds.): *Claiming Space. Locations and Orientations in World Literatures*. New York: Bloomsbury Academic, pp. 1–27.

Fonseca, Carlos (2020): *The Literature of Catastrophe. Nature, Disaster and Revolution in Latin America*. New York: Bloomsbury.

Gallagher, Mary (2002): *Soundings in French Caribbean Writing Since 1950: The Shock of Space and Time*. Oxford: Oxford University Press.

Glissant, Édouard (1997): *Poetics of Relation*. Trans. Betsy Wing: Ann Arbor: University of Michigan Press.

Gumbrecht, Hans Ulrich (2014): *Our Broad Present: Time and Contemporary Culture*. New York: Columbia University Press.

Helgesson, Stefan (2014): "Radicalizing Temporal Difference: Anthropology, Postcolonial Theory, and Literary Time." In: *History and Theory*, 53 (Forum: Multiple Temporalities), pp. 545–562.

Henrikson, Paula/Kullberg,Christina (eds.) (2020): *Time and Temporalities in European Travel Writing*. New York: Routledge.

Kaakinen, Kaisa (2017): *Comparative Literature and the Historical Imaginary. Reading Conrad, Weiss, Sebald*. London: Palgrave.

Lazarra, Michael J./Unruh, Vicky (eds.) (2009): *Telling Ruins in Latin America*. London: Palgrave Macmillan.

Luiselli, Valeria (2019): *Lost Children Archive*. New York: Knopf.

Massey, Doreen (1993): "Politics and Space/Time." In: Keith, Michael/Pile, Steve (eds.): *Place and the Politics of Identity*. London/New York: Routledge, pp. 141–161.

Prieto, Eric (2012): *Literature, Geography, and the Postmodern Poetics of Place*. London: Palgrave Macmillan.

Reiss, Timothy (2002): *Against Autonomy. Global Dialectics of Cultural Exchange*. Stanford: Stanford University Press, 2002.

Saramago, Victoria (2021): *Fictional Environments. Mimesis, Deforestation, and Development in Latin America*. Evanston, Illinois: Northwestern University Press.

Welge, Jobst (2021): "Locations, Orientations and Multiple Temporalities in the Contemporary, 'Global' Latin American Novel." In: Ekelund, Bo G./Mahmutović, Adnan/Wulff, Helena (eds.): *Claiming Space. Locations and Orientations in World Literatures*. New York: Bloomsbury Academic, pp. 193–216.

I Locations and Spatiotemporal Constellations:
 Lives, Literary Fields

Gesine Müller
Spatial Dynamics and Colonial Positioning in Nineteenth-Century Spanish- and French-Language Caribbean Literatures

As a crossroads of wide-ranging influences, with diverse traditions of staging of interwoven spaces, the Caribbean is an insightful region for exploring questions about the literary landscapes of time. Relational conceptions of space, as expressed, for example, in Édouard Glissant's notions of *Antillanité*, *relationalité*, and *tout-monde*, are integral to Caribbean experiential spaces such as colonial Martinique where Glissant was raised. As Jobst Welge recently demonstrated, the contemporary global Latin American novel "connects not only different geographical spaces through different narrative lines; it also juxtaposes different temporalities as they emerge from specific places" (Welge 2021: 194). I would like to apply this perspective to the Caribbean literary production of the nineteenth century. My remarks below will particularly focus on the links between literary spatial/temporal configurations and colonial positions in various (post-)colonial contexts. I will conclude with an example from twentieth-century literature that reveals continuities and differences in conceptions of space/time as well as identity.[1]

As an example of the narrativization of history and identity using spatial metaphors in the nineteenth century, allow me to quote a famous line from Chateaubriand's *Mémoires d'outre-tombe*, which was extensively received in the Caribbean: "I have found myself between two centuries as at the junction between two rivers; I have plunged into their troubled waters, regretfully leaving behind the ancient strand where I was born and swimming hopefully towards the unknown shores where the new generations will land" (Chateaubriand 2014: 5).[2] Additionally, one might anticipate nineteenth-century texts to set the literary

---

[1] The ideas expressed below build on my previous work concerning spatial conceptions in Caribbean literatures, converging in my monograph *Crossroads of Colonial Cultures. Caribbean Literatures in the Age of Revolution* (Müller 2018).
[2] "Je me suis rencontré entre deux siècles comme au confluent de deux fleuves; j'ai plongé dans leurs eaux troublées, m'éloignant avec regret du vieux rivage où je suis né nageant avec espérance vers une rive inconnue" (Chateaubriand 1958 [1848]: 1047).

Note: Unless otherwise noted, all translations are my own.

Gesine Müller, Universität zu Köln

stage in ways that communicate the conflation of cultural identity and national territory preceding the topographical turn. This turn has been conceptualized as a break with this conflation, exemplified by the notion of "displacement" that has supplanted concepts of migration such as exile and diaspora, as suggested by Sigrid Weigel (2002: 156). Ubiquitous connectedness may now be characteristic of the dislocated intellectual world of the Caribbean in the twentieth and early twenty-first centuries – both in regard to spatial dynamics and, often, in regard to the treatment of time layers and their sediments. However, we obviously cannot apply it directly to the nineteenth century, when colonial ties gave the connection a mostly clear directionality, although this framework was repeatedly burst open.

First, we will consider writings by four literary representatives of different colonial realms in the Caribbean: the novel *Stella* by the Haitian writer Émeric Bergeaud, published in 1859; the novel *Outre-mer* by Louis de Maynard de Queilhe of Martinique, published in 1835; the Condesa de Merlín's impressions from her visit to Cuba (*La Havane*), published in 1844; and *La peregrinación de Bayoán* by the Puerto Rican author Eugenio María de Hostos, published in 1863. This gives us four voices from very different colonial spheres: Bergeaud, from Haiti, which had gained its independence from France, contrasts with Maynard de Queilhe, a writer from the French colony of Martinique, which never became independent. Writing from a self-contradictory position that oscillates between the poles of Cuba, Madrid, and Paris, the Condesa de Merlín describes the island where she grew up and which she is now revisiting after many years away. Meanwhile, Hostos, as a representative of the Spanish colonial sphere, is the only one of the three who, even just from the point of view of the language, was situated in a context in which the pursuit of independence had a completely different meaning than it had in the French colonial empire: these Caribbean islands were, after all, the last dependent American enclaves of Spain, the mother country (*Madre Patria España*).

One contemporary author, Maryse Condé, completes the tableau of Caribbean literary examples. Condé hails from Martinique, an island that maintains a colonial status to this day. What distinguishes the ways in which these Caribbean texts stage spaces and times? And what do these distinct positions signify in relation to the corresponding constructions of identity?

1 Émeric Bergeaud: *Stella* (1859)

The novel takes place during the Haitian Revolution (1791–1804), in the last stage of colonial rule, when the state of Haiti was to be founded, a period riven by violent conflicts over the abolition of slavery and the struggle for independence from the colonizing power. Despite all that, Eméric Bergeaud's *Stella* begins with a highly idealized description of nature:

> Connaissez-vous le pays du cèdre et de la vigne,
> où sont des fleurs toujours nouvelles, un ciel toujours brillant;
> où les ailes légères du zéphyr, au milieu des jardins de roses,
> s'affaissent sous le poids des parfums;
> où le citronnier et l'olivier portent des fruits si beaux;
> où la voix du rossignol n'est jamais muette;
> où les teintes de la terre et les nuances du ciel,
> quoique différentes, rivalisent en beauté?
> (Bergeaud 1859: 1)³

This is an excerpt from a poem by Lord Byron that, in turn, borrows from the opening of Goethe's poem "Mignon": "Kennst Du das Land, wo die Zitronen blühn" [*Know'st thou the land where lemon-trees do bloom*]. These Romantic verses were originally rhapsodising the nature and landscape of Italy. Why would Caribbean writers take descriptions of Italian nature by German or English poets and transfer them to Haiti in order to extol what is supposedly their "own"?

The spatial tension that is extolled in this first novel from Haiti, still a very young state and therefore post-colonial, leads to the center of our question, as the territorial beauty of what is later to become the national space is decisive for the cultural positioning here. This is why Bergeaud, in describing the colony of Saint-Domingue, quotes Byron's and Goethe's paradisiac images, in order to emphasize the claim to the founding space that is yet to be established (Thiem 2010: 68). The ode to nature is introduced with the Romantic structural elements of a fairy tale: "Sur une terre fortunée, au sein d'une nature séduisante et prodigue de ses dons les plus précieux" (Bergeaud 1859: 1).⁴ The audience is immediately called upon to visit this island and marvel at its natural beauty (Thiem 2010: 68). Here, "landscape" functions as an aesthetically modeled natural space whose manifestation is contingent upon historically mutable systems of knowledge and renders these systems visible, for they cannot be perceived as such directly. As an object of human perception and practices of appropriation, landscape is an

---

3 "Know ye the land of the cedar and vine? Where the flowers ever blossom, the beams ever shine, Where the light wings of Zephyr, oppress'd with perfume, Wax faint o'er the gardens of Gúl in her bloom; Where the citron and olive are fairest of fruit, And the voice of the nightingale never is mute; Where the tints of the earth, and the hues of the sky, In color though varied, in beauty may vie [. . .]" (Bergeaud 2014: 7).
4 "In a fortunate land, at the heart of a captivating and lavishing environment [. . .]" (Bergeaud 2014: 7).

anthropogenically coded form of nature and can thus be read as a projected space in which a specific historical imaginary, subjective affective dispositions, and both spoken and unspoken notions can take shape and be artistically enacted.

But the crucial element here is the omnipresence of knowledge about Western culture, according to which this beautiful nature must still be tamed and civilized. This, too, finally comes to pass in the final chapter, in which the foundations of civilization constitute the bedrock on which the nation can be formed (Thiem 2010: 69).

> Ils savent qu'on n'est réellement heureux que par l'âme, fort que par l'intelligence, et que ces facultés sublimes ne se développent qu'au contact de la civilisation. La civilisation n'est pas exclusive; elle attire au lieu de repousser. C'est par elle que doit s'opérer l'alliance du genre humain. Grâce à sa toute-puissante influence, il n'y aura bientôt sur la terre ni noirs, ni blancs, ni jaunes, ni Africaines, ni Européens, ni Asiatiques, ni Américaines: il y aura des frères. Elle poursuit de ses lumières la barbarie qui se cache. Partout où celle-ci, de sa voix mourante, conseille la guerre, la civilisation prêche la paix; et quand retentit le mot haine, elle répond amour. (Bergeaud 1859: 324)[5]

This rigorous orientation toward European values means that the African sphere, also evoked in the novel, remains a place of memory alone.[6] Thiem emphasizes rightly that here the actual civilizational values for establishing a cultural identity are directly connected to the European value system, and that the African space is therefore reduced from the status of a dynamic field of action to the purely imaginary status of a memory that has become static. This memory is one-dimensional and does not convey any movement. The author uses this national myth to attempt to lead Haiti out of the position of the Other and into the ranks of Western nations. In *Stella*, nation building takes place as an allegorical spatialization of historical time and events. Its allegorical character expresses itself in abstract figures, but is reduced to a static image (Thiem 2010: 74–76). The treatment of space in the novel is immediately noticeable as a structuring framework. A variety of different spaces arise that are characterized by their own semantic unity and therefore also by their demarcation from each other.

---

5 "They know that one can only be truly happy via the soul and achieve strength with intelligence, and that these sublime faculties can only be developed after contact with civilization. Civilization does not exclude; it attracts rather than repels. It is through it that human bonds must be constructed. Thanks to its all-powerful influence, soon there will be no blacks, no whites, no yellows, no Africans, no Europeans, no Asians, no Americans, but only brothers. Civilization dispels, with all its light, barbarity when it wishes to hide. Wherever barbarity, in its dying voice, counsels war, civilization advocates for peace. When the word hate is uttered, civilization answers love" (Bergeaud 2014: 201).
6 Cf. Thiem 2010: 76.

2 Louis de Maynard de Queilhe: *Outre-mer* (1835)

Maynard de Queilhe is a Béké, a member of Martinique's white Creole upper class, which, in 1835, the year of *Outre-mer*'s publication, was primarily concerned with preserving the old order of things. Its wealth was mostly based on the successful functioning of the plantation economy, which relied on slavery. The *Békés* viewed revolutionary thinking from Europe – philanthropic ideas in general and the abolition of slavery in particular – as a great danger. When the Revolution of July 1830 arrived, it seemed to them as though the nightmare of 1789 was just being repeated all over again. The novel *Outre-mer* paints a picture of a society that is stuck and a Creole caste driven by fear of losing its old privileges. As a member of the literate Creole upper class, Maynard de Queilhe projects plenty of self-assurance in the preface: "Les colons ne se considèrent que comme des passagers sur une terre d'exil; ils ont toujours les ailes entrouvertes, pour regagner leur ancienne patrie" (Maynard de Queilhe 1835: I, 13).[7] At most, we might be able to detect a spatial indecisiveness with regard to the book's audience: "Il est ensuite beaucoup de choses de ce livre qui paraîtront étranges, tantôt aux personnes du pays où je suis, tantôt aux personnes du pays où vous êtes" (Maynard de Queilhe 1835: I, 12).[8] Alienation on both sides of the Atlantic? Not really, because in each case he is talking about the upper class, whether Continental French or, correspondingly, Creole. Although he was born there himself, Maynard de Queilhe had an experience of exile on the Antilles that was marked by longing for the mother country.

The novel has three geographical settings: Martinique as a colony, France as the mother country (*mère-patrie*), and the ship, which is clearly bound for the French mother country. The ship's focus on its destination and the straightness of its route, however, only emphasize the bipolarity between mother country and colony. Crucially, this spatial bipolarity is also reflected in the textual space: first, on the level of the constellation of protagonists, namely good Creoles, evil Blacks, and the supposedly noble mulatto who is unmasked at the end as a rebellious Satan; and second, on the level of the book's literary role models, because the Martinique-born Maynard de Queilhe's reliance on Bernardin de Saint-Pierre, Victor Hugo and Georges Sand is omnipresent, in the sense of René Girard's mimetic theory or, to use the vocabulary of postcolonial theory, as

---

[7] "The colonists only think of themselves as travelers in a land of exile; they always have their wings half-spread, ready to return to their former homeland."
[8] "There are, therefore, many things in this book which will seem strange, whether to the people of the country where I am or to the people of the country where you are."

mimicry.⁹ It is for good reason that Maynard de Queilhe's mimetic proceedings have been compared to the tropical climbing liana plant (Bongie 1998: 319). Lianas shoot into the air without branching; the colonial offshoots cluster around the mother plant. The bipolar spatial structure that is found in *Outre-mer* is also underscored by Martinique's function as an island. This, too, takes place in the context of a nineteenth century trend in island motifs: as with the Île de Bourbon (actually Réunion Island) in George Sand's *Indiana* or Île de France (that is, Mauritius) in Bernardin de Saint-Pierre's *Paul et Virginie*, Martinique is characterized by an island semantics of isolation and exile (Ette 2005: 143). The protagonist Marius laments:

> Une misérable petite île! moins qu'une île, une espèce d'îlet; des fièvres, des serpents et des êtres qui se donnent des coups de fouet, parce qu'ils ne sont pas tous également jaunes, ou parce que les uns le sont trop et les autres pas assez; ou parce qu'il y en a qui ne le sont pas du tout. Misère! Misères! (Maynard de Queilhe 1835: I, 42)¹⁰

3 María de las Mercedes Santa Cruz y Montalvo (Condesa de Merlín): *La Havane* (1844)

The third example – *La Havane*, in which an author confronts her experience of cultural and spatial deracination – is an outlier when compared to the first two works described above. In Gastón Baquero's introduction to Condesa Merlín's literary work, the line "A Cuban who writes is not always a Cuban writer" (1975: 8) already highlights the central problem that any critical engagement with the writer and musician, who was born in Cuba in 1789 and died in Paris in 1852, must confront. The plurality of her names speaks for itself. María de las Mercedes Santa Cruz y Montalvo is better known as Condesa de Merlín or otherwise Comtesse Merlin (Díaz 1994: 58). The fact that she primarily wrote in French may explain her absence from the official canon of nineteenth-century Cuban literature.

---

9 The lack of originality in nineteenth-century literature from the French Antilles – Patrick Chamoiseau and Raphaël Confiant have called it *littérature doudouiste* – is practically a cliché of Franco-Caribbean literary studies. However, this conclusion does not subtract from the cultural-historical wealth available from a close analysis of the mimetic process.

10 "A miserable little island! Not even an island, a sort of islet; fevers, snakes, and people lashing out at each other because they are not all equally yellow, or because some are overly so and others not enough; or because there are some who are not yellow at all. Misery! Miseries!"

Shortly after her birth, her family emigrated to Madrid, and she herself grew up in Cuba with her grandmother, until age twelve, whereupon she followed her family to Spain. There, she married the French Count Antoine Christophe Merlin (1771–1839), a general in the Napoleonic army (Méndez Rodenas 1990: 708). In 1812, after Napoleon's defeat, the Merlins were forced to leave Spain – with the whole French community there – and the couple settled in Paris. During the period from 1813 to 1839, the Creole Santa Cruz y Montalvo became one of the leading *bellesdames* of the Parisian cultural establishment. Her salon at 40 Rue de Bondy attracted important musicians and literati of the era. In 1840, precisely a year after her husband's death – by which point she had been living in France for some 38 years – she traveled to Cuba for several weeks.

As an outcome of that journey, her travelogue *La Havane* was published in three volumes. Whereas the first stops on her trip, several cities on the East Coast of the United States, are consistently described from the distanced perspective of an outsider – the Condesa characterizes herself as "[É]trangère à tous ce qui m'entoure" (Condesa de Merlín 1844: I, 65)[11] – this self-representation and attitude abruptly shifts upon her arrival in Cuba. The author now presents herself as a patriotic Cuban describing her own, familiar country. In the preface, she writes to the Capitán General: "Permettez, général, que je place sous votre égide protectrice cette œuvre conçue par le sentiment patriotique d'une femme; le désir ardent de voir mon pays heureux me l'a seul inspirée" (Condesa de Merlín 1844: I, 5).[12] The book is dedicated "To my compatriots" ("À mes compatriotes"; Condesa de Merlín 1844: I, 7).

Montalvo constantly references the *Crónicas de las Indias*, and particularly Columbus, in her descriptions of the island.[13] At the very beginning, she paraphrases the explorer's *Diario de a bordo*; upon arriving in Cuba, he – like her – believed he had reached the most beautiful country in the world. She invokes its *loci amoeni* on various occasions. This fits with her stylized and exalted portrayal of Cuba's indigenous population, which by then had essentially been annihilated (Díaz 1994: 62):

> À quelque distance, et plus prêt de la côte, je découvre le village de Puerto Escondido; à ces chaumières de forme conique, couvertes jusqu'à terre de branches de palmiers; aux buissons touffus de bananiers qui, de leurs larges feuilles, protègent les maisons contre

---

11 "[A] stranger to everything around me."
12 "Allow me, general, to place this work, conceived by a woman's patriotic feeling, under your protective auspices; it was inspired solely by the ardent desire to see my country happy."
13 In regard to her continuous use of other sources – even exposed as plagiarism in one case – Silvia Molloy writes: "Rediscovery came [. . .] less from what she saw on that trip than from what she read, remembered and imagined" (Molloy 1991: 93, see also Ianes 1997: 214).

les ardeurs du soleil; à ces pirogues amarrées sur le rivage, et à la quiétude silencieuse de l'heure de midi, vous diriez que ces plages sont encore habitées par des Indiens. (Condesa de Merlín 1844: I, 276)[14]

Thus, the Condesa's descriptions of nature feature multiple overlapping layers of time, which are, however, always marked by the tension between the claim of speaking as a Cuban and the European gaze of the "explorer," a tension that also pervades the following quote:

> Lorsque j'aperçois ces palmiers séculaires, qui courbent leur orgueilleux feuillage jusqu'au bord de la mer, je crois voir les ombres de ces grands guerriers, de ces hommes de résolution et de volonté, compagnons de Colomb et de Vélazquez; je les vis, fiers de leurs plus belles découvertes, s'incliner dans leurs reconnaissance devant l'Océan, pour le remercier d'un si magnifique présent. (Condesa de Merlín 1844: I, 269)[15]

Just like the Spanish conquistadors, she views Cuba's greatness and beauty as a gift to the European newcomers. Although her almost stubborn self-stylization as a Cuban is undeniable, some passages simultaneously resonate with a fragile experience of identity, as if she were asking: *Who am I, now that I am here in the tropics? A countess or a Creole? Santa Cruz y Montalvo or the Condesa de Merlín?*[16] On the literary level, this ambivalence is also reflected in the use of possessive pronouns whose antecedents are often difficult to pin down. For example, who are "*our* poets"? Are they French, Spanish, or Cuban? This is not clearly indicated by the text, given that "nos" and "notre" frequently refer to locations on both sides of the Atlantic: "nos plus riches hôtels de Paris" (Condesa de Merlín 1844: I, 74 f.), "notre monde européen" (Condesa de Merlín 1844: II, 49), "nos élégants de salon"

---

14 "Some distance away, and closer to the coast, I come upon the village of Puerto Escondido: from those conical cottages, covered with palm branches all the way down to the ground; from the bushy banana trees whose large leaves protect the houses from the heat of the sun; from these canoes moored along the shoreline; and from the silent quietude of the noon hour, you would say that these beaches are still inhabited by Indians."
15 "When I perceive these age-old palm trees, which bend their proud foliage right down to the edge of the sea, I feel as though I am seeing the shadows of those great warriors, those men of resolution and will, the companions of Columbus and Velazquez; I see them, proud of their most wonderful discoveries, bowing down in their gratitude in front of the Ocean to thank it for such a magnificent gift."
16 Méndez Rodenas 1990: 709. This turmoil also finds a clear expression in her memoirs, published in 1836: "There are two 'I's within myself that constantly struggle with each other, but I always encourage the 'strong' one, not because it is 'stronger' but because it is the more wretched, the one that achieves nothing. (Existen en mi dos 'yo' que luchan constantemente, pero estimulo siempre al 'fuerte,' no por ser el 'más fuerte' sino porque es el más desgraciado, el que nada consigue.)" *Souvenirs et mémoires de Madame la Comtesse Merlin, publiés par elle-même*, Paris, 1836, p. 246, quoted in Méndez Rodenas 1990: 80.

(Condesa de Merlín 1844: II, 54), but also "Nos *guajiros*" (Condesa de Merlín 1844: II, 51; cf. Díaz 1994: 63).

La Havane is an important example of the "unhousedness" that is so characteristic of Cuban literature, and rests on a series of dichotomies: Cuba–France, Spanish–French, local *costumbrismo*–European exoticism, memory–present. To conclude, using George Steiner's terminology, a preliminary close reading of her work conveys a sense of extraterritoriality (Steiner 1972). If we consider the struggle around "Cubanness" in the context of her colonial agenda, the author's true sense of identity is inevitably fractured. Yet the othering perception of the landscape underscores the outsider's view: like Maynard de Queilhe, the Condesa de Merlín stages the Caribbean region as a European construct.

4 Eugenio María de Hostos: *La peregrinación de Bayoán* (1863)

> [. . .] ir a Cuba, al Darién, del Darién al Perú; del Perú al Méjico; de Méjico a La Habana [. . .] y en Nuevitas quedarme para ir a Cat Island (San Salvador de Colón, indiana Guanahaní) y al volver, visitar a los amigos [. . . .], que en tanto empeño tiene en que me prepare, para mi peregrinación a Europa [. . .]. (Hostos 1988: 108)[17]

This quotation, out of the mouth of the homeless protagonist in *La peregrinación de Bayoán*, has an implicit political program: the utopia of a search for a universal Caribbean identity (Thiem 2010: 184). In an obvious allusion to Christopher Columbus's travel journals, the novel, written in the form of a travel diary, begins with notations for October 12th, the day of Columbus's discovery of America. The young Puerto Rican Bayoán, whose name is borrowed "from the first native of Boriquen who doubted the Spaniards' immortality" (according to Hostos, in the novel's guide to names), leaves his home island by ship with the goal, at first only vaguely formulated, of visiting the Caribbean islands and the Latin American mainland (Thiem 2010: 186).

In this novel, the ship, unlike in *Outre-mer*, represents a kind of threshold space. It can be seen as a vehicle that crosses the boundaries of time frames, transporting the protagonist from one level to another, thus allowing an oscillation between time frames and spaces: "El viento empujaba a la fragata, y la

---

[17] "Going to Cuba, to Darién, from Darién to Peru, from Peru to Mexico, from Mexico to Havana [. . .] and staying in Nuevitas to go to Cat Island (San Salvador de Colón, the Indian Guanahaní) and then, when I return, visiting my friends [. . .] and with all this effort preparing myself for my pilgrimage to Europe."

fragata andaba como ando yo, empujado por un viento que aún no sé si lleva a puerto" (Hostos 1988: 192).[18] Bayoán is torn back and forth between the Antilles and Spain (and wants to prove his strength to Spain); his inner struggle has to do with the future direction of his life (Thiem 2010: 199). This ever-present conflict and process of initiation leads him to develop his consciousness, so that at the end, he, who was homeless, clearly realizes where his voyage is going to lead: "America is my homeland" ("América es mi patria"; Hostos 1988: 355; Thiem 2010: 199). Bayoán's pilgrimage structures the literary space: "Yo soy un hombre errante en un desierto, y mi único oasis eres tú [se está dirigiendo a su patria]. Yo soy un peregrino. . . ¿Necesito peregrinar? Pues, ¡adelante!" (Hostos 1988: 18).[19]

His voyage appears as a multidimensional search, an expression of openness but also of foreignness; the pilgrimage motif includes being oriented towards a goal but also the idea of the journey as the goal. This results in a circular structure that is broken in many places. In taking on the pilgrimage as a literary subject, the open status of the pilgrimage is constitutive, which is primarily significant in the way it structures space. The circular structure, which is constitutive for the pilgrimage motif, is no coincidence, given that Hostos's allusion to Columbus's logbook is so crucial. It was after all the return to his starting point in Europe (and the honor the Catholic monarchs accorded him there) that gave meaning and legitimacy to Columbus's voyage of discovery, with its first stop in the Antilles.

Pilgrimage is a very fundamental literary motif in the nineteenth century. The single greatest bestseller of that time was Lord Byron's *Childe Harold's Pilgrimage: A Romaunt*; as l have already mentioned in the context of Bergeaud.[20] Hostos himself expressed a deep admiration for Byron. He was ultimately less interested in freedom, which only concerned Puerto Rico, than in sketching out a complete Spanish-American project that included the beginnings of an Antillean confederation. In Hostos's work, the Caribbean region is conveyed as a multirelational model whose liberating power derives from that same multirelationality. Although the clearly political dimension belongs to an earlier century, the

---

18 "The wind pushed the frigate, and the frigate walked the way that I walk, pushed by a wind about which I still do not know whether it leads to port."
19 "I am a man wandering in a desert, and you [addressing his homeland] are my only oasis. I am a pilgrim. Must I make this pilgrimage? Well then, onward!"
20 Byron was extremely popular, and with the publication of *Childe Harold* in 1812, 1816, and 1818, Byron became famous overnight. The protagonists of such canonical Latin American novels as Jorge Isaacs's *María* and José Mármol's *Amalia* can be found reading the book. How can we explain this fashion? Is it the romantic symbol per se of an unbridled yearning for freedom? Is it the fascination with the sublime image of the ocean: unlimited, timeless, not subject to humankind?

pilgrimage motif can definitely be read as an early form of nomadism, à la Vilém Flusser, or of the rhizomatic migrant, à la Deleuze/Guattari. The most convincing reading is Hostos's anticipation of the ideas of Édouard Glissant, specifically Glissant's concept of *Antillanité*, which is not based on any one-dimensional nationalistic perspective but, rather, on the structure of the mangrove. The dense mangrove forests present us with a topological image that is also of central significance for our final literary example.[21]

5 Maryse Condé: *Traversée de la Mangrove* (1989)

The space–time configurations in the nineteenth-century Caribbean novels examined here tend to be static in nature. Yet their descriptions of the Caribbean region – especially in the works of Hostos and Condesa de Merlín – update the multilayered historical depths inscribed within themselves, revealing their significance largely in relation to the protagonists' and authors' complex, and sometimes fragile, experiences of identity. Against this backdrop, let us now consider a twentieth-century Caribbean novel: Maryse Condé's *Traversée de la Mangrove*, published in 1989.[22]

In the novel, Condé cedes authorship – at least in part – to her protagonist Francis Sancher alias Francisco Alvarez Sanchez, who, as his ex-lover Vilma reports, has worked on a manuscript titled *Traversée de la Mangrove* himself:[23]

> —Tu vois, j'écris. Ne me demande pas à quoi ça sert. D'ailleurs, je ne finirai jamais ce livre puisque, avant d'en avoir tracé la première ligne et de savoir ce que je vais y mettre de sang, de rires, de larmes, de peur, d'espoir, enfin de tout ce qui fait qu'un livre est un livre et non pas une dissertation de raseur, la tête à demi fêlée, j'en ai déjà trouvé le titre: 'Traversée de la Mangrove.'
> J'ai haussé les épaules.
> —On ne traverse pas la mangrove. On s'empale sur les racines des palétuviers. On s'enterre et on étouffe dans la boue saumâtre.
> —C'est ça, c'est justement ça." (Condé 1989: 202–203; cf. Ette 2003: 264)[24]

---

21 For more on the mangrove metaphor, see also the monograph by Juliane Tauchnitz (2014).
22 For more on *Traversée de la Mangrove*, see Ottmar Ette's fundamental interpretation (2003).
23 For more on strategies of authorship in Condé's work, see Gewecke (2000: 171).
24 "You see, I'm writing. Don't ask me what's the point of it. Besides, I'll never finish this book because before I've even written the first line and known what I'm going to put in the

According to some interpreters of this dual authorship structure, a female writer like Maryse Condé was necessary in order to complete the project of a "rhizomatic" identity à la Deleuze and Guattari (1977: 28, see Ette 2003: 284ff.) and render the mangrove roots navigable. Unlike those of ordinary trees, which are anchored deep in the ground – that is, in history – mangrove roots extend laterally above the surface, connected like an offset to a parent plant. In this novel, I also perceive a call for a *identité relationnelle* – as distinguished from an *identité racine* in Édouard Glissant's definition (1990/1997) – yet I believe that the question of the specific space-time network generated by the narrative takes on greater significance.

The book takes place in a self-contained rural microcosm, the remote Guadeloupian village of Rivière au Sel, during the wake for the late Francis Sancher. Each of the novel's twenty chapters is the story of a different narrator, each of whom participates in the wake. Although the locals seem to have previously lived quite solitary and uncommunicative lives in each other's vicinity, their interwoven connections as revealed by the individual stories generate a sense of community. Sancher's mysterious death not only brings together the people at the funeral but makes them realize the dynamic of their web of relationships. The protagonist of Sancher – a center point around which the polyphonic voices circle, centrifuge-style – serves as a blank space in several respects. First, no one knows any specifics of his past. The locals viewed him with suspicion and considered him an outsider for many years until the stories told during the wake reveal they all have specific relationships with him. Second, though he has worked on the manuscript of *Traversée de la Mangrove* and gave up on it, concluding it was a hopeless endeavor, he is the only character who does not get a turn as a narrator. His novel project, as an attempt at a *constructed* identity, is doomed to failure because relational identity can no longer be *described* by a single author (Malena 1999: 69). Here Sancher's death, and thus abandonment of any individual initiative, is the precondition for the group's initiative. Barthes's dictum about the death of the author is literally carried out, except that the author's authority gives way not to the self-referentiality of an anonymous subject-less text, but to polyphony and *mutual* referentiality.

---

way of blood, laughter, tears, fears, and hope, well, everything that makes a book a book, . . . I've already found the title: 'Crossing the Mangrove.'

I shrugged my shoulders.

You don't cross a mangrove. You'd spike yourself on the roots of the mangrove trees. You'd be sucked down and suffocated by the brackish mud.

Yes, that's it, that's precisely it." (Condé 1995: 158).

Because the frame story is restricted to the night of the wake, the narrative time is extraordinarily compact and crowded, which intensifies the sense of synchrony amongst the diverse interpersonal connections. This specific narrative situation conceals a multi-layered temporal dimension: the circle of shared stories is situated at the intersection between an immutable past and a dynamic present, gesturing toward an open-ended future that lies within the players' own power. In the diachronic perspective, as a self-contained history, each story refers back to the past, pointing at individual experiences but also collective ones. In the synchronic perspective, as open communication, the histories (plural!) within the stories become the basis of encounter and of a pluralistic exchange. It is each individual's respective personal history and origins – and not their homogeneity as a group – that enables their distinct perspectives on what they have in common. Specifically, the novel exhibits their memory of the deceased and thus of their shared village, which serves as a miniature stand-in for the whole island and contemporary Guadeloupe.

6 Conclusion

As we have seen, Sigrid Weigel's thesis that the theme of displacement has replaced the conventional migration concepts of exile and diaspora cannot be argued equally for all the novels examined here. And yet the toolkit of spatial theory provides important keys to the basic understanding of postcolonial positioning and constructions of identity. Guadeloupe and Martinique have not lost their colonial status to this day, but have merely been structurally converted into French *Départements*. The political and cultural gravitational pull of French colonialism was far more formative and effective than the Spanish model. Thus, in *Outre-mer*, the concept of exile works strikingly well. The binary opposition between the metropolis and the colony is unbroken there. The novel can be read as a perfect example of the "mapping of empire" in Edward Said's use of the term (Bachmann-Medick 2006: 235).

In *Stella*, the much more complicated spatial structure suggests that the multirelationalism of young Haitian society has far-reaching spatial implications. *Stella* represents colonial independence. The individual spaces in *Stella*, however, appear to be very static. This has to do with the irresolvable contradiction in the Haitian sense of self, proclaiming political independence while simultaneously affirming cultural dependence.²⁵ Because Haiti constitutes a special case, not only in the Caribbean but throughout the Western Hemisphere, it is unsurprising that its spatial perspectives diverge from those of the other novels.

The novels of Maynard de Queilhe and the Condesa de Merlín stage the colonial gaze of the European who attempts to combine varied elements into a broader landscape – and thus into a delimitable unit. Although a fragile identity construction is sometimes evident in the Condesa's at times contradictory positioning, *La Havane* – like *Outre-mer* – represents an affirmation of the colonial status quo, whereas Hostos's novel *La peregrinación de Baoyán* is based on the element of movement. *La peregrinación de Bayoán*'s understanding of the Caribbean archipelago projects an island-based logic and emphasizes the internal relationality of that logic (Ette 2005: 153). In this novel, the Caribbean symbolizes the concept of a "third space" (in Bhabha's usage of that term), which offered itself beyond the "hypnoses [of] Europe and Africa" (Bernabé et al. 2002: 22, cited in Ette 2003: 256). Where *Outre-mer* and *La Havane* present a colonial discourse, oriented towards Europe, and *Stella* puts forward an anticolonial discourse, oriented towards Africa, what we find in *La peregrinación de Bayoán* is a different, postcolonial discourse, one which enables a new kind of spatial conception. *Bayoán* is a truly pan-American discourse, with independence-minded traditions, making reference to the connections across all of the Americas. Although nineteenth-century writings do not manifest the same kind of radical structure of movement that we see in twentieth- and twenty-first-century texts, *La peregrinación de Bayoán* and, to a certain extent, *Stella* as well, do anticipate Glissant's assertion of a relational conception of space. The spatial turn asserts that it refers not to physical space nor to natural space but to socially produced space as a dynamic process. Physics and nature are undeniably important categories for the nineteenth century, and a present-day interpretation would not be possible without them. And yet theories of interconnectedness, relationality, and movement that arose in the late twentieth century raise our awareness of dimensions that were already more present in the nineteenth century than has been assumed. The four narratives of that era convey the intersections that result from the simultaneity of unequal spaces and territories, the ways in which spaces are charged through imperial inscriptions, hidden hierarchies, displaced experiences, and breaks in continuity, phenomena that then become the predominant

---

25 Symptomatic of this is the famous line by Massillon Coicou: "Oh France, we love you, like many, no doubt. / Of your own children will never love you" ("Oui, France, nous t'aimons beaucoup, comme plusieurs de tes propres enfants ne t'aimerons jamais"; Coicou 1892: 113).

theme in Maryse Condé's 1989 novel *Traversée de la Mangrove*. Of course, the notions of identity proposed here are fragmented and decentralized by nature. They call for dissolving authorial authority in favor of a plurality of narrators whose very identities – that is, whose dynamic context – is first constituted by the overlaps and entanglements among their stories. These stories are merged without a single stage direction, as if autonomously, into the microcosmic mosaic, thus demonstrating that the narratives' cohesion and equivalence are not due to an overarching general principle – as would be symbolized, for example, by a superordinate narrator – but can instead be attributed solely to their own joint initiative of *prise de parole*.

Bibliography

Bachmann-Medick, Doris (2006): *Cultural turns. Neuorientierungen in den Kulturwissenschaften*. Reinbek bei Hamburg: Rowohlt-Taschenbuch-Verlag.

Baquero, Gastón (1975): "Introducción a la novela." In: Baez, Vicente (ed.): *La Enciclopedia de Cuba, Vol. 3: Novela, costumbrismo*. San Juan/Madrid: Enciclopedia y clásicos cubanos, pp. 1–21.

Bergeaud, Émeric (2014): *Stella*, translated by Adriana Umaña Hossman. N.p.: Markus Wiener. (*Stella*, edited by Beaubrun Ardouin. Paris: E. Dentu, 1859).

Bernabé, Jean/ Chamoiseau,Patrick/ Confiant,Raphaël (2002 [1989]): *Éloge de la Créolité*. Paris: Gallimard.

Bongie, Chris (1998): *Islands and Exiles. The Creole Identities of Post/Colonial Literature*. Stanford: Stanford University Press.

Chateaubriand, François-René de (2014): *Memoirs from beyond the Tomb*, translated by Robert Baldick. London: Penguin Classics. (*Mémoires d'outre-tombe* [1848], edited by Maurice Levaillant. Paris: Gallimard, 1958).

Coicou, Massillon (1892): *Poésies nationales*. Paris: Goupy et Jourdan.

Condé, Maryse (1995): *Crossing the Mangrove*, translated by Richard Philcox. New York: Anchor Books. (*Traversée de la Mangrove*. Paris: Mercure de France, 1989).

Condesa de Merlín, Maria de las Mercedes Santa Cruz y Montalvo (1844): *La Havane*. 3 vols. Paris: Amyot.

Deleuze, Gilles/Guattari, Félix (1977): *Rhizome: Introduction*. Paris: Minuit.

Díaz, Roberto Ignacio (1994): "Merlin's Foreign House. The Genres of La Havane." In: *Cuban Studies*, 24, pp. 57–82.

Ette, Ottmar (2005): "Von Inseln, Grenzen und Vektoren. Versuch über die fraktale Inselwelt der Karibik." In: Braig, Marianne et al. (eds.): *Grenzen der Macht – Macht der Grenzen. Lateinamerika im globalen Kontext*. Frankfurt am Main: Vervuert, pp. 135–180.

Ette, Ottmar (2003): "Crossing the Mangrove." In: *Literature on the Move*, translated by Katharina Vester. Amsterdam: Rodopi, pp. 255–294.

Gewecke, Frauke (2000): "Der Titel als Chiffre einer Subversion. 'Moi, Tituba, sorcière . . . Noire de Salem' von Maryse Condé." In: Mecke, Jochen/Rothe, Arnold (eds.): *Titel – Text – Kontext. Randbezirke des Textes. Festschrift für Arnold Rothe zum 65. Geburtstag*. Glienicke/Berlin: Galda + Wilch, pp. 159–177.

Glissant, Édouard (1997): *Poetics of Relation*, translated by Betsy Wing. Ann Arbor: University of Michigan. (*Poétique de la relation*. Paris: Gallimard, 1990).

Hostos, Eugenio María (1988 [1863]): "La peregrinación de Bayoán." In: Hostos, Eugenio María: *Obras completas*, ed. Julio López. Río Piedras: Editorial de la Universidad de Puerto Rico.

Ianes, Raúl (1997): "La esfericidad del papel. Gertrudis Gómez de Avellaneda, la condesa de Merlín y la literatura de viajes." In: *Revista Iberoamericana*, LXIII, 178–179 (January to June), pp. 209–218.

Malena, Anne (1999): *The Negotiated Self. The Dynamics of Identity in Francophone Caribbean Narrative*. New York: Lang.

Maynard de Queilhe, Louis de (1835): *Outre-mer*, 2 vols. Paris: Renduel.

Méndez Rodenas, Adriana (1990): "A Journey to the (Literary) Source. The Invention of Origins in Merlin's Viaje a La Habana." In: *New Literary History*, 21, 3, pp. 707–731.

Molloy, Sylvia (1991): *At Face Value. Autobiographical Writing in Spanish America*. Cambridge: Cambridge University Press.

Müller, Gesine (2018): *Crossroads of Colonial Cultures. Caribbean Literatures in the Age of Revolution*. Berlin/Boston: De Gruyter.

Steiner, George (1972): *Extraterritorial: Papers on Literature and the Language Revolution*. London: Faber and Faber.

Tauchnitz, Juliane (2014): *La Créolité dans le contexte du discours international et postcolonial du métissage et de l'hybridité. De la mangrove au rhizome*. Paris: L'Harmattan.

Thiem, Annegret (2010): *Rauminszenierungen. Literarischer Raum in der karibischen Prosaliteratur des 19. Jahrhunderts*. Berlin/Münster: Lit.

Weigel, Sigrid (2002): "Zum 'topographical turn.' Kartographie, Topographie und Raumkonzepte in den Kulturwissenschaften." In: *KulturPoetik*, 2, 2, pp. 151–165.

Welge, Jobst (2021): "Locations, Orientations and Multiple Temporalities in the Contemporary, 'Global' Latin American Novel." In: Ekelund, Bo G./Mahmutović, Adnan/Wulff, Helena (eds.): *Claiming Space. Locations and Orientations in World Literatures*. New York: Bloomsbury Academic USA, pp. 193–216.

Sarah Burnautzki
Dissolution of Time and Space in *Memórias postumas de Brás Cubas*

1 Time and Space – Two "Misplaced Ideas"?

In a seminal essay from 1973, Brazilian literary theorist Roberto Schwarz develops the concept of "misplaced ideas." He puts forward the influential proposition that "foreign" ideas such as European liberalism entered inevitably into a relationship of discrepancy with social and political reality in Brazil, in as much as they were not "appropriate" to the Brazilian economic system which was based on the exploitation of slave labor and oriented toward the export market.[1] I am concerned here first and foremost with the spatial metaphor, the latent normative notion of the "right" and the "wrong place" of ideas that Schwarz employs to describe patterns of interaction between Latin American and European cultures.[2] Indeed, the relations of different literatures to one another within theoretical discussions of literature and literary history are often expressed in spatial and temporal terms. "Center" and "periphery," the idea of "being ahead of one's time" and literary 'belatedness' are highly ambivalent metaphors in this context, which can both critically highlight or naturalize and legitimize relations of inequality and domination.[3]

---

[1] Schwarz's reflections have been controversial in Brazil: Already after the publication of his essay, sociologist Carvalho Franco argued that slavery and liberalism, as well as free capitalist market economy, were not only compatible, but rather closely intertwined in Brazil and accused him of falling into that dualism of Europe and Brazil, centre and periphery, which he actually wanted to fight, with the idea of 'misplaced ideas' (Carvalho Franco 1976 cit. in Palti 2006: 153–156).
[2] For a comprehensive and critical discussion of the essay, see Palti (2006).
[3] Sociologist Manuela Botacă points out that the boundary-setting power with which Europe has historically designed diverse fluctuating cognitive and imperial maps to legitimize the asymmetrical difference between its self-definition and its absolute Other has always been temporally, spatially, and ontologically structured. According to her, the evolutionist notion that humanity had to undergo a linear development of several successive stages from an original state of nature to Western civilization justified a temporal demarcation and the notion that essential differences between Europeans and non-Europeans could be explained via insurmountable natural categories such as primitive-civilized, irrational-rational, traditional-

Sarah Burnautzki, Universität Heidelberg

I would like to combine the critical questioning of temporal and spatial concepts as theoretical operators with my reflections on Machado de Assis's novel *Memórias postumas de Brás Cubas* (The Posthumous Memoirs of *Brás Cubas*, 1881), which in some respects enters into a dissonant relationship with its immediate literary environment shaped by evolutionist theories of European provenance. Influenced by European evolutionist theories, which conceive of Brazilian civilization as evolutionarily 'backward' on an imaginary timeline that at the same time allows European civilization to be imagined as 'modern,' Brazilian intellectuals in the nineteenth century searched for the adequate literary expression of Brazilian reality and elevated naturalism to the model of their national identity.[4] Machado de Assis's unique push against the aesthetic dogmatism of his contemporaries[5] can be plausibly interpreted as a literary strategy oriented not toward local regionalism but toward international models (such as Cervantes, Shakespeare, Sterne, and others), thus claiming to measure itself against the "Greenwich Meridian," another (Eurocentric) spatial metaphor with which Pascal Casanova expresses the unequal struggle for the legitimate definition of world literature in the international literary space.[6] What remains problematic is the latently hierarchizing perpetuation of inequality relations as a never fully catchable temporal and spatial distance inherent in this latently Eurocentric and deterministic theoretical perspective.

But how can the hegemonic implications of the metaphors of time and space be transcended? Can the categories of time and space be "dissolved" or replaced by others? As the example of the *Memoirs* shows, narrative work on the categories of time and space is also productive for the critical reflection of

---

modern, entitled both a spatial and an ontological demarcation within cognitive maps (Botacă 2010: 29).

4 For an overview of the literary debates of the "geração de 1870" and its struggle for an authentic national identity and national literature, see Ventura 1992.

5 Influenced by positivism, his contemporaries experimented with French naturalism in search of an "estilo tropical," such as Araripe Junior, or undertook, like Sílvio Romero, the attempt to make evolutionism the method of literary criticism, as is especially evidenced by his ostentatiously racist treatment of Machado's work.

6 Although Casanova develops a sophisticated model in Bourdieu's wake and, drawing on the Marxist concept of capital, describes the unequal distribution of symbolic capital in world literature, her approach remains Eurocentric. According to her approach, structurally disadvantaged authors of peripheral literatures use specific literary strategies in the struggle for recognition in order to make up for the literary backwardness of their respective national literature in the context of an international perspective. However, even this approach is not free of normative, evaluative implications and teleological premises (Casanova 1999).

literary theory and points to possibilities of overcoming the normative implications and teleological premises associated with the concepts of time and space.

2 Abolition of Time and Space through the Construction of a Paradoxical Narrative Situation

Machado de Assis's *Memórias postumas de Brás Cubas* is a novel of the late 19th century and contains virtually no descriptions of landscape. At best, it can be considered metaphorically as a "journey through time," insofar as the fictional narrating author Brás Cubas *recalls* his past life, thus *traveling in it* in a metaphorical sense, and making it the *quasi-present subject* of the plot. Yet the question of the novelistic construction of space and time has broader implications for this novel as well: as categories subject to historical change, space and time are not regarded as coordinates objectively located in the "world" but rather as constitutive components and *products of cognitive processes* and thus as significantly involved in the construction of symbolic orders of knowledge (see Bruns 2017: 5). Just as the concrete spatial or landscape design of a novel can provide information about the construction of symbolic orders of a certain time, the intentional fading out of spatial references, the reduction of spatial representations, or the drastic renunciation of referential effects must therefore also be determined as aesthetic procedures that can be questioned in terms of function and meaning. The direct connection between the categories of space and time as instruments of perception, cognition, and thus of the constitution of meaning and knowledge suggests that a signal function is inherent in the renunciation of a referential framework for the novelistic space. Time plays a special role in Brás Cubas' memoirs, that much is certain. As early as the 1980s, Paula Speck pointed out that the most important insight into the *conditio humana* may not be conveyed here through the level of action, but rather made possible through formal procedures, especially those that convey temporal structures (see Speck 1981: 7).

Let us first turn to the narrative structures in terms of time and space and examine the novel's narrative situation. The classic autodiegetic situation, which is characteristic for memoirs, a literary subgenre of autobiography, allows for an assumed identity in the threefold sense of author, narrating and experiencing self, a primarily temporal gradation of the narration in two dimensions or narrative levels[7]: The frame plot of the *narrating* I and the internal plot of the *experiencing* I. Although considered as identical to each other, both I's share neither the same time nor the same place within the fiction. In a significant departure from autobiography however, the situation in *Memórias postumas de Brás Cubas* has an ironic double meaning. On the one hand, the typical situation of memoirs, i.e., the expected identity between author, narrator, and protagonist, is subverted, insofar as the *figure* of Brás Cubas presents itself as a *fictitious author* and a narrator who positions himself at an ironic distance from the real author Machado de Assis as well as from the expectations of an audience that trusts the reading pact of autobiographical genres.[8] On the other hand, this ironic twist comes to a climax in as much as the narrator presents himself as *dead* at a significant point at the beginning of the novel: "eu não sou pròpriamente um autor defunto, mas um defunto autor" (Machado de Assis 1971: 513).[9] This statement has a programmatic character. While fictional autobiography, that is, the presence of a narrative function that playfully identifies itself as the author, is not a rare literary artifice, the *dead narrator*, who speaks without the condition of the possible success of his speaking, is a remarkable contradiction, a paradoxical sign, that contradicts what is generally expected – in this case, the realist-naturalist "doxa" – in that it announces an unexpected poetological innovation.[10] We are dealing with a text that runs counter to mimetic principles and, in renouncing a referential shaping of the novelistic space, sets into motion the overthrow of outmoded perceptual contexts and orders of knowledge. The narrator Brás Cubas speaks *although* he is dead, which significantly recodes the *meaning* of time and space: The first narrative level, on which the action begins, becomes a 'beyond' with regard to the categories of time and space, and thus a negative entity, a 'non-place' from which cannot logically be narrated, or which must elude referential approximation through linguistic means. Unlike living narrators, who can be fictionalized in time and space, the dead narrator does not locate himself in relation to his statement, but *de-locates* himself in timelessness and otherworldliness. In contrast, the second narrative

---

[7] Speck even identifies a third level, that of the reader: "However, it is possible to discern a third temporal succession within the novel: that of the represented 'reader.' Machado creates this 'reader' within the fiction itself by using a battery of techniques that go back to Cervantes and Sterne" (Speck 1981: 10).
[8] On the now much criticized notion of *pacte autobiographique*, see Lejeune (1975).
[9] "I am not exactly an author recently deceased, but a deceased man recently an author" (Machado de Assis 2020: 5).
[10] For an in-depth analysis of auto-thanatographic narrations, see Weinmann (2018, here 138–143).

level, which contains the internal plot of the experiencing Brás, represents a 'this world' that in principle seems to be subject to earthly temporality.

What function does this constellation of the wordly and other-worldly narrative levels fulfill? Semantically, the incessant alternation between the two levels takes on the paradoxical meaning of a transgression of death. Both levels, which logically exclude each other, are narratively brought into a temporal and spatial overlapping relationship. This has the pragmatic effect of a refunctionalization of language, which no longer aims primarily at an effect of realism, but generates an alternative poetic-experimental "space" – more specifically, the text – in which the narrative becomes self-referential and largely detaches itself from the conventional frame of reference of space and time. In the following, I would like to illustrate how the dissolution of space and time takes place narratively and how the narrative levels are brought into a relationship of mutual superimpositions.

3 Anti-realistic Time and the Spatial Structure of the Frame Story

First, it should be noted that the novel does not (or cannot) completely dispense with referential techniques of representation. Rather, the program of turning away from realistic spatial design is carried out progressively insofar as referential and anti-referential techniques alternate with each other. The realistic illusion of a linguistically representable reality, the past life of the protagonist Brás Cubas as it 'really' was, thus comes into conflict with an aesthetic product that gradually takes over space and time, the text of the narrator Brás, who reflects on himself while writing, in relation to which the adverbs of spatial deixis function predominantly in a self-referential way.

The radical renunciation of realistic descriptions is probably most evident in the aesthetic design of the otherworldly place of narration. Lacking any spatial and temporal dimension and virtually devoid of movement, Brás' otherworld corresponds neither to Christian ideas nor does it represent a travelable "realm of the dead" in the Dantean sense, but rather an abstract "non-place" withdrawn from description, a narratological difficulty that the narrator solves by relativizing the significance of this problem and at the same time directing attention to the text in its aesthetic form: "[. . .] *evito contar* o processo extraordinário que empreguei na composição destas Memorias, trabalhadas cá no outro mundo. Seria curioso, mas nimiamente extenso, e aliás desnecessário ao entendimento da obra. A obra em si mesma é tudo [. . .]" (Machado de Assis

1971: 513).[11] Further mentions of the place of enunciation are always kept vague, containing only indirect hints regarding the afterlife and explicit commentaries referring back to the text of the *Memórias*: "Agora, porém, que estou cá do outro lado da vida, posso confessar tudo" (Machado de Assis 1971: 515).[12] The shaping of time in *Brás Cubas* neither serves to create realistic probability effects nor to attest to the historical veracity of the narrative. Rather, the exposure of narrative time, that is, the time of the reading process, can be observed here as well, with a simultaneous turning away from mimetically narrated time. In the act of writing, the narrator reflects ironically, he spends not so much time as eternity: "realmente, expedir alguns magros capítulos para êsse mundo sempre é tarefa que distrai um pouco da eternidade" (Machado de Assis 1971: 583).[13]

The alternation of referential and anti-referential modes of structuring time is evident on both narrative levels and illustrates the significant change to which the temporal dimension of the novel is subject. On the level of the frame story of the dead narrator, the problem of the possibility of narration in the afterlife must first be solved, which also experiences a negative solution, namely by omission: Brás largely "dispenses" with a concrete representation of the otherworldly situation and does not even attempt to create a verisimilar illusion of "eternity." In temporal terms, too, the afterlife remains an abstract "nonplace," withdrawn from immediate description, and the temporality of the afterlife is only indirectly addressed.

4 Anti-realistic Time and Space Structure of the Inner Story

Yet also for the second, worldly narrative level, the internal story, a very restrained use of descriptive procedures is to be noted. The few specifically located places in the plot, predominantly in Brazil but also in Europe, fulfill only a minimal referential function. Places that *appear as real*, such as "Rio de

---

11 "I will refrain from relaying the extraordinary process that I employed in composing these *Memoirs*, crafted here in the otherworld. It would be of interest, but tediously lengthy, and superfluous to one's understanding of the work. The work in itself is all" (Machado de Assis 2020: 3).
12 "Now, however, that I am on the other side of life, I can confess it all" (Machado de Assis 2020: 8).
13 "[. . .] and dispatching a few meager chapters into the other world is invariably a bit of a distraction from eternity" (Machado de Assis 2020: 153).

Janeiro," "Tijuca," or even "Coimbra," are named but not described, so that the semantic component of the local deixis remains one-dimensional. "Rio de Janeiro" does appear as a real and inhabitable place, insofar as Brás Cubas, for example, is able to "return" there after his obligatory study visit to Europe. Yet narrative set pieces of the scheme of returning home, which is topical in the genre of the "Bildungsroman," such as the reunion with family members, serve here only as an ironic pretext to turn the narration back on itself and to subordinate the narrated to the process of narration. In this sense, the narrator stylizes his return to Rio de Janeiro in a parodic way as a "rebirth":

> Vim. Não nego que, ao avisar a cidade natal, tive uma sensação nova. Não era efeito da minha pátria política; era-o do lugar da infância, a rua, a tôrre, o chafariz da esquina, a mulher de mantilha, o prêto do ganho, as cousas e scenas da meninice, buriladas na memória. Nada menos que uma renascença. O espírito, como um pássaro, não se lhe deu da corrente dos anos, arrepiou o vôo na direção da fonte original, e foi beber da água fresca e pura, ainda não mesclada do enxurro da vida.
> Reparando bem, há aí um lugar-comum. Outro lugar-comum, tristemente comum, foi a consternação da família. Meu pai abraçou-me com lágrimas. (Machado de Assis 1971: 544)[14]

In a cliché-like manner, the narrator describes a "renaissance" which he himself, however, exposes as a banal narrative commonplace, as a "lugar-comum," and thus directs attention away from the referential-semantic level to the rhetorical aspect of his narration, which he allows to become the primary, the explicit object of reference with the help of the local deixis "aí" / "there" ("Reparando bem, há aí um lugar-comum"). To this he adds another commonplace, "outro lugar-comum." Subordinate to the now foregrounded interest in trivial expressions thus appears the substantive referential field of the second commonplace, the hypocrisy of family feelings, "my family's affliction." exposed *incidentally* and *as incidental*. In this way, the narrative space undergoes a transformation of its referential functions, in consequence of which the *places* of action supposedly referring to 'reality' are occupied by primarily textual common *places* referring to –

---

[14] "I came, I'll not deny that, upon sighting the city of my birth, I felt a new sensation. This was not the effect my political homeland; it was that of the place of my childhood. This street, that tower, the fountain on the corner, women in mantillas, hired-out slaves working odd jobs, the things and scenes of boyhood, engraved into memory. Nothing less than a rebirth. My spirit, like a bird, paid no mind to the current of the years, turned the course of its flight toward the primordial font and went to drink of its fresh, pure water, which was yet to mingle with the torrent of life.
Upon further consideration, there's a commonplace there. Another commonplace, sadly common, was my family's affliction. My father embraced me in tears" (Machado de Assis 2020: 66).

themselves.[15] As the narration 'withdraws' from real-appearing places/spaces and turns to the text as an aesthetic product, the latter takes up more and more space and gains in visibility. The self-reflexive function gains the upper hand over the referential function. As will be shown, the temporal organization of the novel also follows the program of the suspension of time and space outlined here.

On the level of the internal plot, a temporal anchoring of the narration in a historical time span extending from 1805 to 1869 can be discerned. However, historical events only come up at the margins of the narration, and, aside from the Napoleonic wars in distant Europe, no historical dates of Brazilian history are mentioned, no reference occurs to the ongoing economic, social and political crises, or to the obvious historical dates such as the independence of the Brazilian empire. The less importance is given to historical time, the more "time" becomes an ostensible and implicit theme in Brás Cubas' memoir. This occurs through the thematization of time and topics marked by temporality such as "memory," "passing of life," and "death." Thus, at the level of the experiencing self, the theme of time is omnipresent and is found again in the narratives of his own death, of the death of his mother and father, of Marcela, Nhá-Lolo, Dona Plácida, and Quincas Borba, but also in the motif of the pendulum clock and, in particular, the lost watch which stands for lost lifetime (cf. Speck 1981: 8) and is closely related to the motifs of lost love and earthly failure in politics – all of which structure the narrative flow *in terms of time*.

Yet by constantly thematizing the finitude of time, the narrative also refers to its own temporality, recognizable in its own progress and passing, reinforced by the various techniques of incessant intervention in the narrative process. In this way, the narrative's progression through time as such is upended and becomes self-reflexive, as in chapter 102, titled "A Respite" ("De Repouso") in which the narrator *tells of not telling* and instead taking a rest: "Mas êste mesmo homem, que se alegrou com a partida do outro, praticou daí a tempos. . . Não, não hei de contá-lo nesta página; fique êsse capítulo para repouso do meu vexame. Uma ação grosseira, baixa, sem explicação possível. . . Repito, não contarei o caso nesta página" (Machado de Assis 1971: 605–606).[16] By dealing excessively with the passing of time, "withdrawing" from places/spaces that *appear real*, and turning to the text as an aesthetic product, the narration reduces the

---

15 For a more in-depth analysis of the importance of commonplaces in Machado's short story "Teoria do Medalhão," see João Cézar de Castro Rocha (2015: 200–203).
16 "But that same man who rejoiced at the departure of his rival was soon to commit. . . No, I won't recount it on this page; let this chapter serve as a respite for my vexation. A callous, low act, with no possible explanation. . . I repeat, I won't speak of it on this page" (Machado de Assis 2020: 203).

illusion of "being *about something*" and instead *takes place* as an aesthetic action that also *performs itself in time*. Narrated time and narrative time become congruent and, in the performative presentation and experience of the text, overcome the fictional death of the narrator. Numerous other techniques such as ironic forth- and back-references as well as extravagant typographical devices reinforce the self-reflexive character of the text by turning the spatial and temporal dimensions of narration back on the text.

5 Temporal and Spatial Distortion of the Narration

In relation to the realist narrative convention that assumes a meaningful linkage of events, Brás Cubas' narration employs distorting procedures of reshaping referential relations, deforming causal connections and disrupting the linear course of the narration. By narratively distancing himself from the narrative object of the main plot, Brás Cubas' life, the narrator goes on narrative sidetracks.[17] At the same time, he opens up secondary metaliterary narrative spaces and narrative loops. As digressions or self-reflexive points of view within the narration, these sidetracks open up new perspectives from which the aesthetic perception of the main plot itself, as a referentially guaranteed chain of events, becomes questionable and appears increasingly illusory. For the narrator's life and for the course of the plot, the central object of the sequence of chapters 26 to 57 is Brás Cubas' volatile love affair with Virgília Dutra, the daughter of the influential Court Council. His initially reserved interest, their first meeting and the initiation of a marital union, Brás' distancing due to sudden disinterest, which turns into boundless passion when he meets her again, now married to his rival Lobo Neves, and his secret love affair with her, represent the actual content of the main plot. But the far more extensive and thus more important narrative space is taken up by the digressions, often aphoristic reflections and subplots that seem to detach themselves from the main plot and stretch the continuity of the main plot almost to breaking point. Thus, Brás' consent to his father's plan, which comprises only a few sentences, is followed immediately by an almost accidental visit to Dona Eusébia, a former domestic servant of

---

[17] For a detailed analysis of the techniques of defamiliarizing and de-structuring of the plot through techniques of digression and interpolation of other narrative strands, see Eustis (1979).

Brás' deceased mother, who lives in the countryside, the consequences of which bring the main plot about Virgília to a complete standstill for several chapters:

> Vencera meu pai; dispus-me a aceitar o diploma e o casamento, Virgília e a Câmara dos Deputados. – As duas Virgílias, disse êle num assomo de ternura política. Aceitei-os; meu pai deu-me dos fortes abraços. Era o seu próprio sangue que êle, enfim, reconhecia. – Desces comigo? – Desço amanhã. Vou fazer primeiramente uma visita a D. Eusébia [. . .] Meu pai torceu o nariz, mas não disse nada; despediu-se e desceu. Eu na tarde dêsse mesmo dia, fui visitar D. Eusébia. (Machado de Assis 1971: 550)[18]

The supposedly insignificant visit to Dona Eusébia now introduces Brás to her daughter, the pretty, imperceptibly limping Eugênia, for whose sake he postpones his return to Rio. He is inclined to fall in love with her because of her naturalness, and is given to extensive musings about Eugênia's physical (and genealogical) defect, which makes him forget Virgília completely:

> Amanheceu chovendo, transferi a descida; mas no outro dia, a manhã era límpida e azul, e apesar disso, deixei-me ficar, não menos que no terceiro dia, e no quarto, até o fim da semana. Manhãs bonitas, frescas, convidativas; lá embaixo, a família a chamar-me, e a noiva, e o Parlamento, e eu sem acudir a cousa nenhuma, enlevado ao pé da minha Venus. (Machado de Assis 1971: 554)[19]

It is not until eight chapters later that the main plot involving Virgília is taken up again in chapter 37. Brás returns to Rio, meets Virgília in her father's house, and the fledgling relationship is summarized in a few sentences:

> E logo me apresentou à mulher – uma estimável senhora, – e à filha, que não desmentiu em nada o panegírico de meu pai. Juro-vos que em nada. Relede o capítulo XXVII. Eu, que levava idéias a respeito da pequena, fitei-a de certo modo; ela, que não sei se as

---

18 "My father had won; I was ready to accept the candidacy and the marriage, Virgília and the Chamber of Deputies. 'The two Virgilias,' said he, in a flush of political tenderness. I accepted them; my father gave me two hearty embraces. Finally, he could recognize his own blood. 'Are you coming down to the city with me?' 'I'll go tomorrow. First, I'll pay a visit to Dona Eusébia' My father looked down his nose but said nothing; he bade me farewell and went down to the city. As for me, that afternoon I went to visit Dona Eusébia" (Machado de Assis 2020: 80).

19 "The morning brought rain, and I put off my return; but on the next day the morning was clear and blue, and in spite of that I stayed, as I did on the third day, and the fourth, and through the end of the week. Lovely, fresh, inviting mornings; down below was my family calling me, and my bride-to-be, and Parliament; I was deaf to it all, enraptured at the feet of my crippled Venus" (Machado de Assis 2020: 87).

tinha, não me fitou de modo diferente; e o nosso olhar primeiro foi pura e simplesmente conjugal. No fim de um mês estávamos íntimos. (Machado de Assis 1971: 556)[20]

Already in the following chapter 38 the course of the main action abruptly breaks off again: "- Venha cá jantar amanha, disse-me o Dutra uma noite. Aceitei o convite. No dia seguinte, mandei que a sege me esperasse no Largo de S. Francisco de Paula, e fui dar várias voltas. Lembra-vos ainda a minha teoria das edições humanas?" (Machado de Assis 1971: 556).[21] A longer secondary plot then begins which includes a coincidental encounter with Marcela, his socially unbefitting early love, now disfigured by smallpox. Only three chapters later he is taken back by memory to the visit to the Dutras, in the context of which the episode of the disagreeable encounter with Marcela again gains relevance for the main plot: Brás' dislike of Marcela culminates in a hallucination that *ad hoc* "contaminates" his feelings for Virgília, and out of a momentum of weariness he severs ties with her. A contingent, purely associative, hallucinated *connection* with the main plot emerges from the episodic minor plot which, however, *actually affects* the main plot – a phenomenon that Brás unemotionally refers to as the metaphysical law of "solidariedade do aborrecimento humano" (Machado de Assis 1971: 560)[22] – and which not only refracts ironically the arbitrariness and superficiality of human relationships but at the same time points to the arbitrariness (the artificiality) of narration.

Through the temporal and spatial distortion of the narration, it becomes clear that the fiction dispenses with the aesthetic *illusion*, namely the impression that the narrative is based on *seemingly logical*, causal connections. The narrative, which meanders associatively from one secondary setting to another, leads into yet another spatial and temporal narrative dimension, into self-reflexive poetic spaces of thought, which make the originally pursued main plot seem increasingly void and make the textual product all the more clearly perceptible in terms of time and space.

---

[20] "[. . .] he introduced me to his wife – an estimable lady – and his daughter, who did not belie my father's panegyric in the slightest. I swear to you, not in the slightest. Reread Chapter XXVII. I, who had my ideas about the girl, gazed at her in a certain way; she, who may have had ideas of her own, returned the gaze in kind; and our first look was purely and simply conjugal. After a month's time we were on intimate terms" (Machado de Assis 2020: 92).
[21] "'Come dine with us tomorrow,' Dutra said to me one night. I accepted the invitation. The following day, I had my coach wait for me at the Largo de São Francisco de Paula, and I went out for a stroll. Do you still recall my theory of human editions?" (Machado de Assis 2020: 93).
[22] "[T]he solidarity of human disgruntlement" (Machado de Assis 2020: 102).

6 Misplaced Ideas, Belated Literatures: Overcoming Restrictive Coordinates of Space and Time

In the course of my reflections on spatio-temporal conceptions of literature, the question of the possibility of lifting the dominant implications of temporal and spatial concepts is central. Accordingly, an examination of the poetological program of turning away from realistic time and space in the *Memórias postumas de Brás Cubas* may lead us to some conclusions I will now briefly outline.

While Brazilian intellectuals, under the influence of evolutionist theories, attempted to reduce their nation's supposed civilizational "backwardness" through literary affiliation with European naturalism, *Brás Cubas's Memoirs* indicate more than just a different "tempo" in regard of literary history. By playfully shaping time and space, the text becomes self-referential, pointing beyond both the mimetic principles of realism and naturalism as well as the restrictive relation of centre and periphery, no longer reproducing the case of an unsurmountable posteriority.

By fictionalizing an impossible narratological "non-place" – the beyond – in the *Memoirs*, Machado de Assis simultaneously metaphorizes the "otherworldly" position of Brazilian literature in the global context – an insight central to Roberto Schwarz' readings of Machado (*Ideias fora do lugar*, 1973/1992; *Um mestre na periferia do capitalismo*, 1990/2000). However, the impossible narrative situation allows for more: by breaking with mimetic principles based on realistic representations of time and space, the text overcomes dominant narrative conventions while challenging problematic hierarchical orders of knowledge – such as the relations naturalized by the categories of space and time. Through the self-referential unfolding of the paradoxical narrative situation, the simultaneously *logically impossible* and yet *narratologically possible* discourse, the narrator performs a revolution of the spatial and temporal coordinates of the reading experience. At the same time, what does *take place*, is the overcoming of the structural marginalization implemented by the spatial schema of centre and periphery. Following the metaliterary scope of this insight, space and time are not objective categories but functions of perception and narration, consequently fictional products, and as fictional they can be directly experienced aesthetically. At the same time, the narrative demonstrates that "ideas" and "literary strategies" have neither a fixed identity nor an asserted meaning but can be generated in different literary contexts and charged with different meanings, making the notion of the "belatedness" of ideas seem obsolete.

The textual treatment of the function and meaning of the categories of time and space, as the analysis of the *Memórias* was able to show, also makes a critical contribution as an aesthetic elaboration of temporal and spatial coordinates to the questioning of restrictive hierarchical structures of space and time.

Bibliography

Botacă, Manuela (2010): "Grenzsetzende Macht. Geopolitische Strategien europäischer Identitätsbildung." In: *Berliner Journal für Soziologie*, 20, pp. 24–44.

Bruns, Claudia (2017): "'Rasse' und Raum. Überlegungen zu einer komplexen Relation." In: Bruns, Claudia: *"Rasse" und Raum. Topologien zwischen Kolonial-, Geo- und Biopolitik: Geschichte, Kunst, Erinnerung*. Wiesbaden: Reichert Verlag, pp. 1–43.

Carvalho Franco, Maria Sylvia de (1976): "As ideias estao no lugar." In: *Cadernos de Debate* 1, pp. 61–64.

Casanova, Pascale (1999): *La République mondiale des Lettres*. Paris: Seuil.

Castro Rocha, João Cézar de: *Machado de Assis. Towards a Poetics of Emulation*, East Lansing: Michigan State University Press, 2015.

Eustis, Christopher (1979): "Time and Narrative Structure in 'Memórias Póstumas de Brás Cubas'." In: *Luso-Brazilian Review*, 16, 1, pp. 18–28.

Lejeune, Philippe (1975): *Le pacte autobiographique*. Paris: Le Seuil.

Machado de Assis, Joaquim Maria (^{2}1971 [1959]): *Machado de Assis. Obra Completa em três volumes*, Vol. 1. Rio de Janeiro: Editora José Aguilar.

Machado de Assis (2020): *The Posthumous Memoirs of Brás Cubas*. Transl. by Flora Thomson-DeVeaux. New York: Penguin Books.

Palti, Elías José (2006): "The Problem of 'Misplaced Ideas' Revisited: Beyond the 'History of Ideas' in Latin America." In: *Journal of the History of Ideas*, 67, 1, pp. 149–179.

Schwarz, Roberto (1973/1992): "As ideias fora do lugar." In: *Estudos Cebrap* 3, reprinted in *Misplaced Ideas*. London/New York: Verso, pp. 19–32.

Schwarz, Roberto (1990/2000): *Um mestre na periferia do capitalismo: Machado de Assis*. São Paulo: Duas Cidades/Editora 34.

Speck, Paula K. (1981): "Narrative Time and the 'defunto Autor' in 'Memorias postumas de Bras Cubas'." In: *Latin American Literary Review*, 9, 18, pp. 7–15.

Ventura, Roberto (1991): *Estilo Tropical. História cultural e polêmicas literárias no Brasil 1870–1914*. São Paulo: Companhia das Letras.

Weinmann, Frédéric (2018): *"Je suis mort." Essai sur la narration autothanatographique*. Paris: Le Seuil.

Anne Brüske

Recreating the World of the Cuban Revolution: Geopolitical Imagination and Entangled Spaces in the Graphic Memoir *Adiós mi Habana* (2017)

1 Cuba and Comics – Postsocialism and Postcolonialism

The figuration of the island is one of the most recurrent topoi connected to the Caribbean and especially Cuba, reiterating in Cuban texts *desde dentro y desde fuera* the tension between isolation and connection, remembering and forgetting, geography and culture. José Lezama Lima, for instance, discusses Cuban "insularismo" as a motor for poetic and cultural openness, Antonio Benítez Rojo's poststructuralist thought conceives of Cuba as one of the many islands giving birth to the Caribbean meta-archipelago, and numerous narrative texts written in- and outside Cuba insist on islandness as both a material fact and a tool to deconstruct the national canon.[1] Similarly, thanks to its literary representations, Havana, once dubbed the "Paris of the Caribbean," has become famous for its ruins and its material, moral, and social decay in the aftermath of the *período especial* of the 1990s.[2]

Undoubtedly, philosophical texts and written narratives are most powerful in producing spaces. Comics and, more generally, graphic narratives, however, offer even more complex perspectives on Cuba as a material and imagined space. For, in contrast to classical text-only narratives they draw on both images *and* text in order to produce fictional space. It is this multimodal narration appealing to the reader on various channels that has lent comics their reputation as an apt medium for mass communication and education. From 1959 on, following Fidel Castro's credo for art, media, and literature, "Dentro de la revolución todo, contra

---

[1] Cf. Lezama Lima (1997), Benítez Rojo (1998). Cf. also Graziadei (2017: 65–68).
[2] Exner (2017), Pérez Medrano (2019), Obejas (2009). For a reflection on and beyond the 'ruins' of Havana cf. also Birkenmaier/Whitfield (2011).

Anne Brüske, Universität Regensburg

https://doi.org/10.1515/9783110762273-004

la Revolución, nada,"[3] the Cuban Revolution used *historietas* in magazines such as *Mella* to mold its readerships according to the model of "the new man"[4] reshaped by Ernesto Guevara and to implant its imagination of Cuba as an autarchic postcolonial, social, and internationalist space. Examples for these attempts at emphasizing Cuba's anti-imperialist and anti-colonial stance are the comic series *Pucho* (~1955–) and *Supertiñosa* (~1959–) by Virgilio Martínez Gaínza (1931–2008) and *Elpidio Valdés* (1970–) by Cuban artist Juan Padrón (1947–2020), one of the most widely distributed comic and cartoon productions, evolving around the eponymous fictional hero from the Spanish-Cuban war of independence (1895–1898).[5] Alongside domestic productions, the so-called *muñequitos rusos*, animation films imported from the USSR and other Eastern European countries and screened on Cuban national television from the 1960s to the 1990s, aimed at constructing Cuba as part of a globally connected socialist space.[6]

Interestingly, showcasing Cuba as a socialist and independent postcolonial space is not restricted to the Revolution's honeymoon years (1960–1963) and the so-called *Quinquenio gris* (1971–1976) whose post-Stalinist politics promoted the *gleichschaltung* of culture, arts, and education.[7] In transnational graphic narratives created and published *desde fuera* at the beginning of the 21st century, the production of Cuba as a locally, regionally, and globally entangled space also plays an important role for the re-definition of the Cuban nation and Cuban space. Pursuing more diverse pedagogic goals, these graphic narratives draw a different and, at times, nuanced picture of Cuba, its Revolution, and the forms of (post)socialism and anti-colonial internationalisms promoted by its political elite.

The focus of my contribution is this different take from outside that reconsiders Cuba as a space of cultural and political entanglements between the Caribbean, the United States, and the Soviet Union, and as part of a post- and anticolonial 'Global South.' Telling stories of migration from and to Cuba, graphic memoirs *desde fuera*, from outside Cuba, such as *Sexilio* (2004) by Jaime Cortez, *Cuba. My Revolution* (2010) by Inverna Lockpez, *Adiós mi Habana* (2017) by Anna Veltfort, *Apuntes para un viaje a Alemania* (2016) by Carlos Aguilera und Damián Menéndez reflect upon these entanglements both in their

---

3 Castro Ruiz (1961). "Within the Revolution, everything, against the Revolution, nothing" (translation A.B.).
4 Cf. Guevara (1978 [1965]).
5 Cf. Mogno (2008).
6 Cf. Pérez Cano (2020: 61), Puñales-Alpízar (2012: 25), Porbén (2015: 123).
7 Cf. Story (2020).

textual and graphic elements.[8] They are characterized by interconnections and productive frictions, e.g., with regard to their publication contexts, their language, and their plots that involve Cuba, the U.S., and other places. Drawing on Veltfort's *Adiós mi Habana*, a U.S.-Cuban graphic memoir written and illustrated by a German American who lived in Havana from 1962 to 1972, I aim to unravel the imagined worlds and geopolitical imaginaries that are crafted through the connection of individual micro-perspectives (life stories), national perspectives (Cuban society and policies), and global perspectives. My goal is to expose how these autobiographic graphic memoirs critically (re)construct Cuba's entanglements, power structures and geopolitical imaginaries by means of their respective production of social space and time, shedding light on Cuba's position on the intersection between the Global South, North, and East, or, in a cold-war terminology, between the First, the Second, and the Third World.

2 Graphic Narratives, the Production of Space, and Geopolitical Imaginaries

But what is social space anyway, and how do graphic narratives contribute to our understanding of social space, imagined worlds, and geopolitical imaginaries?

Following French sociologist Henri Lefebvre in *La Production de l'espace* (1974) I consider "space" a relational, multitemporal, and multiscalar phenomenon that is a result of the dialectical negotiation between the triad of spatial practices (*perçu*), representations of space (*conçu*) and spaces of representation (*vécu*).[9] This means that space is constituted in our minds while we shape material land- and cityscapes (e.g., by building cities or destroying ecosystems), while we represent geographical space in maps, political texts or urban planning, and transform, symbolize, or while we imagine space in artistic, spiritual, or religious practices.[10] From Lefebvre's post-Marxist point of view, space ought to be conceptualized as a social phenomenon and a process that relies both on ideas and on material circumstances, such as conditions of production and reproduction, and that varies depending on cultural and historic contexts. Produced in our minds by a complex interplay of representations, imagination,

---

8 For an analysis of Lockpez' *Cuba. My Revolution* and Veltfort's *Adiós mi Habana* cf. Pérez Cano (2020). Cf. Cortez (2004), Lockpez (2010), Morejón Arnaiz/Aguilera (2020), Veltfort (2017).
9 Lefebvre (2000 [1974]: I, 14 and 11, 17 cf. also II, 11: 161–162).
10 Lefebvre (2000 [1974]: I, 15: 42–43 [italics in the original]).

and matter, social space is also characterized by its palimpsest-like multitemporality (we integrate actual and remembered space into our understanding of space, material spaces frequently feature different layers), its multi-scalarity (we combine our perceptions, concepts, and lived experience on different scales such as the local, the national, the transnational, and the global), and its relationality (more often than not we do not produce spaces as separate entities but as interrelated and entangled realms).

If we transfer such an understanding of social space to media and texts, fictional space is characterized by the same threefold dialectic of spatial practices, representations of space, and spaces of representation. At the same time, the production of fictional space through narration is conditioned by its mediality, for instance, the linearity of a written text or the sequentiality of a graphic narrative in comparison to the contiguity of a simple picture.[11] Compared to the novel that operates mostly with the text channel, in graphic narratives, the images, organized in panels and sequences of panels, provide a visual production of space alongside with verbally narrated space, the product of the negotiation between graphically and verbally created space depending on the nature of the text-image relationship.[12] This multi-modal production of space occurs, in accordance with Wolfgang Iser's reader response theory[13] and its elaboration for graphic narratives by Scott McCloud, in the act of reception.[14] In the process of "closure,"[15] panels and sequences are integrated into a story and, with them, 'drawn' and 'written' fictional spaces into an overarching multimodal production of space.[16] This multimodally crafted space emerges from the relationship between narrated space and the space of narration, the narratological perspectivization of fictional spaces, and semantic patterns of spatial order – categories that are also central to classical narrative texts.[17] Furthermore, intertextual and intermedial references contribute to the production of fictional space by enriching, determining, or overdetermining it culturally, medially, and politically.[18]

---

11 Cf. Lessing (1788), Lotman (2006: 529).
12 For different relations between graphic and textual representation cf. Abel/Klein (2016: l99–100). A more elaborate theory on the different dimensions of spatial production in comics or graphic narratives is presented in Schüwer (2008).
13 Cf. Iser (1976).
14 McCloud (1994: 63), cf. Abel/Klein (2016: 84ff).
15 McCloud (1994: 63)
16 For a fruitful theory on the creation of space and its different aspects in graphic narratives for instance integrating affective aspects in reader responses to panels and their visual representation of narrated spaces cf. Schüwer (2008: 87–207, esp. 197).
17 Cf. Brüske (2020: 138–154).
18 Cf. Kristeva (1967: 440–441, Hescher (2016: 77–83).

To be sure, the production of fictional space by media interacts with the production of the nonfictional social spaces we live in. Not only is fictional space created in cultural media such as literature and graphic narratives, but it also has an impact on how we produce nonfictional everyday spaces. This applies to all scales, from the micro scale to the geopolitical macro-scale. Responding to changing conceptions of belonging and migration, diaspora or exile texts and other cultural media contribute to creating "[transnational] imagined communities"[19] and their social spaces forming narratives in which different layers of time and space overlap. Going beyond local or national scales, as Arjun Appadurai argues in *Modernity at Large* (1996) those imaginations engender "imagined worlds,"[20] i.e., ideas of how the world is constituted as a global social space, their anthropological function as a social practice being to put a deterritorialized world in order, to recontextualize it as a global space and to re-signify previous patterns of order.[21] In this process, the material "image," i.e. the graphic novel, and the "imagined," its overall narrative, which both draw on pre-existing "imaginaries" become the central means of reterritorialization by which a seemingly deterritorialized world is re-embedded into cultural patterns of interpretation:[22]

> The interplay of the materiality of "images," the creativity of "the imagined," and the social groundedness of the "imaginary" creates fictive realities, which at the same time become social facts that institute any given social formation as the imaginary is perceived to provide its central foundational condition of possibility.[23]

Compared to the classic medium of the novel, graphic novels lend special weight to concrete, visually comprehensible, and globally circulating images. They seem thus especially suited to transport narratives of "imagined worlds" and disclose their corresponding "geopolitical imaginaries."[24] In connection

---

19 Anderson (^{6}2006 [1983]), Sökefeld (2006: 267).
20 Appadurai (1996: 33): "These landscapes thus are the building blocks of what (extending Benedict Anderson) I would like to call imagined worlds, that is, the multiple worlds that are constituted by the historically situated imaginations of persons and groups spread around the globe [. . .]. An important fact of the world we live in today is that many persons on the globe live in such imagined worlds (and not just in imagined communities) and thus are able to contest and sometimes even subvert the imagined worlds of the official mind and of the entrepreneurial mentality that surround them."
21 Cf. Appadurai (1996: 31).
22 Cf. Appadurai (1996: 31, 33), Epple/Kramer (2016: 42, 49–50).
23 Epple/Kramer (2016: 47). Cf. also Appadurai (1996): "The image, the imagined, the imaginary – these are all terms that direct us to something critical and new in global cultural processes: *the imagination as a social practice.*"
24 Cf. Epple/Kramer (2016).

with the creative realm of the "imagined," geopolitical imaginaries, "providing beliefs [. . .] and thus creating forms of social consensus"[25] have a cohesive impact on society. Accordingly, they do not so much depict a global world order as co-produce it and allow reflection on it.[26] In the following, I will discuss how "imagined (global) worlds" are produced as social spaces in transnational Cuban graphic memoirs by the combination of text and image. Taking *Adiós mi Habana* as an example, I will more specifically investigate the memoir's Cuban-centered imagined global spaces and its underlying geopolitical imaginaries that are (re)constructed from a post-Cold War and postcolonial perspective.

3 The Production of Space in *Adiós mi Habana*: Cuba in a Global World

The graphic memoir *Adiós mi Habana*, written and illustrated by Anna Veltfort (*1945), looks back at the beginnings of the Cuban Revolution from a distance of more than 40 years. Published first in Spanish in Madrid in 2017 after 10 years of creation, it tells the story of Connie, a German-American living in Havana from 1962 to 1972. Covering the early years of the Cuban Revolution it provides insight into the social and political projects of the post-1959 era, Cuba's material culture and Cuba's geopolitical positioning in this time.

The coming-of-age years of young Connie in Havana form the heart of the autobiographical graphic narrative. It is framed by a series of paratexts such as Veltfort's acknowledgements, her preface, a prologue by the Madrid-based Cuban publisher and writer Antonio José Ponte, as well as an all-text epilogue and a section of notes which document Veltfort's textual and visual sources. These paratexts attest to the historicity of the events depicted in the memoir while also emphasizing the individual perspective Veltfort develops in the

---

[25] "The imaginary, by providing beliefs or religious emblems and thus creating forms of social consensus, guarantees both the maintenance of the functional infrastructure of society in the present and its continuity in the future" (Epple/Kramer 2016: 46).
[26] "[According to Iser, the acts of fictionalization] represent modes of a literary or aesthetic "world construction" that comes to create structures that do not pertain to the social, historical, cultural and literary systems, realities, or environments to which they refer, but do have a considerable impact on the understanding and perception of these realities, and therefore assume an important regulatory role in social life" (Epple/Kramer 2016: 47).

interplay between her younger Cuban self Connie, herself as a mature U.S.-based narrator as well as the author and illustrator.[27]

Adiós mi Habana features large portions of verbal narration in both dialogues and explanatory textboxes, a plain language, a rather realistic, clear drawing style, and a predominantly vivid coloring. Subdivided into seven chapters, the memoir draws its audience's attention to certain key subjects and locations by introducing each chapter with a gaze through a bull's-eye, thusly preconfiguring the readers' production of Cuban social spaces and an imagined global world (Figure 1).

Figure 1: Chapter titles in Anna Veltfort (2017): *Adiós mi Habana. Las memorias de una gringa y su tiempo en los años revolucionarios de la década de los 60*. Madrid: Verbum, with permission by the author.

The gaze through the bull's eye also symbolizes the multitemporal superimpositions of perspective in the narration. It corresponds mostly to the retrospective view of the first-person narrator and illustrator – not to the view of the adolescent protagonist –, representing a selection of past events that are transposed into the

---

27 Interestingly, Veltfort recently stated in an interview that she wanted to portray the Revolution and Cuba of the 1960s from as unadulterated a perspective as possible, pointing to her realistic drawings and the historical documents displayed in the memoir. This comment exemplifies the complex tensions between referentiality and fictionality in autobiographical media in general and perhaps more specifically the frictions between an individual subjective and a collective, perhaps more holistic perspective in the graphic memoir drawing on both text and images (cf. Henken/Veltfort 2021).

present of the narrator and her readership. Moreover, in its visual and textual production of space, the graphic memoir operates on two levels. On the one hand, it uses the autobiographical plot and individual perspective of the transnational migrant Connie, mediated through the narrator's graphical and textual account, to create Cuba as a social space. On the other hand, it connects this autobiographical plot with a more collective and political spatio-poietic narrative interested in reconstructing and reevaluating Cuban socialism and anticolonial internationalism in their local, national, and global manifestations from a spatio-temporal distance. By interweaving the levels of individual life story, Cuban socialism, and Cuban internationalist and anticolonial aspirations, Veltfort's graphic memoir creates Cuba as a locally defined space in a global world and as a part of heterogenous geopolitical imaginaries of the 1960s. For this purpose, the graphic memoir uses not only its plot or, according to Gérard Genette's terminology, *histoire*, but also heavily draws on phenomena of intertextuality and intermediality, both on the level of *histoire* and *discourse*.[28] Hence, in what follows I first discuss the production of the narrated space of *Adiós mi Habana* through the autobiographical plot. Then, in a second step, I focus on the multiscalar production of space through intertextual and -medial references that contextualize the plot on a national and a global scale.

4 Narrating Autobiographical Cuban Space(s) from a Transnational Angle

In *Adiós mi Habana*, the narrated space, i.e., the fictional space created by the memoir's *histoire* and its discursive representation, is constituted by the autobiographical plot. The text foregrounds the spatial practices, spatial concepts, and spatial imaginations of the protagonist, represented through the filter of the narrator. The plot centers on Connie's youth in revolutionary Havana, her involuntary coming-out as a lesbian, and the conflicts she faces given the repressions of the Revolution towards intellectuals, homosexuals, and non-Cuban citizens. As spatial practices of national and global scope, Connie's migrations structure the graphic memoir. They emphasize the multitemporality of Veltfort's spaces – the superimposition of the narrator's remembered spaces and present views on the protagonist's past spaces – as well as the relationality of the subspaces of California, Cuba, New York City, and Canada, to name but a few. At the same time, Connie's spatial practice of traveling (*espace perçu*) embeds

---

28 Cf. Genette (1972).

those places in the geopolitical contexts of the post-WWII and the cold war era and inscribe the memoir into the cultural tradition of Caribbean diasporas. As a child, Connie migrates from post-war Germany to the U.S.; as a teenager, she enters Cuba, a socialist bastion in the emerging Global South, via Mexico due to the Cold War travel restrictions and the U.S. embargo on Cuba; and as a young adult, she must leave Cuba via detours to get back to the United States. The reiterated visual representation of ships and crossings, a recurrent motive in Caribbean diaspora narratives, the gaze through the bull's eyes, and the structure of the first chapter insist on the importance of these practices of traveling while commenting on them visually e.g., through their colorings, for instance representing Connie's traumatic transit through Mexico in a nightmarish blue.[29] Whereas Connie's peregrinations can be read as practices of involuntary spatial appropriation, the depiction of young Connie starting over with her family in different places in California and in Cuba emphasizes the dimension of lived space (*espace vécu*). This lived space is co-constituted by the political and conceptual dimension of space (*espace conçu*) as expressed in the textual and visual discourse of *Adiós mi Habana*. On a discourse level, for example, the memoir links Connie's new beginnings for example with information and documents concerning the civil rights movement and the strong anti-communist politics of the McCarthy era, with autobiographic details on the communist engagement of her stepfather Ted Veltfort, and with Connie's participation in the historic protests by NAACP members against Woolworth's segregationist policy in San Francisco in 1960.[30]

Throughout the book, the graphic memoir combines Connie's local microperspective with the transnational geopolitical contexts of the 1960s, emphasizing the interconnections of geopolitical contexts with, and their consequences for, a locally based individuum. In the same vein, the reflection on Cuba as a socially and geopolitically intertwined space takes center stage. Cuba is presented as a place that has left an indelible mark on the protagonist and continues to represent a political preoccupation for the narrator and creator of the memoir. This fundamental importance of Cuba and especially Havana is implied by the memoir's circular structure: its *récit* begins with Connie's arrival at the port of Havana and ends 10 years later at the same place with her giving farewell to the personified city that has become a home for the "gringa" and

---

29 Cf. Veltfort (2017: 15–62, esp. 28–31).
 The first chapter of the memoir begins with Connie's arrival in Havana, but then turns back in time to focus Connie's first migration to the USA and her nightmare-like transit through Mexico to Cuba in 1962, highlighted by the blueish coloring of this Mexican episode.
30 Cf. Veltfort (2017: 25).

constitutes one of the hidden protagonists of the memoir: "¡Adiós, Gringa!" – "¡Adiós mi Habana..!"[31] It is through Connie's written and drawn activities, movements, and everyday spaces in the Havana of the 1960s that the memoir produces the Caribbean metropolis as a lively, yet contradictory and contested urban space. On a visual level, it represents the urban space through realistic drawings inspired by corresponding historical photographs of Havana and sketches by Veltfort from the 1960s or by personal diaries.[32]

Showing and telling Connies's everyday spaces and places, divided into the comfortable spaces reserved to "foreign technicians," the oftentimes modest dwellings of the Cuban population, and Havana public spaces, the memoir draws a differentiated picture of early revolutionary Habana and its (intellectual) youth. Cuba is depicted as a space marked by harsh contradictions, as the episodes of revolutionary fieldwork reaching out to the rural poor in the Sierra Maestra show in which Connie and her fellow students at the University of Havana participate.[33] Furthermore, Havana, a *pars pro toto* for Cuba as a nation and as an isolated yet interconnected island space, appears shattered into different fractions and torn apart by opposing forces. As a U.S. American citizen, a university student, and a lesbian, Connie experiences exclusion from the potentially creative and resistant differential spaces of education and culture, which the Cuban Revolution tries to homogenize into abstract institutional space of power by 'cleaning' for instance the university of Havana (chapter 2) or intellectual circles (chapter 5) from 'counterrevolutionaries.' The Revolution sets the heteronormative ideal of the "hombre nuevo" as the standard of its cultural and educational policy: "Con la revolución todo, contra la revolución nada."[34] Instead of realizing the "right to the city"[35] as a right to participation, the Revolution favors the perpetuation of intersectional exclusion along old (ethnicity) and new fault lines (sexuality, performance).

---

31 Veltfort (2017: 217). Cf. Veltfort (2019: 209): "GOODBYE, GRINGA!" "GOORDBYE, MY HAVANA. . .!"
32 Cf. Veltfort used photographs of Havana which acquaintances sent her from Cuba and field diaries from the Sierra Maestra (cf. Veltfort 2017: Agradecimientos, 11), her own sketches of the city and of interiors as exposed in the interview with Ted A. Henken (2021) as well as other sketches by eyewitnesses as indicated in the notes (cf. e.g. Veltfort (2017: 222).
33 Cf. chapter 3 "La Sierra Maestra," Veltfort (2017: 99–131).
34 Veltfort (2017: 168). "Within the Revolution, everything, against the Revolution, nothing" (translation A.B.).
   Note the error in Veltfort's quote of Fidel's 1961 discourse on the liberties and limits of artistic expression that says: "Dentro de la revolución todo, contra la revolución nada" (cf. Castro Ruiz 1961).
35 Cf. Lefebvre (1967).

Two aspects of Connie's life story and her corresponding spaces evidence these divisions: Connie's coming-out and the Revolution's spatial order regarding Havana's foreign population. In September 1967, two men attack Connie and her partner on the Havana Malecón at night and accuse them of sexual misconduct. This forced coming-out as a lesbian represents a significant moment in Connie's coming-of-age process (chapter 3).[36] As a key event in Connie's life, the attack and its sequels epitomize Havana's socio-spatial and ideological fragmentation and advancing *gleichschaltung*, for the homophobic attack forms the prelude to a series of people's court and intra-university trials against the two young women. As potential 'counterrevolutionaries,' they are threatened with expulsion from university as well as a court sentence. On the story level, the narrative connects the attack and its tiring aftermath with the film *Morgan* (1967, Karel Reisz), a comedy critical of communism, by having some panels show the two women's visit to the cinema, and then, on the opposite page, depicting the Malecón in a panoramic take and the incipient attack in a long shot in idealizing blue tones. On the following double page – alternating half-total, close-up, and American shot[37] – the general red coloring of the panels as well as the red stars symbolizing pain indicate the gravity of the assault. First, the text is reduced to a few uncommented interjections uttered during the fight in speech bubbles; the narrator's discourse only reappears after the attack in the last panel of the double page with a panoramic shot of the Hotel Cuba Libre at night, a landmark of modern Havana, localizing the events both visually and textually: "CRUZAMOS EL MALECÓN Y EN SILENCIA TOMAMOS UNA CALLE LATERAL."[38]

From an intersectional perspective, the episode exposes Havana to be a heteronormative male-dominated space, from the streets of the city to the institutions of the Revolution (and into the private sphere), for it is not the attackers but their victims who are hauled before the Revolution's legal authorities for causing public nuisance. The real scandal for the Revolution, the graphic memoir suggests, consists in the visibility of women in public space who do not conform to the heteronormative rationale of the Revolution and who dare to appropriate this purportedly neutral "abstract space" of power.[39] Although the Revolution officially

---

36 For a short analysis of this episode cf. Pérez Cano (2020: 70).
37 For an overview on camera distance and its effects in film or comics cf. Lewis (2012: 90–94).
38 Veltfort (2017: 134–139, here 137). Cf. Veltfort (2019: 129): "WE CROSSED THE MALECÓN & HURRIED UP A SIDESTREET."
39 Lefebvre (2000 [1974]: 60–65). This episode also illustrates the spatial separation shedding the Cuban from the foreign population of the island and the special relationship between Cuba

alleges to create "differential spaces"[40] of equal opportunity and tolerance in terms of ethnicity, class, and gender, it nevertheless perpetuates a heteronormative spatial order through its apparatus of power. As various episodes in *Adiós mi Habana* show, this politics of space results in the displacement of marginalized population groups to private interiors, to the outskirts of the city or to the labor camps of the Revolution – and in subversive strategies to escape the dictates of the Revolution.[41]

Another striking aspect is the way the Revolution treats Havana's foreign population, reproducing the geopolitical order of the Cold War and strictly separating the Cuban population from the foreign population through urban planning. *Adiós mi Habana* comments on the special status of foreign technicians or diplomats by providing extensive and detailed overview pages with an illustrated *Who's Who* of the foreign leftist intelligentsia and their privileged living conditions, which it implicitly contrasts with the humility and confinement of Cuban dwellings.[42] The connection between geopolitics and Cuban immigration policies becomes evident on the *histoire* level in the privileged, albeit politically precarious, position of invited foreigners and their families in Havana: in 1969, Connie's family is forced to leave the country due to her stepfather's political proximity to the Soviet Union; as a U.S. citizen, later, Connie cannot to find work after graduating from the University of Havana without renouncing to her U.S. passport.[43] The Revolution's spatial concept of the material and cultural separation of the Cuban from the foreign population determines the life of the protagonist, who, as a transnational and local border crosser, tries to mediate between the isolated parallel world of the foreign community, organized by the Cuban Institute for Friendship with Peoples ICAP (Instituto Cubano de Amistad con los Pueblos), and the Cuban population's everyday spaces. However, even Connie's success in mediating those spaces is limited. While she can create a protected private space in which heterodox encounters are possible, eventually the Cuban authorities thwart her plans to escape with her Cuban partner to London, and Connie must leave Cuba. In addition to this immediate autobiographical setting, the narrator's discourse refers to events of global political significance, linking them to Connie's life. Thus, the Playa Girón invasion (1961),

---

and the United States: Connie's parents do hardly acknowledge her summonses while her nationality complicates the trials.

40 Lefebvre (2000 [1974]: 60–65). For an explication of "differential" and "abstract spaces" in Lefebvrian throught applied to postcolonial contexts (cf. Brüske 2018: 182–183).
41 Cf. Veltfort (2017: 90–93, 122–123, 159–160).
42 Cf. also Veltfort (2017: 41–45, 53, 68–69).
43 Cf. Veltfort (2017: 155, 203).

the October Crisis (1962), the war in Vietnam, and the invasion of Czechoslovakia (1968) by Soviet troops are mentioned in the text and represented visually while Connie's autobiographical account carves out their importance for education, economy, and culture in Cuba.[44]

5 Producing Multiscalar "Imagined Worlds" and "Geopolitical Imaginaries" through Intertextuality

This depiction of multiscalar entanglements points to an important spatio-poietic technique in *Adiós mi Habana*, the production of fictional space via intertextuality, pertaining most often to the intersection between *espaces de representation* and *représentations de l'espace*. Whereas autopoietic references are scarce in *Adiós mi Habana*, the graphic memoir sports myriad intertextual and intermedial references.[45] These references contextualize Connie's spatial practices, representations of space, and imaginations of space in the material culture of the early Revolution quoting international pop songs and their lyrics, films or photographs and other well-circulated images. For instance, they show Connie's fellow students' thirst for banned music such as albums by Bob Dylan and Joan Baez or the Beatles as well as the repression connected to their consumption.[46] Above all, however, these references deploy their spatio-poietic effect via the dimensions of artistic *espace vécu* and representative *espace conçu*. Being both representations of space and spaces of representation they characterize Veltfort's Havana on different scales: on the local micro-scale as a contested space between the Revolution's official doctrine and 'sub-' or 'countercultures,' on a national scale as an anti-colonial and socialist nation, and on a global geopolitical scale as part of the socialist Second World and the uprising Third World. Approaching techniques of graphic journalism,[47] *Adiós mi Habana* employs historical material, such as iconic photographs of the revolutionaries Fidel Castro or Che Guevara, for instance "Guerrero heroico" (1960) by Alberto Korda or the

---

44 Cf. Veltfort (2017: 26, 46–52, 93, 163–164).
45 It is not the process and context of the graphic memoir's creation but the coming-of-age process of the artist as an individuum in-between spaces that takes center space here.
46 Cf. Veltfort (2017: 82, 175–176).
47 Cf. Hangartner (2016: 298–299).

picture of Guevara's corpse in Bolivia (1967),[48] clips from Cuban or North American newspapers and magazines, political speeches, or other texts to document and create the Cuba of the 1960s and 1970s. These documents belong in part to a global archive of images that have been circulating since the 1960s and 1970s while others originate from the author's and illustrator's personal archive which she has been publishing since 2007 on her website *El Archivo de Connie*.[49] The graphic memoir combines these historic documents with Connie's autobiographical narrative in large collages that frequently occupy double pages.[50] The memoir uses the interplay between the different strands of verbal and visual narration to evidence the entanglements between the dimension of the individual, the local, the national, and the global. Doing so, the memoir tends to resort to a three-step-argumentation that first represents a global political event, secondly perspectivizes this event with regard to Connie's individual situation, and thirdly portrays its local or national reverberations in Cuba. In order to connect the three dimensions, the collages play with different shades of coloring, for instance choosing red as the basic color for each panel of a sequence. The collages also arrange quoted images and texts in a kaleidoscope-like structure, always positioning the individual autobiographical plot in a central position. In combining historical documents and individual biography, the graphic memoir unfolds an ironic critique of the Cuban Revolution and, more generally, of cold war politics from a spatiotemporal and post-socialist distance. This critical composition of texts, historical documents, and images represents an attempt to recreate Cuban social space in the 1960s and 1970s and to offer its audience the possibility to experience Havana and Cuba by way of their medium-triggered imagination. At the same time, it points to the ideological space of narration from which the coming-of-age story is told. Anna Veltfort is writing and drawing from outside Cuba, but unlike a whole generation of Cuban Americans she is not either firmly anchored in the harsh anti-Cuba rhetoric of the United States.

The use of historical documents in the three-step technique intertwining global political events, individual perspective and local/national consequences is particularly prominent in chapters 2 and 5 ("La universidad de la Habana," "La ofensiva revolucionaria"). The chapters focus on the Revolution's repressive measures to 'cleanse' public and private space of undesirable individuals.

---

48 Cf. Veltfort (2017: 73, 154). On the iconization and adaption of photographs showing Guevara cf. also Pouzol (2016).
49 Cf. Veltfort (2007). The website itself was not available at the time of publication, but has been archived digitally by the University of Miami within the "Veltfort Collection."
50 For example, cf. Veltfort (2017: cover page, 36–37, 46–47, 57, 80–81, 128–129, 154–155, 158–159, 162–164).

In "La depuración," a subsection of Chapter 2, the narrator's discourse links the establishment of the infamous UMAP labor camps[51] to the Tricontinental Conference (officially: Primera Conferencia de Solidaridad de los Pueblos de África, Asia y América Latina) which followed the Bandung Conference (1955) in Havana in 1966. The conference gathered political and anticolonial leaders from the Global South such as Amílcar Cabral (Guinea-Bissau, Cabo Verde) and Nguyen Van Tien (Vietnam), foregrounding the revolutionary processes in Cuba and Vietnam and the solidarization of the non-aligned states of Asia, Africa, and the Americas against imperialism and colonialism in the Organization of Solidarity of the People of Africa, Asia, and Latin America (OSPAAAL).[52] The sequence of panels condemning the UMAP camps and showing the paradox of their mere existence in an anti-colonial nation[53] begins with a double-page dedicated to the establishment of the labor camps (Figure 2).[54]

In the foreground of the page, the narrator's discourse depicts the disappearance of one of Connie's friends on the streets of Havana in a sequence of three colorful panels. The sequence bears the title "UMAP [.] UN DÍA DE NOVIEMBRE DE 1965, NUESTRO AMIGO GUSTAVO VENTOSO DESAPARECIÓ"[55] in a white textbox. Textboxes placed beneath or between the panels as well as the panels themselves provide details about the disappearance and report rumors of labor and re-education camps. The background panels, obliquely cropped and colored in shades of red with black lines contrast practices of surveillance, punishment, and subversive appropriation of space in the UMAPS with the praise of camps by Cuban politicians. On the upper left, Fidel is depicted in a dialogue with three other Cuban officials reconstructing the 'invention' of the UMAP: "¡SÍ! LA LLAMAREMOS LA UMAP. ¡UNIDADES MILITARES DE AYUDA A LA PRODUCCIÓN!" and explaining their target groups: "LOS ANTISOCIALES," "LA LACRA," "LOS RELIGIOSOS."[56] On the upper right, there is a partial

---

51 The UMAP camps, i.e. Unidades Militares de Ayuda a la Producción or Military Units To Aid Production, were labor camps existing from 1965 and 1968 that were meant to 're-educate' so-called counterrevolutionaries by forcing them to do agricultural labor in state farms.
52 Cf. Mahler (2018: e.g., 2–3). The Tricontinental Conference also provided Cuba a platform as a (Latin) American player in the face of its US-triggered exclusion from the Organization of American States from 1962 till 2009.
53 Veltfort (2017: 90–93).
54 Veltfort (2017: 90–91).
55 Veltfort (2017: 90). Cf. Veltfort (2019: 82): "UMAP [.] ONE DAY IN NOVEMBER 1965, OUR FRIEND GUSTAVO VENTOSO DISAPPEARED."
56 Veltfort (2017: 90). Cf Veltfort (2019: 82): "YES! WE'LL CALL IT THE UMAP, UNIDADES MILITARES DE AYUDA A LA PRODUCCIÒN!" and: "THE SOCIAL MISFITS," "THE DEADBEATS," "THE RELIGIOUS."

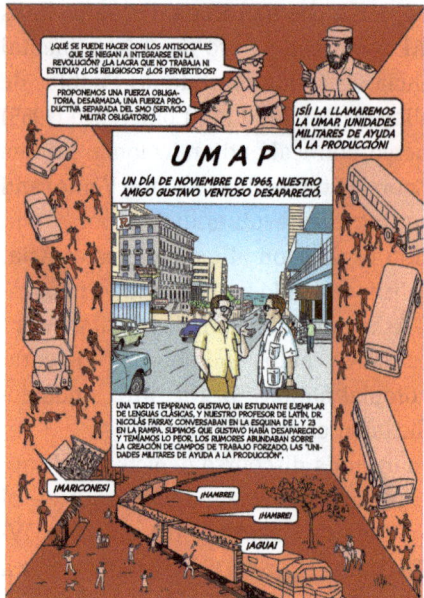 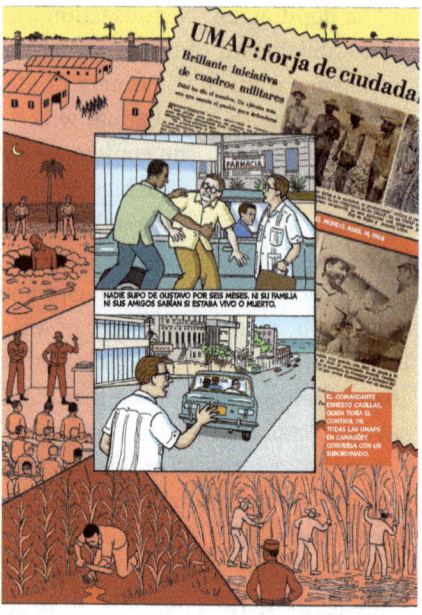

Figure 2: "UMAP [.] UN DÍA DE NOVIEMBRE DE 1965, NUESTRO AMIGO GUSTAVO VENTOSO DESAPARECIÓ." Anna Veltfort (2017): *Adiós mi Habana. Las memorias de una gringa y su tiempo en los años revolucionarios de la década de los 60.* Madrid: Verbum, pp. 90–91, with permission by the author.

reproduction of an article from the Cuban newspaper *El Mundo* (1901–1969) of April 14, 1966, calling the UMAP camps a "brillante iniciativa de cuadros militares" and a "forja de ciudad[anía]."[57] The reproduction shows photos both of camp inhabitants at work and of Ernesto Casillas, an official in charge of the UMAP in Camagüey. Scenes of camp life are depicted on the remaining page surface, commented by short intradiegetic interjections in white speech bubbles, showing the prisoners' inhumane treatment, insults and indoctrination, their

---

[57] Veltfort (2017: 91). "A brilliant initiative of military leaders/cadres," "a forge of citizenship" (translation A.B.). Those clips are also restored on *El Archivo de Connie* and referred to in the notes section. Cf. Veltfort (2017: 222), Veltfort (2007–:

https://wayback.archive-it.org/16782/20210527203441/http://www.annaillustration.com/archivodeconnie/wp-content/uploads/20210527202009/20210527203402/UMAP-20210527201966.pdf).

hard work, as well as their despair.[58] Whereas the background panels in shades of red give context information on the foundation and functioning of the UMAP and the newspaper clip lends these graphic representations historical authenticity, the central positioning of the *histoire* elements, emphasized by the diagonal gutter lines of the background panels, concretizes the UMAP's immediate threat to the civilian population's psychological or physical integrity and focuses on individual and collective suffering in the "heterotopia" of the camp.[59]

In an ironic commentary on these local and national repressive spatial practices, the subsequent double-page spread focuses on a meeting of global importance (Figure 3): the Tricontinental Conference, held in January 1966, only a few months after the UMAP were founded.[60] Its structure is similar to the previous double page. The colorful panels that carry the story are placed in a central position while the irregular and more uniformly colored background panels provide context information of national and global scope. The narrator's discourse, placed in textboxes above and beneath the first central panel showing Connie's mother Leonore interviewing a conference participant, briefly describes the international conference, Cuba's role, and Leonore's attitude as foreign correspondent for the German newspaper *Das andere Deutschland*, while in a second panel, positioned beneath, Connie and her fellow students speculate about their friend Gustavo's fate.

The background explicates the collective-political spatial dimension. From a distance of almost 50 years, it reveals the contradictoriness of global anti-colonial engagement and internal repression. More specifically, by dividing the background panels into two unequal parts, the graphic memoir pinpoints the opposition between the revolutionary impetus of the international conference during which Cuba claimed global leadership in the struggle against colonial oppression and the forced disappearance of dissidents. The upper two-thirds, in shades of yellow and green, consist of a collage of photos taken at the Tricontinental Conference, newspaper clippings from the socialist newspapers *Hoy*, *Revolución* and the newly founded organ of the Cuban government *Granma*, as well as a *Who's Who* of anti-colonial leaders such as Che Guevara, Amílcar Cabral, and Ben Barka, depicted in bull's eye-shaped circles. On the right page,

---

[58] Cf. Veltfort (2017: 222). The sketches of the camp are drawn from work by ex-prisoners published in the 1984 documentary *Conducta Impropia* by Néstor Almendros and Orlando Jiménez Leal.
[59] For the concept of heterotopias as contrasting spaces, cf. Lefebvre (2000 [1974]: II, 14: 189–190).
[60] Veltfort (2017: 92–93).

Figure 3: "LA CONFERENCIA TRICONTINENTAL." Anna Veltfort (2017): *Adiós mi Habana. Las memorias de una gringa y su tiempo en los años revolucionarios de la década de los 60.* Madrid: Verbum, pp. 92–93, with permission by the author.

excerpts from Fidel Castro's closing remarks of January 15, 1966, are presented in a white speech bubble that originates from the reproduction of a photograph of the conference's concluding discussion.[61] This iconic take on Fidel towering over the lectern in front of portraits of Ho Chi Minh, Patrice Lumumba, and Augusto César Sandino and on the Tricontinental Conference as a moment of nascent Third World solidarity and joint Global South politics has circulated around the globe.[62] As an image of anti-colonial internationalist solidarity under Cuban leadership, in the context of the graphic memoir, it has the discursive function to

---

[61] The recreation of the conference picture seems to stem from a photograph credited to the Cuban national newspaper *Granma*. A digital copy is available in an article from January, 3, 2022, on the webpage of the independent news channel TeleSur: "Primera Conferencia Tricontinental: Un hito de solidaridad" (2022).

[62] On the "propaganda machine" of the Tricontinental and its circulation of posters, magazines, books, and radio programs cf. Mahler (2021).

reconstruct the "imagined world" (Appadurai) of the Cuban Revolution in the 1960s and the corresponding Cubano-Centric "geopolitical imaginary" while commenting on the Revolution's flaws and failures from the post-1989 and outside-Cuba perspective of the memoir's audience. The memoir reproduces the beginning of Fidel's concluding remarks in which he conjures Cuba's fellow countries from Asia, Africa, and the Americas to stand together underlining their "COMMON INTEREST" and their "COMMON ANTI-IMPERIALIST STANCE":[63]

> NO SE NOS ESCAPA LA TRASCENDENCIA DE ESTE ACTO QUE CULMINA EN LA NOCHE DE HOY. [. . .] HA SIDO ESTA UNA GRAN VICTORIA DEL MOVIMIENTO REVOLUCIONARIO. NUNCA HABÍA TENIDO LUGAR UNA REUNIÓN DE TAL AMPLITUD Y DE TAL MAGNITUD, EN QUE LAS REPRESENTACIONES REVOLUCIONARIAS DE 82 PUEBLOS SE REUNIERAN PARA DISCUTIR PROBLEMAS DE INTERÉS COMÚN. NUNCA UNA REUNIÓN TAN AMPLIA, PORQUE AQUÍ HAN ESTADO REPRESENTADOS LOS PUEBLOS DE TRES CONTINENTES, LOS MOVIMIENTOS REVOLUCIONARIOS DE LOS PUEBLOS DE TRES CONTINENTES, QUE TIENEN UNA COMÚN POSICIÓN ANTIMPERIALISTA, QUE REPRESENTAN LA LUCHA DE SUS PUEBLOS, DESDE DISTINTAS IDEAS O POSICIONES FILOSÓFICAS, O DESDE DISTINTAS CREENCIAS RELIGIOSAS, REPRESENTATIVAS EN MUCHAS OCASIONES DE DISTINTAS IDEOLOGÍAS, PERO QUE TIENEN ALGO DE COMÚN. . .[64]

The lower third of the image is a continuation of the graphic discourse about the UMAP deployed on the previous two pages. In shades of red again, it shows episodes of rebellion, repression, and subversion, such as the shooting of a protesting Afro-Cuban prisoner as well as the improvised celebrations with which the prisoners appropriate the hostile space of the camp.

By arranging anti-colonial solidarization and internal de-solidarization in separate yet contiguous sequences of panels and connecting them discursively, the narrator's co-composition of textual and visual discourse engages in a critique and a re-evaluation of the Revolution's concepts and practices. It is the distance in time and the information gathered retrospectively that allows the

---

63 Veltfort (2017: 93, 2019: 85).
64 Veltfort (2017: 93, 2019: 85): "THE IMPORTANCE OF THIS EVENT WHICH HAS COME TO A CLIMAX TONIGHT, DOES NOT ESCAPE US. . . THIS HAS BEEN A GREAT VICTORY FOR THE REVOLUTIONARY MOVEMENT. NEVER HAS THERE BEEN A GATHERING OF SUCH DIMENSIONS AND OF SUCH MAGNITUDE, A GATHERING IN WHICH THE REVOLUTIONARY REPRESENTATIONS OF 82 PEOPLES HAVE MET TO DISCUSS PROBLEMS OF COMMON INTEREST. NEVER HAS THERE BEEN SUCH A LARGE MEETING, BECAUSE THE PEOPLES OF THREE CONTINENTS HAVE BEEN HERE; THE REVOLUTIONARY MOVEMENTS OF THE PEOPLES OF THREE CONTINENTS WHO HAVE A COMMON ANTI-IMPERIALIST STANCE; WHO REPRESENT THE STRUGGLE OF THEIR PEOPLES WITH DIFFERING PHILOSOPHICAL IDEAS OR POSITIONS, OR WITH DIFFERING RELIGIOUS BELIEFS; WHO ON MANY OCCASIONS REPRESENT DIFFERING IDEOLOGIES. BUT THEY HAVE SOMETHING IN COMMON. . ."

narrator to posit that the Revolution employs practices of repression similar to those once employed by the colonial power apparatus of the Spanish. This criticism coalesces in the episode of the killing of the Afro-Cuban prisoner, suggesting undertones of racism by visually depicting his murderer as a Euro-descendent Cuban Criollo. The graphic memoir parallels the Revolution's repressive practices with those of the former slaveholding society, revealing the continuity of colonial hegemonies that the Cuban Revolution asserts to have abolished. It thus calls into question (the mere possibility) of an effective solidarization of Cuba with Africa. The victim's name, Elegguá, adds to the implicit critique of post-1959 racism: Elegguá is the name of one of the most important Afro-Cuban orishas, keeper of the crossroads, and a syncretic fusion of a Yoruba deity and the Catholic saint San Antonio de Padua. The murder of the prisoner Elegguá by the Cuban Revolution can then be interpreted as the elimination of Afro-Cuban cultures, very much in contradiction with the Revolution's official discourse.[65] It also constitutes a form of cultural and biological racism, which Fidel Castro declared a common point of struggle at the Tricontinental Conference, continuing just after the excerpts quoted in *Adiós mi Habana*:

> [. . .] lo más común que une hoy a los pueblos de estos tres continentes y de todo el mundo, que es la lucha contra el imperialismo, la lucha contra el colonialismo y el neocolonialismo, la lucha contra el racismo [. . .][66]

The sequence of the UMAP shooting at the bottom of the double page and the iconic photograph of the Tricontinental Conference on the top of the right page form a both discursive and visual dialogue, the shooting episode representing the hidden subtext to the official anti-colonial positions pronounced by Fidel Castro. Interestingly, like most of the photographs used for the graphic memoir, also the picture of Fidel at the Tricontinental Conference is not inserted into the collage as an identical reprint. Veltfort rather recreates the photograph by redrawing the contours of objects and persons but adding different colorings. This technique of recreating iconic images rather than just reprinting them produces an effect of 'reversed alienation': Thanks to their transformation into

---

65 On the shortcomings of the Cuban Revolution in terms of antiracism cf. e.g. Zurbano Torres (2015), Mahler (2021). Whereas the Revolution made a point in addressing the Afro-Cuban community in the early period, insisting for example on the ethnographic work by Fernando Ortiz or Miguel Barnet's publication of Esteban Montejo's testimony *Biografía de un cimarron* (1966), its politics rapidly proved insufficient while the issue was declared to be resolved (cf. Mahler 2021).
66 Castro Ruiz (1966). "What the peoples have most in common to unite the people of three continents and of all the world today is the struggle against imperialism, the struggle against colonialism and neo-colonialism, the struggle against racism." (translation A.B.).

pictures similar in style and colors to the other graphic elements of the memoir the photographic documents insert themselves smoothly into its graphic world and lend the autobiographical story and its spaces 'documented' authenticity. Via the dimension of space of representation and representations of space they contribute to the production of an overall Cuban and global space in the graphic novel. Hence, the autobiographical plot, the documentary character, and their spatio-poietic potential interlock in the composition of the memoir and in its anticipated reader response.[67]

The juxtaposition of the UMAP and Tricontinental Conference, uttering severe criticism with regard to the revolutionary Cuba's national practices and global imaginaries, is embedded in the narration of the practices of "cleansings" ("LAS GRANDES PURGAS DE 1965") at the University of Havana.[68] Also the larger account of Cuba's *gleichschaltung* by excluding undesirable subjects from public institutions tightly integrates historical visual and textual material, such as short comic strips from *Alma Mater*, *Mella*, and *Juventud Rebelde*, official journals of the Young Communist League (UJC) and student union FEU (Federación Estudiantil Universitaria).[69] For instance, the memoir reproduces a 1965-cartoon from *Mella* in which the dog Pucho, one of Virgilio Martínez' most popular characters, ridicules intellectuals and exposes the Revolution's utilitarian attitude to art.[70]

In conjunction with the memoir's autobiographical plot these historical documents enable the audience to enter the protagonist's experienced space in Cuba and to view the Revolution's spatial project with a critical eye given its repressive character for both individual subjects and the collective of the Cuban population. From a global perspective, the narrator's discourse documents and reiterates – by reproducing propaganda material that employs anti-capitalist, anti-individualist, and anti-North American stereotypes to 'educate' the Cuban

---

[67] In a similar structure, Chapter 5, "La ofensiva revolucionaria," relates both verbally and visually the international Congreso Cultural de La Habana (1968) to Cuban domestic policies and their consequences for Cuba's population: As a result of internal cleansings in the Communist Party of Cuba (PCC) Connie's pro-Soviet stepfather is dismissed, while due to the so-called "revolutionary offensive" all hospitality and craft businesses are shut down. Later, this chain of events completed by Fidel's approval of the Soviet invasion of Czechoslovakia (global), the persecution of non-conformists in the "Operación Hippie," the Caso Padilla (national), and the protagonist's simultaneous illness with hepatitis after serving as a laborer in the countryside (individual/local); cf. Veltfort (2017: 154–158).
[68] Cf. Veltfort (2017: 78–96, here 78).
[69] Cf. e.g. Veltfort (2017: 87, 95, 96).
[70] Cf. Veltfort (2017: 96).

population – the geopolitical fault lines of the Cold War that still hold for Cuba in 2017, at the time of the narration.

Ultimately, the intermedial references embed *Adiós mi Habana* as a "mosaic of quotations"[71] in a network of verbal and visual discourses while simultaneously possessing a significant spatio-poietic function. First of all, they produce the individual space of the memoir's protagonist Connie, and second, they reproduce, contextualize, and document the social, spatial, and cultural concepts of the Revolution. Third, by using globally circulating images and historical documents, they evoke associations of Cuba and the geopolitical order of the Cold War in their 21st century audiences. Moreover, the interweaving of intermedial references with individual, local, national, and geopolitical perspectives underscores the complex relationality of Havana and Cuba as part of the Americas, the anticolonial movement, and the Cold War bloc world. Veltfort's spatial production is then to be seen as an expression of the geopolitical imaginary of the Cold War world from a retrospective viewpoint. By means of the autobiographical character Connie and her transgressions of boundaries, it creates a globally entangled imagined space defying the era's block logic.

6 Producing Multiscalar "Imagined Worlds," Retrieving "Images" from the Archive

In summary, the production of multiscalar fictional space in the graphic memoir *Adiós mi Habana* operates on two levels. On the first, the narrated spaces and "imagined worlds" the characters live in attempt to reconstruct Connie's individual understanding of her world and time as well as collective geopolitical imaginaries. So, the memoir presents the "imagined local/national/global worlds" of the 1960s and 1970s from Connie's perspective as a transnational subject *and* from the perspective of the Cuban Revolution unveiling thusly contemporary geopolitical imaginaries. The process of reproducing these specific spaces in the memoir relies on historical documents, "images" that lend the represented "imagined worlds" and "imaginaries" of the time authenticity. On a second level, the spaces of narration from which the narrator/illustrator 'speaks' in the 2010s are deeply imbricated with the memoir's narrated spaces from the 1960s and 1970s. Impacting on the audience's perception and assessment of the post-1959 characters' "imagined worlds" and "geopolitical imaginaries" from

---

[71] Kristeva (1967: 440–441): "tout texte se construit comme mosaïque de citations."

a postcolonial and postsocialist perspective, they contribute to an overall production of fictional space in the memoir in which different layers of time and understandings of space overlap in a spatiotemporal palimpsest.[72] Therefore, the "images," showcased and framed by the narrator's graphic and textual discourse, rather than solely authenticating the "imagined worlds" of the protagonist and contemporary "geopolitical imaginaries," serve to deconstruct the imagined communities and the Revolution's geopolitical imaginaries.

As discussed above, intertextuality – the crosslinking of Connie's autobiographical account with different types of documents – plays an important role in creating *Adiós mi Habana*'s spaces and reflecting on the multiscalar entanglements of the 1960s and 1970s world from a transnational angle. This leads to the question of Veltfort's sources and images, and more specifically to the question of the archive. Most of the documents reproduced in *Adiós mi Habana* can be found either in *El Archivo de Connie* or they are referenced in the memoir's note section making them traceable and verifiable, on the one hand.[73] On the other hand, their insertion into the autobiographical and the larger political narrative may be interpreted as complementary to the safeguarding and communicative function of the online archive. Since the mid 2000s, Veltfort has been collecting "[d]ocumentos, fotografías, música y publicaciones de la vida cultural y universitaria de La Habana en la década de 1960 y algo de la década de 1970,"[74] attesting to the repression of homosexual and other marginalized groups. Making these documents available to the Cuban community *fuera* had become a priority to the author after the nascent rainbow washing tendencies of the Cuban government in the 2000s, i.e. the efforts to downplay structural homophobia within the Revolution and to promote open-mindedness through the creation of institutions such as the Centro Nacional de Educación Sexual (CENEX) in 1989.[75] Following Aleida Assmann, collecting historical and cultural

---

72 For a new conceptualization of the connection between the postsocialist and the postcolonial cf. Koobak, Tlostanova, and Thapar-Björkert (2021: 3): "As analytical terms, both postcolonialism and postsocialism are concerned with legacies of imperial power, dependence, resistance, and hybridity, therefore pointing to multiple productive convergences between the two. Yet, postcolonialism is commonly equated with the global South, rarely addressed through postsocialist perspectives, while at the same time postsocialism is often only associated with Central and East Europe, post-Soviet countries in the Caucasus and Central Asia, and China – sites that are always already interwoven with a (post)colonial world order and almost never seen as decolonising."
73 Veltfort (2017: 221–226).
74 Veltfort (2007–: "Documents, photographs, music, and publications of the cultural and university life in the Havana of the decade of the 1960s and some of the decade of the 1970s."
75 Cf. Henken/Veltfort (2021).

documents in archives can be conceptualized as a way of remembering passively.⁷⁶ However, rather than just safekeeping a dormant knowledge about Cuba in its local, national, and global entanglements, *El Archivo de Connie* has contributed to reactivating this half-forgotten and half-repressed knowledge and to reanimating the discussion about Cuba and its Revolution in the 1960s and 1970s within an active community as the comments section below the blog entries show. The graphic memoir then goes one step further by reframing a certain amount of the digitized documents through its autobiographical lens and by reaching out to a larger audience.

Finally, it is safe to say that *Adiós mi Habana*, as an act of autobiographically inspired transnational imagination, offers its audience a very particular and well-informed view on early post-1959 Cuba. Linking individual, local, national, and global perspectives, it criticizes the shortcomings and marginalization engendered by the Revolution and shows Cuba's complex global entanglements as both an isolated and a connected island. Adopting the peculiar perspective of a U.S. American women traveling to and from Cuba, it differs from the majority of texts on emigration, exile, and diaspora. Unlike *Apuntes para un viaje a Alemania* or *Cuba. My Revolution* it eschews "looking back in anger";⁷⁷ rather exhibiting nostalgia and constructive criticism the memoir ponders on the protagonist's and the text's implicit, yet fundamental question: "¿Y TODAVÍA PODREMOS SER REVOLUCIONARIAS?" or: "Can we still be revolutionaries?"⁷⁸

Bibliography

Abel, Julia/Klein, Christian (eds.) (2016): *Comics und Graphic Novels. Eine Einführung*. Stuttgart: J.B. Metzler.
Anderson, Benedict (⁶2006 [1983]): *Imagined Communities. Reflections on the Origin and Spread of Nationalism*. London: Verso.
Appadurai, Arjun (1996): *Modernity at Large. Multural Dimensions of Globalization*. Minneapolis: University of Minnesota Press.
Assmann, Aleida (2008): "Canon and Archive." In: Erll, Astrid/Nünning, Ansgar (eds.) (2008): *Cultural Memory Studies. An International and Interdisciplinary Handbook*. Berlin/New York: De Gruyter, pp. 97–107.
Benítez Rojo, Antonio (1998): *La isla que se repite*. Barcelona: Casiopea.
Birkenmaier, Anke/Whitfield, Esther (eds.) (2011): *Havana Beyond the Ruins. Cultural Mappings after 1989*. Durham: Duke University Press.

---

76 Cf. Assmann (2008: 99).
77 Gewecke (2001: 554): "Blick zurück im Zorn."
78 Veltfort (2017: 207, 2019: 199), Henken/Veltfort (2021).

Brüske, Anne (2018): "Spatial Theory, Post/Colonial Perspectives, and Fiction. Reading Hispano-Caribbean Diaspora Literature in the US with Henri Lefebvre." In: Bauer, Jenny/ Fischer,Robert (eds.) (2018): *Perspectives on Henri Lefebvre. Theory, Practices and (Re) Readings*. Berlin/Boston: De Gruyter, pp. 178–206.

Brüske, Anne (2020): *Zwischen De- und Reterritorialisierung. Raumproduktion US-karibischer Diasporaliteraturen*. Habilitationsschrift, University of Heidelberg.

Castro Ruiz, Fidel (1961): "Discurso pronunciado por el comandante Fidel Castro Ruiz, primer ministro del gobierno revolucionario y secretario del PURSC, como conclusión de las reuniones con los intelectuales cubanos, efectuadas en la Biblioteca Nacional el 16, 23 y 30 de junio de 1961." In: <http://www.cuba.cu/gobierno/discursos/1961/esp/f300661e.html> (Last accessed on 07/ 04/2022).

Castro Ruiz, Fidel (1966): "Discurso pronunciado por el Comandante Fidel Castro Ruiz, primer secretario del comite central del Partido Comunista de Cuba y primer ministro del gobierno revolucionario, en el acto clausura de la primera Conferencia de solidaridad de los pueblos de Asia, África y América Latina (tricontinental), en el Teatro Chaplin, La Habana, el 15 de enero de 1966." In: <http://www.cuba.cu/gobierno/discursos/1966/esp/f150166e.html> (Last accessed on 07/ 04/2022).).

Cortez, Jaime/ Hebert,Patrick (2004): *Sexile = Sexilio*. Los Angeles: Institute for Gay Men's Health.

Epple, Angelika/ Kramer,Kirsten (2016): "Globalization, Imagination, Social Space. The Making of Geopolitical Imaginaries." In: *forum for interamerican research*, 9, 1, pp. 41–63.

Exner, Isabel (2017): *Schmutz. Ästhetik und Epistemologie eines Motivs in Literaturen und Kulturtheorien der Karibik*. Paderborn: Fink.

Genette, Gérard (1972): "Discours du récit." In: *Figures III*. Paris: Seuil, pp. 67–278.

Gewecke, Frauke (2001): "Kubanische Literatur der Diaspora (1960–2000)." In: Ette, Ottmar/ Franzbach, Martin (eds.) (2001): *Kuba heute. Politik, Wirtschaft, Kultur*. Frankfurt/Main: Vervuert, pp. 551–616.

Graziadei, Daniel (2017): *Insel(n) im Archipel. Zur Verwendung einer Raumfigur in den zeitgenössischen anglo-, franko- und hispanophonen Literaturen der Karibik*. Paderborn: Fink.

Guevara, Ernesto "Che" (1978 [1965]): *El hombre nuevo*. México D.F.: UNAM.

Hangartner, Urs (2016): "Sachcomics." In: Abel, Julia/Klein, Christian (eds.) (2016): *Comics und Graphic Novels: Eine Einführung*. Stuttgart: J.B. Metzler, pp. 291–303.

Henken, Ted A./Veltfort, Anna (2021): "'Can We Still Be Revolutionaries?' Anna Veltfort interviewed by Ted A. Henken." In: *No Country Magazine*. <https://nocountrymagazine.com/can-we-still-be-revolutionaries-anna-veltfort-interviewed-by-ted-a-henken/> (Last accessed on 07/ 04/2022).

Hescher, Achim (2016): *Reading Graphic Novels: Genre and Narration*. Berlin/Boston: De Gruyter.

Iser, Wolfgang (1976): *Der Akt des Lesens. Theorie ästhetischer Wirkung*. München: Fink.

Koobak, Redi/ Tlostanova,Madina/Thapar-Björkert, Suruchi (2021): "Introduction. Uneasy Affinities Between the Postcolonial and the Postsocialist." In: Koobak, Redi/ Tlostanova, Madina/Thapar-Bjӧrkert, Suruchi (eds.) (2021): *Postcolonial and Postsocialist Dialogues. Intersections, Opacities, Challenges in Feminist Theorizing and Practice*. London/ New York: Routledge, pp. 1–10.

Kristeva, Julia (1967): "Bakhtine, le mot, le dialogue et le roman." In: *Critique. Revue générale des publications françaises et étrangères*, XXIII, 239, pp. 438–465.
Lefebvre, Henri (1967): "Le droit à la ville." In: *L'Homme et la société*, 6, pp. 29–35.
Lefebvre, Henri (2000 [1974]): *La production de l'espace*. Paris: Anthropos.
Lessing, Gotthold Ephraim E. (1788): *Laokoon, oder über die Grenzen der Mahlerey und Poesie. Mit beylaeufigen Erlaeuterungen verschiedener Punkte der alten Kunstgeschichte*. Berlin: Voss.
Lewis, Jon (2012): *Essential Cinema. An Introduction to Film Analysis*. Boston: Wadsworth.
Lezama Lima, José (1997): "Coloquio con Juan Ramón Jiménez." In: Lezama Lima, José (ed.) (1997): *Ensayos latinoamericanos*. Mexico: Editorial Diana, pp. 165–192.
Lockpez, Inverna/ Haspiel, Dean (2010): *Cuba. My Revolution*. New York: Vertigo.
Lotman, Jurij (2006): "Künstlerischer Raum, Sujet und Figur (1970)." In: Dünne, Jörg/Günzel, Stephan (eds.) (2006): *Raumtheorien. Grundlagentexte aus Philosophie und Kulturwissenschaften*. Frankfurt/Main: Suhrkamp, pp. 529–545.
Mahler, Anne Garland (2018): *From the Tricontinental to the global South. Race, Radicalism, and Transnational Solidarity*. Durham/London: Duke University Press.
Mahler, Anne Garland (2021): "The Tricontinental Racial Justice Movement." In: *Lefteast*. <https://lefteast.org/the-tricontinental-racial-justice-movement/> (Last accessed on 07/04/2022).
McCloud, Scott (1994): *Understanding Comics [The Invisible Art]*. New York: Harper Perennial.
Mogno, Diego (2008). "Historietas cubanas. Medio siglo de sátira, aventura, humorismo, educación y propaganda en Cuba." In: Ostuni, Hernán (ed.) (2008): *Historia de la historieta latinoamericana. Cuba – Chile – Uruguay*. Buenos Aires: Ediciones La Bañadera del Comic, pp. 3–44.
Morejón Arnaiz, Idalia/Aguilera, Carlos A. (2020): *Escenas del yo flotante. Cuba: escrituras autobiográficas*. Leiden: Bokeh.
Obejas, Achy (2009): *Ruins*. New York: Akashic.
Pérez Cano, Tania (2020): "La memoria como espacio de libertad. Autobiografía y testimonio en las narrativas gráficas *Cuba, my Revolution*, de Inverna Lockpez y *Adiós mi Habana*, de Anna Veltfort." In: *Studia Romanistica*, 20, 2, pp. 57–73.
Pérez Medrano, Cuauhtémoc (2019): *Ficción herética. Disimulaciones insulares en la Cuba contemporánea*. Universitätsverlag Potsdam.
Porbén, Pedro P. (2015): "Revolución 'cómica'. Historietas y políticas de afectos en Cuba posrevolucionaria." In: *Iberoamericana*, XV, 57, pp. 117–130.
Pouzol, Camille (2016): "'Che' Guevara. La novela gráfica: cuando la historieta construye el mito." In: *Tebeosfera*, 3, 5. <https://www.tebeosfera.com/documentos/che_guevara._la_novela_grafica_cuando_la_historieta_construye_el_mito.html> (Last accessed on 07/04/2022).
"Primera Conferencia Tricontinental: Un hito de solidaridad" (2022). In: <https://www.telesurtv.net/news/primera-conferencia-trincontinental-objetivos-logros-20200102-0025.html> (Last accessed on 07/04/2022).
Puñales-Alpízar, Damaris (2012): *Escrito en cirílico. El ideal soviético en la cultura cubana posnoventa*. Santiago: Editorial Cuarto Propio.
Schüwer, Martin (2008): *Wie Comics erzählen. Grundriss einer intermedialen Erzähltheorie der grafischen Literatur*. Trier: WVT.
Sökefeld, Martin (2006): "Mobilizing in Transnational Space. A Social Movement Approach to the Formation of Diaspora." In: *Global Networks*, 6, 3, pp. 265–284.

Story, Isabel (2020): *Soviet influence on Cuban culture, 1961–1987. When the Soviets Came to Stay*. Lanham/Boulder/New York/London: Lexington Books.

Veltfort, Anna (2007–): "El Archivo de Connie. Documentos, fotografías, música y publicaciones de la vida cultural y universitaria de La Habana en la década de 1960 y algo de la década de 1970." In: <http://archivodeconnie.annaillustration.com/ via:https://wayback.archive-it.org/16782/20210527160803/http://archivodeconnie.annaillustration.com/> (Last accessed on 07/04/2022).

Veltfort, Anna (2017): *Adiós mi Habana. Las memorias de una gringa y su tiempo en los años revolucionarios de la década de los 60*. Madrid: Verbum.

Veltfort, Anna (2019): *Goodbye, My Havana. The Life and Times of a Gringa in Revolutionary Cuba*. Stanford University Press.

Zurbano Torres, Roberto (2015): "Racismo vs. socialismo en Cuba. Un conflicto fuera de lugar (apuntes sobre/contra el colonialismo interno)." In: *Meridional*, 4, pp. 11–40.

II **Literary Landscapes and Temporalities: Regions and World(s)**

Miriam Lay Brander
Timescapes of the Desert: Multiple Temporalities in Guimarães Rosa's *Grande Sertão*

Since the publication of Euclides da Cunha's study *Os sertões* in 1902 the semi-desert landscapes in the Northeast of Brazil have acquired a renown which its position far from the economic and cosmopolitan centers would not lead one to expect. While, in the context of Portuguese colonial expansion, the term *sertão* (literally: "hinterland" or "backcountry") was commonly used to refer to not yet explored inland areas, the term maintained a dichotomous relationship with Brazil's coastal cities and continued to be associated with barbarism and backwardness in Brazilian intellectual history after independence in 1822 (Saramago 2021: 37). This idea of Brazil's hinterlands shares a decisive feature with what in several Latin American countries, from the colonial period until the first half of the nineteenth century, has been understood as desert: "an elemental void [. . .] a *tabula rasa* in which history was always about to begin and had to be constructed, a virgin space waiting for projects to be brought to fruition in it" (Uriarte 2020). According to Javier Uriarte's argument, the desert as a topos of wilderness and potentiality becomes "concrete, tangible, present" (Uriarte 2020: 2) in the second half of the nineteenth century when the governing elites subject these regions to "desertification" by causing destruction and death through war as a means of modernization. Uriarte borrows the title of his book *The Desertmakers* precisely from Euclides da Cunha, who, in his essay "Fazedores de desertos" [Desert-makers] (1901) criticizes the exploitation of Brazilian interior's soils, first through its native inhabitants and their practices such as slash-and-burn agriculture, and later by the colonists who continue this depletion of soils, and thus increase poverty. The desert, then, is not conceived of as a product of nature anymore, but as the result of humans acting upon nature. Likewise, in Euclides' work *Os sertões*, which tells the story of the War of Canudos (1896–97) between the Brazilian Army and the rebel town Canudos, the destruction of natural space links the city-dwelling soldiers and the rebellious habitants of the backcountry.

Note: Unless otherwise indicated, all translations are my own.

Miriam Lay Brander, KU Eichstätt

https://doi.org/10.1515/9783110762273-005

The state project of modernization is an attempt to impose the temporality of progress, which characterizes the city, across the entire territory (Uriarte 2020: 18). In this process of desertification, fluidity and mobility, including hydraulic forces, must be controlled, the waters' course must be channeled in order to be converted into "natural resources" (Scott 1998: 13). In this sense, according to Uriarte, "Euclides' project is an attempt to stop movement in order to subsequently direct and resignify it, making it useful and productive" (Uriarte 2020: 223). In contrast to Euclides's utilitarian approach, movement is the central figure of Guimarães Rosa's novel *Grande Sertão: Veredas* published more than half a century later. As I would like to show, Guimarães Rosa's *sertão* evades state control by maintaining its *Eigenzeit* (Nowotny 1990), an "intrinsic time" which cannot be subjugated either through war or through narration. The unpredictability and impenetrability of this region goes along with the narrator's vain attempt to convert his contingent experiences of the intricate ways of the *sertão* into a coherent whole.

Although Guimarães Rosa's *sertão* is at a geographical distance from the Northeast's inland areas which form the setting of da Cunha's work, associations of underdevelopment and potentiality which have shaped the social perception of the regions designated as *sertão* also constitute the imaginary background of *Grande Sertão: Veredas*. Curt Meyer-Clason, who has translated Guimarães Rosa's novel, one of the longest books in the Brazilian canon, into German, describes the region, which is also the homeland of the author, with the following words:

> Sertão – that is mountain ranges and valleys, moors and marshlands, canyons and summits. Tertiary formations, underground rivers which make their way to the surface as wells, desert strips with some cactuses growing there. The habitants of the Sertão are half nomad, rough drovers; their resting places are the village, the oasis in the plane, a piece of farmland, the fazenda – the estate – low situated watering places, the groves of the shady burití palmtree protected by steep slopes. (Meyer-Clason 1984: 150)

When Guimarães Rosa published his novel in 1956, the *sertão*, which had hardly opened to international markets, continued to be the symbol of Brazilian nationalism, as which da Cunha had coined Brazil's hinterland in his literary report at the beginning of the 20th century. While numerous critics, following this view, have interpreted the novel as a representation of contemporary Brazil (Campos Soares 2012: 136), Antonio Cândido adds another dimension by seeing the documentation of the "vida sertaneja" elevated to a universal level thanks to fiction (Cândido 1983: 295) and thus reading the novel as an expression of Brazilian super-regionalism (Cândido 1972). Other critics have deduced the universality of *Grande Sertão: Veredas* from comparing the novel to other classics of European literature (see the contributions in Coutinho 1983). In addition to the national and the universal dimension, ecocritical readings have highlighted the material contours of Rosian *sertão*, the vivid description of which as a geographical region of north-western Minas Gerais is the result of the author's own exploration of its physical characteristics, flora and fauna (Saramago 2020, 2021). For Victoria Saramago, it is precisely Rosa's intent to make "this region visible and sayable in the perceptions and practices that constitute politics" (Saramago 2021: 45), that is, to make the features of Minas Gerais's *sertão* appear in the common sphere of experience. The great international resonance of Rosa's novel contributes to the universal significance of the region, fueling the conviction that the *sertão* should be preserved as both biosphere and memory place.

Indeed, Guimarães Rosa carries the tension between localism and universalism, which is so characteristic for numerous works of 20th century Brazilian literature, to an extreme. At the same time, he transcends this dichotomy, which has been a constant in the criticism of Rosian work, through an interplay of multiple semantic dimensions. As Silviano Santiago has emphasized only a few years ago, the novel's monstruous complexity escapes any interpretation which tries to read it within a certain tradition (Santiago 2019) – an observation that can explain the huge corpus of literary criticism the novel has engendered since its publication. Without trying to domesticate *Grande Sertão: Veredas*, I attempt to approach the novel through its – by no means less complex – temporality. As Paul Ricœur (1983) has stated in *Temps et récit*, "le faire narratif re-signifie le monde dans sa dimension temporelle"[1] by selecting certain elements from the sheer abundance of temporal perceptions and combining them into a whole.[2] In this sense, Guimarães Rosa's *sertão* becomes readable as a cluster of material, symbolical, and metaphysical features which are put together and re-signified in the act of narration. Departing from this premise, I examine how the local and the universal dimension of the *sertão* are inscribed in the interplay between the representation of geographical environment, individual experience, and reflexive abstraction. I would like to argue that by interweaving these dimensions through narration, Guimarães Rosa constructs a complex temporality locating the *sertão* both in timeless prehistory as well as experienced past and immediate present.

---

1 "[T]he narrative act re-signifies the world in its temporal dimension" (Ricœur 1983: 122).
2 The efforts for preserving Guimarães Rosa's *sertão* as described by Victoria Saramago can be considered what Ricoeur calls *mimesis III* or re-figuration (Ricœur 1983: 77): the impact of fictional narration on the reader's imaginary which, in turn, shapes social imaginary in the sense of Cornelius Castoriadis, that is, the way in which a society deals with its physical and biological conditions (Castoriadis 1975: 319).

1 From Euclides da Cunha, *Os sertões* (1902) to *Grande Sertão: Veredas*

The image of one of the four sub-regions in the Northeast of Brazil was largely coined by a single text: In *Os sertões*, Euclides da Cunha tells the story of the civil war between the First Brazilian Republic and the residents of the village of Canudos in the state of Bahia, which found a brutal end when the Brazilian army massacred almost all the habitants of the village. The book, which elicited a broad response in Ibero-America, marks a temporal distance between the time of the primitive Northeast, with its residents' inclination to religious fanaticism and violence, on the one hand, and what the author calls civilization, on the other (Nicolazzi 2010). Da Cunha equates the region not only with a reflux in Brazilian history (da Cunha 2010: 316) but places it outside of history, historiography, and the space of civilization: "terra de ninguém, lugar da inversão dos valores, da barbárie e da incultura"[3] (Ventura 1998). Consequently, the semi-desert region for da Cunha is located inside and yet outside of the nation, when passing through it, the protagonists of his book get the impression of finding themselves "fora do Brasil" (da Cunha 2010: 422). Although situated within Brazilian territory, the *sertão* seems to not embody the values of the nation, but rather its defects. However, while marking the village of Canudos as a metonomy of a sick nation that needs to be healed, da Cunha, at the same time, recognizes in this backward region the potential for a future race of great resilience thanks to its adaptation to the rough climate of the *sertão*. This ambivalent vision of the region's residents is metonymically personified by the *jagunço*, an armed member of gangs in the service of rivalling politicians:

> Era o tipo completo do lutador primitivo – ingênuo, feroz e destemeroso – simples e mau, brutal e infantil, valente por instinto, herói sem o saber – um belo caso de retroatividade atávica, forma retardatária de troglodita sanhudo aprumando-se ali com o mesmo arrojo com que, nas velhas idades, vibrava o machado de sílex à porta das cavernas. (Da Cunha 2010)[4]

As the result of an "ethnic anachronism" (da Cunha 2010: 422), the *jagunço* incorporates the Other who is kept at a spatial and temporal distance from the observer. In the words Anne McClintock has used to describe imperial discourse,

---

[3] "[N]o-man's-land, place of the inversion of values, barbarism, and of unculture."
[4] "He was the full-blown type of primitive fighter, fierce, fearless, and naive, at once simple-minded and evil, brutal and infantile, valiant by instinct, a hero without being aware of the fact – in brief, a fine example of recessive atavism, with the retrograde form of a grim troglodyte, stalking upright here with the same intrepidity with which, ages ago, he had brandished a stone hatchet at the entrance to his cave" (da Cunha 1944: 220–221).

"[g]eographical difference across *space* is figured as a historical difference across *time*" (McClintock 2015: 40).

Johannes Fabian (Fabian 1983: 30–31) has described this "time of the other" as *mundane* or *typological time*: these categories serve anthropologists to create their object of research by labelling certain societies or elements of their own society as "archaic" or "primitive" and thus opposing them to their own present and local environment. In this sense, da Cunha's *sertão* stands for the separation between past and present, modern and savage, between culture and nature, between history and its negation (Nicolazzi 2010).

This view of an uncivilized other which Faustino Sarmiento had already prominently expressed by depicting the life of the Argentinian gaucho Facundo Quiroga in 1845 was symptomatic of the positivist thinking and evolutionism which marked the second half of the 19th century in numerous Ibero-American countries. When Guimarães Rosa writes *Grande Sertão: Veredas* more than 50 years later, the *sertanejo* does not constitute a threat to the modern society following the occidental model anymore. Rather, the novel is the result of a nostalgic turning towards rural settings as a response to increasing industrialization and rural exodus since the beginning of Getúlio Vargas' dictatorship (Depieri Amorim 2013: 6–7). The reality of the *sertão* as the epitome of an archaic Brazil turns into a counterbalance to the modern experience of acceleration emanating from urban rhythms of industrialization.

In accordance with this nostalgic attitude, the narrators' perspective in *Grande Sertão: Veredas* is one from within. While Leopoldo M. Bernucci compares Euclides with foreign travellers, whose gaze recalls important moments experienced by ethnographers such as Léry, Saint-Hilaire, Spix and Martius (Bernucci 1995: 51), Guimarães Rosa's *sertão* is not alien to the narrator and main protagonist of his novel. *Grande Sertão* is the story of landowner Riobaldo who, in a fictional monologue addressed to a listener of superior social status, tells of his forays through the *sertão*, first as a *jagunço* and later as a hard-baked gang leader. His account of violent conflicts between hostile gangs, of marches lasting for days, as well as a variety of encounters and love affairs, is linked to an engagement with the old antagonism between good and evil, between God and the Devil, to whom Riobaldo tries to sell his soul without any success. The first part of the novel consists of a series of anecdotes which serve the first-person narrator as a basis for reasoning on classical themes of European philosophy such as love and hate or life and death. Without finding satisfying responses to his questions, Riobaldo begins to tell his life. After the death of his Indian mother, he lives on the farm of his godfather Selorico Mendes, from where gang leader Zé Bebelo recruits him as a *jagunço*. After the first fight with the hostile gang led by Hermógenes Riobaldo leaves Zé Bebelo's crew to join fearsome gang leader Joca Ramiro whose gang member Diadorim alias Reinaldo becomes a close friend of Riobaldo. Both together decide to leave Joca Ramiro's troop in order to join the gang of Titão Passos who had fought at archenemy Hermógenes's side before. When Hermógenes kills Joca Ramiro numerous *jagunços* join forces under the leadership of Zé Bebelo, whose life Joca Ramiro had saved earlier, to fight a fierce battle against the murderer of the great gang leader. During this time, Riobaldo has two love affairs which provoke Diadorim's jealousy: one with the prostitute Nhorinhá and another with Otacília, with whom Riobaldo gets engaged later. The two big gangs ally for a short time to fight against the government troop, but Zé Bebelo's gang soon leaves the battlefield and reaches Veredas-Mortas, where Riobaldo takes over leadership in the fight against Hermógenes on behalf of Zé Bebelo. In a last bloody battle, Diadorim and Hermógenes engage in a direct fight with each other, in which both lose their lives. In this moment, Riobaldo learns that Diadorim is no other than Maria Deodorina da Fé Bittancourt Marins, Joca Ramiro's daughter, who has revenged her father's life, paying for this with her own.

The great number and cruelty of the battles depicted in *Grande Sertão* have caused some critics to read the novel in a direct line with da Cunha's *Os Sertões*, whose central topic, the War of Canudos, is considered one of the most tragic episodes in 19th century Latin American history. For Javier Uriarte, following James C. Scott (Scott 1998), war is an instrument of the Brazilian state to make the opaque space of the *sertão* legible by simplifying its territory and population. However, the men of the *sertão* evade this visibility, protected by the desert and its irregular landscape where strangeness and mystery predominate (Uriarte 2020: 239). While war, in da Cunha's essay, can then be considered as an ordering intervention of the state to enforce modernization, the violence we find in *Grande Sertão* is much more irrational, unpredictable, and contingent and cannot simply be explained with the necessity of war (Campos Soares 2012: 141).[5] At the same time, it would be too short-sighted to read extreme violence in Guimarães Rosas's *sertão* as a symptom of lawlessness and hence of political and social backwardness. It is true that certain passages of the novel seem to confirm such an interpretation by juxtaposing the archaic environment of the *sertão* and contemporary technological progress:

> Lá era, como ainda hoje é, mata alta. Mas, por entre as árvores, se podia ver um carro-de-bois parado, os bois que mastigavam com escassa baba, indicando vinda de grandes

---

[5] Jean-Paul Bruyas states that this conception of violence might have been influenced by the author's personal experience during Second World War, when he was consul in Germany, where he observed quite closely the excessive violence of a disastrous war (. . .).

distâncias. Daí, o senhor veja: tanto trabalho, ainda, por causa de uns metros de água mansinha, só por falta duma ponte. Ao que, mais, no carro-de-bois, levam muitos dias, para vencer o que em horas o senhor em seu jipe resolve. Até hoje é assim, por borco. (Guimarães Rosa 1994: 136–137)[6]

This contemporaneousness of the non-contemporaneous, which is reinforced by the temporal distance between the scenery described and the present of narration, situates the *sertão* in a not-so-distant past – Riobaldo's uncle, who speaks here, identifies himself as contemporary witness. Other passages reveal a stratum of time which cannot be located historically. The encounter with a group of strangely armed creatures, for example, makes Riobaldo state that "Nos tempos antigos, devia de ter sido assim. Gente tão em célebres, conforme eu nunca tinha divulgado nem ouvido dizer, na vida" (Guimarães Rosa 1994: 544).[7] If the evoking of ancient times makes resonate da Cunha's vision of the *sertão*, statements such as "Os gerais desentendem de tempo" (Guimarães Rosa 1994: 148)[8] definitely seem to situate the region in pre-historic timelessness.

However, the diligence with which the narrator describes and reflects the battles including their strategic particularities makes it difficult to read them as a symptom of the primitivism evoked in the previously cited passages. Felipe Bier, in his study on *Grande Sertão: Veredas*, argues that the particularity of violence in Guimarães Rosa's novel is the result of a tight relationship between a specific historical process and a modern concept of sovereignty. Conforming to this hypothesis, Bier identifies two historical stratums in *Grande Sertão*: the first decades of the *República Velha* at the end of the 19th and the beginning of the 20th century with its dominance of the plantation economy, and the years in which the novel was written half a century later, and in which the rise of capitalism and its juridical institutions cause a crisis of oligarchic forms of governance (Bier 2015). Following up on this thesis, I would like to show that Guimarães Rosa, instead of perpetuating the idea of a prehistoric society in the semi-desert Northeast, deconstructs the opposition between the archaic and the modern by reshaping da Cunha's *sertão* as an allegory for temporal and spatial

---

6 "There was high forest there, as there still is today. But, through the trees, you could see an oxcart waiting, the oxen chewing their cud with little slavering, which showed that they had come a long distance. As you see, Sir: so much work just to cross a few meters of gentle water, all for want of a bridge. Added to which, they had taken many days to come by oxcart the distance you cover in hours with your jeep. Even today it is still the same crawling along" (Guimarães Rosa 1963: 84).
7 "That is the way it must have been in olden times. Such strange people, I had never seen or heard of before in my life" (Guimarães Rosa 1963: 314).
8 "The gerais have no notion of time" (Guimarães Rosa 1963: 91).

passage. Thus, Guimarães Rosa's *sertão* does not appear as atemporal anymore, but as subject to the passage of time, as the following observation by Riobaldo can show: "Aqueles distritos que em outros tempos foram do valentão Volta-Grande. Depois, mesmo Goiás a baixo, a vago. A esses muito desertos, com gentinha pobrejando. Mas o sertão está movimentante todo-tempo – salvo que o senhor não vê" (Guimarães Rosa 1994: 741).[9]

The invisibility of the *sertão* in the sense that its transformations cannot be grasped in measured values constitutes a counterpart to the state's practices of simplification described by Scott as an "attempt to make a society legible, to arrange the population in ways that simplified the classic state functions of taxation, conscription, and prevention of rebellion" (Scott 1998: 2). If those attempts already fail in *Os sertões* (Uriarte 2020: 206–265), they seem absurd in *Grande Sertão: Veredas*. The processes of historical development in Guimarães Rosa's *sertão* are so slow and inconspicuous that they can easily be overseen. However, even this region cannot escape completely from processes of modernization, albeit within a mode of *longue durée*, to use Fernand Braudel's term to designate the long-term scope of historical development. Nevertheless, far from adopting an evolutionist approach, Guimarães Rosa constructs a complex landscape of time in which individual perceptions of time interact with narratological time, metaphysical time, temporal cycles of nature and local social life, and, finally, with universal time.

2 A Narrative Timescape

In Riobaldo's physical and narrative passage through the *sertão*, time and space are closely intertwined. Riobaldo's journey is not only a travel through different temporal strata, but also highlights the complexity of individual and collective temporal experience. When approaching this temporal complexity unfolding in a certain spatial context, Barbara Adam's concept of timescape can be helpful: "a cluster of temporal features each implicated in all the others, but not necessarily of equal importance in each instance" (Adam 2006: 143). The term *scape*[10] includes the inseparability of time and its geographical,

---

9 "Those districts which in former days had been the domain of the Ruffian Volta-Grande. Afterwards, we wandered down in Goiás itself, with its many deserts and poverty-stricken people. But the sertão is moving all the time – even if you cannot see it" (Guimarães Rosa 1963: 420).
10 The term was originally coined by Arjun Appadurai to describe complex connectivities through transnational cultural flows in times of globalization. He distinguishes five scapes

historical, political as well as social context and can therefore help make visible inscriptions of time into a certain geographical space. While Adam has coined the timescape concept in the context of social science, it can be useful to grasp complex temporalities in literary works as it includes the following aspects, which can all easily be found in *Grande Sertão: Veredas*:
- *Time frame* – bounded, beginning and end of day, year, lifetime, generation, historical/geological epoch;
- *Temporality* – process world, internal to system, ageing, growing, irreversibility, directionality;
- *Timing* – synchronization, co-ordination, right/wrong time;
- *Tempo* – speed, pace, rate of change, velocity, intensity: how much activity in given timeframe;
- *Duration* – extent, temporal distance, horizon: no duration = instantaneity, time point/moment;
- *Sequence* – order, succession, priority: no sequence = simultaneity, at same time;
- *Temporal modalities: past, present and future* – memory, perception/experience and anticipation. (Adam 2008: 8–9)

In Guimarães Rosa's novel, these temporal aspects are located on several macroscopic levels, which are all intertwined: the time of Riobaldo's experience, the *Eigenzeit* of the *sertão*, and universal time.[11] Moreover, we could add other levels of time which, however, are less developed in the novel: a metaphysical time as articulated in Riobaldo's referencing to heaven as "fim de fim" (Guimarães Rosa 1994: 22–23) as well as in his quest for the devil, which, however, becomes obsolete when Riobaldo finds out that the devil does not exist, at least not in the form of a transcendent reality; the timelessness of popular tales or songs (Guimarães Rosa 1994: 730) which Riobaldo has heard and which he does not localize temporally or, when doing so, localizes in ancient times[12]; a prospective time which becomes evident in the narrator's hope for better times and which lets da Cunha's evolutionist approach resonate: "Ah, vai vir um

---

(ethnoscapes, technoscapes, financescapes, mediascapes, ideoscapes) which represent global, de-territorialized spaces in constant fluidity (Appadurai 2008.)
[11] I take part of these categories from Arsillo, however, I do not adopt his distinction between an «immovable time of the sertão» and «the movable time of the narration» (Arsillo 2012: 285). Rather I state that the *sertão*, just as Riobaldo's life, is subject to transformation and the passage of time.
[12] "Do que houve e se passou, uma vez, no Carujo, um arraial triste, em antigos tempos" (Guimarães Rosa 1994: 718).

tempo, em que não se usa mais matar gente" (Guimarães Rosa 1994: 24).[13] This hopeful perspective also characterizes Riobaldo's motivation to come to the *sertão* as a young man who anticipated to find in the Northeast of Brazil a perspective for his life: "Eu tinha vindo para ali, para o sertão do Norte, como todos uma hora vêm. Eu tinha vindo quase sem mesmo notar que vinha – mas presado, precisão de agenciar um resto melhor para a minha vida" (Guimarães Rosa 1994: 398).[14] Such an expectant attitude towards a region that had been labelled as backward and barbarian has an ironic effect, but it appears less naïve when we consider that Riobaldo, thanks to his probation in a violent and dangerous environment, in which he was able to progress to the position of a gang leader, has achieved the status of a big landowner. He thus seems to impersonate the fulfilment of da Cunha's vision of a new strong Brazilian society arising from the depths of a savage region and its mestizo residents.

All the temporal dimensions mentioned above confluence in Riobaldo's first-person narrative turning objective time into individual experience (Teixeira Pereira 2020: 245). As the novel is not divided into chapters, the thread of the narrator's monologue is never broken which makes the individual time expressed in Riobaldo's account appear as continuous flux. His narrative style is not chronological, but follows the turns and gaps of the narrator's memory, who himself reflects on his meandering way of telling[15]:

> Não acerto no contar, porque estou remexendo o vivido longe alto, com pouco caroço, querendo esquentar, demear, de feito, meu coração, naquelas lembranças. Ou quero enfiar a idéia, achar o rumozinho forte das coisas, caminho do que houve e do que não houve. As vezes não é fácil. Fé que não é. (Guimarães Rosa 1994: 242)[16]

However, the difficulty of telling for him does not lie in the temporal distance which separates his long-ago experiences from the present. It is rather the cunning of the past things which intermingle in his memory and escape from their place in chronology because of their sheer multitude and their belonging to different periods of time what makes telling so difficult.

---

13 "Ah, there will come a time when men no longer kill each other" (Guimarães Rosa 1963: 16).
14 "I had come there, to the sertão of the North, as everyone does sooner or later. I had come almost without noticing that I was doing so, compelled by the need to find a better way of life" (Guimarães Rosa 1963: 236).
15 Depieri interprets this lack of lineal time in narration as an attribute of orality and hence, as presence of an indigenous element (Depieri Amorim 2013).
16 "I'm not telling it very well because I am stirring the ashes of things lived long ago, with few embers left, trying to warm my heart once more on those remembrances. Or I am trying to pick up the thread, to follow the real course of events, what happened and what didn't. Sometimes it is not easy. Take my word that it isn't" (Guimarães Rosa 1963: 148).

Contar é muito, muito dificultoso. Não pelos anos que se já passaram. Mas pela astúcia que têm certas coisas passadas – de fazer balancê, de se remexerem dos lugares. O que eu falei foi exato? Foi. Mas teria sido? Agora, acho que nem não. São tantas horas de pessoas, tantas coisas em tantos tempos, tudo miúdo recruzado. (Guimarães Rosa 1994: 253–254)[17]

What is found throughout Riobaldo's monologue is the difference between an individual that tells and one that experiences. The distinction between old, mature Riobaldo, who looks back on his life, and young Riobaldo becomes evident in passages where the narrator mentions insights which he did not have as a *jagunço*: "Ah, naqueles tempos eu não sabia, hoje é que sei (Guimarães Rosa 1963: 57)[18]; "Agora, eu velho, vejo: quando cogito, quando relembro, conheço que naquele tempo eu girava leve demais, e assoprado" (720).[19] Yet, he has not found answers to all the questions which came up during his younger years: "Eu era dois, diversos? O que não entendo hoje, naquele tempo eu não sabia" (700).[20] The quest for answers to the great questions of life constitutes a continuum between the experiencing and the telling individual, connecting past and present, desert and civilization. In some, albeit few cases, the experienced past is presented even superior to the present in terms of knowledge, when, for example, Riobaldo refers to his knowledge of the schemes and tricks of the *jagunço* world: "Esse Hermógenes – belzebu. Ele estava caranguejando lá. Nos soturnos. Eu sabia. Nunca, mesmo depois, eu nunca soube tanto disso, como naquele tempo" (249).[21] In passages like this, Guimarães Rosa valorizes the knowledges of the *jagunço* as a basis for reflecting on farther-reaching, philosophical questions and therefore provides a first hint for the universal significance of the *sertão*.

---

17 "Telling something is a very, very difficult business. Not because of the years that have gone by, but because certain things of the past have a way of changing about, switching places. Was what I have said true? It was. But did it happen? Now I'm not so sure. So many hours and people, so many things at so many times, all mixed up together" (Guimarães Rosa 1963: 154).
18 "Ah, in those days I didn't know it, but today I do" (Guimarães Rosa 1963: 36).
19 "Now that I am old I see it : when I think it over, when I recollect, I recognize that at that time I was acting rashly, vaingloriously" (Guimarães Rosa 1963: 408).
20 "Was I two different persons? At that time I did not know something I still do not understand" (397).
21 "Hermógenes-Beelzebub. There he was poised in the shadows. I knew it. Never again, not even afterwards, did I experience this feeling so strongly as at that time" (Guimarães Rosa 1963: 152).

3 Time of Riobaldo's Experience

The nexus between the past of Riobaldo's experience and the present of narration also becomes evident when the narrator evokes the possibility of visiting the places he knew as a *jagunço*: "Aqueles foram meus dias. Se caçava, cada um esquecia o que queria, de de-comer não faltava, pescar peixe nas veredas... O senhor vá lá, verá. Os lugares sempre estão aí em si, para confirmar" (Guimarães Rosa 1994: 31).[22] Again, this statement could be read as evidence for the timelessness of the *sertão*, were there not the passages which describe the transformations this region has undergone.

Apart from the passages which refer to the relation of past and present, numerous passages are dedicated to the temporal rhythms and daily routines of the *jagunço* life as well as Riobaldo's personal perception of time including his hours spent with Diadorim ("Eu estava todo o tempo quase com Diadorim," Guimarães Rosa 1994: 31–32).[23] A recurring spatio-temporal figure is the aimlessness of the gang's forays and the unsteadiness of the *jagunço* life: "Dias inteiros, nada, tudo o nada – nem caça, nem pássaro, nem codorniz. O senhor sabe o mais que é, de se navegar sertão num rumo sem termo, amanhecendo cada manhã num pouso diferente, sem juízo de raiz? Não se tem onde se acostumar os olhos, toda firmeza se dissolve" (Guimarães Rosa 1994: 443–444).[24] This spatial restlessness goes hand in hand with temporal volatility as expressed in the premature death of many *jagunços* due to their dangerous lifestyle: "A E bastantes morreram, no final. Esse sertão, esta terra" (Guimarães Rosa 1994: 452).[25] It becomes evident here that it is not the individual behavior or misfortune that led to death, but the determinist force of the desert. Fate and geographic environment are inextricably linked to each other. However, Riobaldo's fictional biography will show that it is possible to overcome this geo-determinism and to move up to a civilized life. Yet, it would be too simplistic to read Riobaldo's social rise as an allegory for the advancement of Brazilian civil society, as the multiple intersections and reversions of past and present show.

---

[22] "Those were the days for me. We hunted, each forgot what we wanted to forget, there was no shortage of grub, we fished in the streams. Just go there, you'll see. The places are all still there to bear me out" (Guimarães Rosa 1963: 21).
[23] "I was with Diadorim most of the time" (Guimarães Rosa 1963: 22).
[24] "Then whole days, nothing-not a thing-no game, no birds, no partridge. Do you know what it is like to traverse the endless *sertão*, awaking each morning in a different place? There is nothing to which to accustom the eyes, all substance dissolves" (Guimarães Rosa 1963: 261).
[25] "Freedom is like this, movement. Many of them died in the end. This sertão, this land."

To return to temporal references in the novel, it is often about finding the right moment for setting out ("tempo de partida," Guimarães Rosa 1994: 522–523) or attacking the enemy – the aspect of "timing" in Adam's terminology. When waiting for the latter for a long time, Riobaldo reports losing his sense of time ("Mas eu não percebi o vivo do tempo que passava," Guimarães Rosa 1994: 348). While Riobaldo experiences waiting for the enemy as a time vacuum ("vazio do tempo," Guimarães Rosa 1994: 806), he describes being trapped by him as a "time within time" ("um tempo no tempo," Guimarães Rosa 1994: 485, see also 585).

This monotony of the *jagunço*'s routine is disrupted, besides some love affairs, through at least three events: The first is his twofold ascent within the gang hierarchy, in each case accompanied by a change of name: first to Tatarana and later to Urutu-Branco, which both stem from Tupy vocabulary and can therefore be read as references to indigenous rituals of initiation as reflected in Riobaldo's great changes of life (Depieri Amorim 2013: 8). A second turning point is the message of gang leader Joca Ramiro's death after a rain period which Riobaldo describes as monotonous. The greatest caesura, however, is the moment in which Riobaldo realizes that the devil, to whom he had desperately been trying to sell his soul, does not exist, or, at least, only in the form of an illusion, which, in turn, seems to confirm his existence as a reality constantly feigning itself. This insight makes him fall into a "time gully" ("buracão de tempo," Guimarães Rosa 1994: 602), a metaphor in which resonates Michel de Certeau's "trou de temps" (Certeau 1975: 221): an absence of meaning that opens a rift in time. This loss of consciousness and sense then turns into a greater capability of reflection:

> Sabendo que, de lá em diante, jamais nunca eu não sonhei mais, nem pudesse; aquele jogo fácil de costume, que de primeiro antecipava meus dias e noites, perdi pago. Isso era um sinal? Porque os prazos principiavam. . . E, o que eu fazia, era que eu pensava sem querer, o pensar de novidades. Tudo agora reluzia com clareza, ocupando minhas idéias, e de tantas coisas passadas diversas eu inventava lembrança, de fatos esquecidos em muito remoto, neles eu topava outra razão; sem nem que fosse por minha própria vontade. (Guimarães Rosa 1994: 604–605)[26]

---

[26] "From then on I never daydreamed again; the easy habit by which I used to foretaste my days and nights was lost to me forever. Was it a sign that the term had begun? What I was doing was thinking without volition, thinking on new things. Everything now shone clearly, filling my thoughts. I found myself remembering many different things in the past, long forgotten things, and I saw them in a new light, without express desire on my part to do so" (Guimarães Rosa 1963: 346).

Not only Riobaldo's gang members notice the transformation of their leader, but also his narrative style changes. On the level of both experience and telling, aphorisms, maxims and sayings become more frequent, which testifies to a higher capability of abstraction. What these literary small forms have in common is that they abstract from a series of single experiences and observations a rule which, in turn, can be applied to place concrete situations in a larger context.[27] In this sense, Riobaldo's metaphysical disillusion, which, at the same time, is an enlightenment in terms of wisdom, paves the way for a broader perspective that situates the *sertão* in a universal context.

4 Time of the *Sertão*: From Local to Universal Time

While most of the elements of the timescape constructed in *Grande Sertão* coincide with Riobaldo's individual experience, others refer to cycles of nature: "tempo do pendão do milho" (Guimarães Rosa 1994: 31)[28]; "tempo da cana" (Guimarães Rosa 1994: 74)[29]; "tempo de comprar arroz" (Guimarães Rosa 1994: 140)[30]; "Tempo [. . .] das águas" (Guimarães Rosa 1994: 427).[31] The cyclic nature of these time sequences implies a certain variability with simultaneous stability, a movement that is reflected in human life: "Mas a natureza da gente é muito segundas-e – sábados. Tem dia e tem noite, versáveis, em amizade de amor" (Guimarães Rosa 1994: 248).[32] Yet, what prevails over daily routine in Guimarães Rosa's novel is the unpredictability of the *sertão*: "Sertão é isto: o senhor empurra para trás, mas de repente ele volta a rodear o senhor dos lados. Sertão é quando menos se espera" (Guimarães Rosa 1994: 402)[33]; or "Sertão –

---

27 On the signification of small literary forms in *Grande Sertão*, see Lay Brander (2020: 185–208).
28 "[W]hen the corn is in tassel," (Guimarães Rosa 1963, 21).
29 "[T]he cane harvest season" (47).
30 "[T]ime for those who could not plant rice to buy it" (86).
31 "[T]he wet season" (253).
32 "But one's nature is full of contradictions. There is day and night, inconstancy, in the friendship of love" (151).
33 "The sertão is like that: you think you have left it behind you, and suddenly it surrounds you again on all sides. The sertão is where you least expect it" (238).

se diz –, o senhor querendo procurar, nunca não encontra. De repente, por si, quando a gente não espera, o sertão vem" (Guimarães Rosa 1994: 541).[34]

Aphoristic formulations like these go far beyond single observations and experiences, in two respects. First, they are the result of a process of abstraction fusing Riobaldo's individual experiences (or what he has learned from hearsay in his immediate environment) to more general statements. Second, they are not limited to the geographic region in Brazil's Northeast anymore but add a universal dimension to the landscape roamed by Riobaldo. From a narrative perspective, aphorisms often serve Riobaldo to condense his insights, whereby they do not convey practical advice, but serve to notice the contingency of life as well as the relativity of morally correct behaviour (Lay Brander 2021: 185–208). This becomes evident, for example, in the following maxim in which Riobaldo reflects on his acting as a *jagunço* out of the temporal distance of narration: "Digo: o real não está na saída nem na chegada: ele se dispõe para a gente é no meio da travessia" (Guimarães Rosa 1963: 52).[35] This commentary highlights the two conflicting aspects which characterize Riobaldo's learning process: To gain wisdom does not mean to reach a predetermined learning goal ("chegada," "arriving"), but to make the right decisions in the windings of life ("travessia," "journey") epitomized in the twisted paths of the *sertão*: "E que: para cada dia, e cada hora, só uma ação possível da gente é que consegue ser acerta" (Guimarães Rosa 1963: 393–394).[36] If the devil does not exist, good and bad are not absolute categories anymore, but spatio-temporal relativities. Instead of metaphysical forces, the *sertão* in its telluric dimension becomes the ruling authority whose order lies precisely in its disorder, in its arbitrariness.

If the paths – "veredas" – of the *sertão* symbolize Riobaldo's moral quest, this does not mean that his struggle for morally correct action takes place in an allegorical space, as some interpreters of the novel view Guimarães Rosa's *sertão*. Indeed, there are mythical places like, for example, "Veredas-Mortas," which we look for in vain on the map. With these imaginary places, the author seems to take up da Cunha's ghostly *ipueiras* or "lagoas mortas" (da Cunha 2010: 12),[37] which refer to a remote past in which the first settlers of the *sertão* built a hydraulic infrastructure.

---

[34] "The sertão, they say, you never find by looking for it. Suddenly, when you least expect it, the sertão appears" (312).
[35] "I mean, the truth is not in the setting out nor in the arriving : it comes to us in the middle of the journey" (Guimarães Rosa 1994: 85).
[36] "Every day, at every hour, there can be only one possible step which is the right one" (Guimarães Rosa 1994: 693).
[37] "[D]ead lakes" (da Cunha 1944: 11). Da Cunha describes them in this way: "Some of these *ipueiras* show the trace of exertions put forth by the sons of the hinterland. On their borders,

Although da Cunha transforms these testimonies of first human acting on the *sertão* through a "rhetoric of ghostliness" (Uriarte 2020: 245) he confers them a material dimension. In contrast, some of Riobaldo's statements such as "The sertão has no places in it" (Guimarães Rosa 1963: 291)[38] or "The sertão – it is inside of one (Guimarães Rosa 1963: 257)[39] could suggest that this region does not exist in geographical terms. However, this universality is disrupted in the innumerable realistic depictions of the landscapes of Minas Gerais's *sertão* and its people. Guimarães Rosa's *sertão* is neither a merely allegorical, nor a merely geographic space, but includes the levels of both local experience and universal validity. On the one hand, it is geographically localizable and describable, on the other hand, it is a prototype that comprises all places on the world where violence and insidiousness reign, as the following statements following the pattern "Sertão is where. . ." show.

> [S]ertão é onde manda quem é forte, com as astúcias. Deus mesmo, quando vier, que venha armado! (Guimarães Rosa 1994: 19)[40]
>
> Sertão é onde homem tem de ter a dura nuca e mão quadrada. (Guimarães Rosa 1994: 148)[41]
>
> Sertão é isto: o senhor empurra para trás, mas de repente ele volta a rodear o senhor dos lados. Sertão é quando menos se espera [. . .]. (Guimarães Rosa 1994: 402)[42]

Although, in these definitions the shrewdness and violence of the *sertão* prevail, the rough landscapes also bear positive connotations. One day, when Riobaldo marching at Diadorim's side is overwhelmed by a feeling of joy, he interprets this feeling as an effect of his geographic environment: "Sertão foi

---

erected like floodgates between the slopes, are crude walls of barren rock. They put one in mind of the monuments of a primitive people buried in obscurity. The common patrimony of those who here have to struggle with the privations of a fierce climate, they date in general from a remote past. They afford us a picture of those who first braved the vicissitudes of an expedition into these parts. They still stand there, indestructible; for the backwoodsman, even though he might be a lonely wayfarer, never failed to lift a stone to stay the structure at its swaying points of junction" (da Cunha 1944: 12).

38 "O Sertão é sem lugar" (Guimarães Rosa 1994: 500).
39 "Sertão: é dentro da gente" (Guimarães Rosa 1994: 435).
40 "[S]ertão is where the strong and the shrewd call the tune. God himself, when he comes here, had better come armed!" (Guimarães Rosa 1963: 13).
41 "[S]ertão has its own criminal code. The sertão is where a man must have a stiff neck and a hard fist" (Guimarães Rosa 1963: 91).
42 "[S]ertão is like that : you think you have left it behind you, and suddenly it surrounds you again on all sides. The sertão is where you least expect it" (Guimarães Rosa 1963: 238).

feito é para ser sempre assim: alegrias!" (Guimarães Rosa 1994: 719).[43] Here as well, the *sertão* has to be read as a metaphor for the whole life.

Guimarães Rosa's *sertão* can thus be localized one moment geographically, the next in the interior of man, the next at any place and, finally, comprises the whole world. This relationship between *sertão* and the world is reversable: "O Sertão é do tamanho do mundo" (Guimarães Rosa 1994: 96)[44] and the whole world is a *sertão*: "E nisto, que conto ao senhor, se vê o Sertão do mundo" (Guimarães Rosa 1994: 484).[45] In both versions, Riobaldo elevates his local and individual experience to a universal level by equating the space in which it takes place with the whole world.

In *Grande Sertão: Veredas*, Guimarães Rosa constructs a complex timescape combining geographical space and temporal aspects including *time frame* (cycles of nature, routines of the *jagunço* life), *temporality* (maturing of Riobaldo, civilisatory transformation of the *sertão*), *timing* (being in the right place and doing the right thing in the right moment), the alternation of *tempo* (acceleration of the action in episodes of battle) and *duration* (periods of standstill and waiting) as well as *sequence* (unchronological telling) and *temporal modalities* (Riobaldo's memories and anticipations, past of experience – present of narration). To this list, following Adam's model, I would like to add *irruption of time* as another aspect significant in both historical processes (see Braudel's term *événement*) and Guimarães Rosa's novel. Irruptions of time in *Grande Sertão: Veredas* do not modify the landscape, but change social constellations, such as the composition and hierarchy of gangs, or mark epistemic turning points in Riobaldo's vision of his environment. It is thus thanks to the shocking insight that the devil does not exist that the *sertão* can advance to a universal metaphor. If human life is not determined by metaphysical categories, it is nothing more and nothing less than paving one's way through a chaotic and unpredictable landscape. And even Riobaldo's social setting, although putting an end to his spatial movement, does not end his quest for answers to the big questions of life. This aimlessness has a positive connotation: "O rio não quer ir a nenhuma parte, ele quer é chegar a ser mais grosso, mais fundo" (Guimarães Rosa 1994: 621).[46]

---

43 "The sertão was made to be like that always: bright and happy!" (Guimarães Rosa 1963: 408).
44 "The sertão is as big as the world" (Guimarães Rosa 1963: 60).
45 "And in what I am telling, we see the Sertão of the world" (my translation).
46 "A river does not want to go anywhere; what it wants is to grow bigger and deeper" (Guimarães Rosa 1963: 354).

Os sertões already had shifted "away from the state's legibilizing and simplifying discourse toward one of greater ambivalence" by throwing the narrator, who ceases to identify himself with the state, back upon himself (Uriarte 2020: 237). In *Grande Sertão: Veredas*, Guimarães Rosa develops this complexity further bringing into dialogue a multiplicity of temporal features. By rejecting a teleological vision of time, Guimarães Rosa offers an alternative model to da Cunha's linear, evolutionist approach, in two respects. First, contrary to the latter's spatialization of time, Guimarães Rosa emphasizes the movability of the landscape, not only in terms of unpredictability, but also of its transformation within a *longue durée*. Second, by equating the *sertão* with the world, Guimarães Rosa not only deconstructs the center-periphery-relation between the coastal cities and the hinterlands but places the *sertão* in a relation of simultaneity with the rest of the world. The time of Guimarães Rosa's *sertão* is not only past and potential future, but also universal time; just as the *sertão* is anywhere, its past events can happen at any time. This universal dimension creates another form of timelessness, not in the sense of primitivism, but in the sense of humanism. The habitant of the *sertão* is no more the uncivilized other, but the modern individual finding its way in a world of lost beliefs and uncertainties: "O diabo não há! É o que eu digo, se for... Existe é homem humano. Travessia" (Guimarães Rosa 1994: 875).[47]

Bibliography

Adam, Barbara (2006): *Time*. Reprinted. Cambridge: Polity Press (Key concepts).
Adam, Barbara (2008): "The Timescapes Challenge: Engagement with the Invisible Temporal." In: Edwards, Rosalind (ed.) (2008): *Researching Lives Through Time: Time, Generation and Life Stories*. Leeds: University of Leeds (Timescapes Working Paper Series, 1), pp. 7–12.
Appadurai, Arjun (2008): *Modernity at large. Cultural dimensions of globalization*. Minneapolis, Minn.: Univ. of Minnesota Press (Public worlds, 1).
Arsillo, Voncenzo (2012): "The veredas of Time. Dialectics of Time Images in Grande Sertão: Veredas by João Guimarães Rosa." In: Leite, Ligia Chiappini Moraes (ed.) (2012): *Studies in the Literary Achievement of João Gimarães Rosa, the Foremost Brazilian*. Lewistin, NY: Mellen, pp. 284–294.
Bernucci, Leopoldo M. (1995): *A imitação dos sentidos. Prógonos, contemporâneos e epígonos de Euclides da Cunha*. São Paulo: Edusp.
Bier, Felipe (2015): *O resto do sertão. História e modernidade em "Grande sertão: veredas."* Curitiba: Editora Appris.

---

[47] "There is no devil! What I say is, if he did... It is man who exists. The passage" (Guimarães Rosa 1963: 492).

Bruyas, Jean-Paul (1983): "Técnica, estruturas e visão em *Grande Sertão: Veredas.*" In: Coutinho, Eduardo (ed.) (1983): *Guimarães Rosa.* Rio de Janeiro: INL/Civilização Brasileira, pp. 458–477.
Campos Soares, Claudia (2012): "*Grande sertão: veredas*: a crítica revisitada." In: *Letras de hoje*, 47, 2, pp. 136–145.
Cândido, Antonio (1973): "Literatura y subdesarrollo." In: Fernández Moreno, César (ed.) (1973): *América Latina en su literatura.* Mexico: Siglo XXI, pp. 335–353.
Cândido, Antonio (1983): "O homem dos avessos." In: Coutinho, Eduardo (ed.) (1983): *Guimarães Rosa.* Rio de Janeiro: INL/Civilização Brasileira, pp. 294–299.
Castoriadis, Cornelius (1975): *L'institution imaginaire de la société.* Paris: Seuil (Collection Esprit).
Certeau, Michel de (1975): *L' écriture de l'histoire.* Paris: Gallimard (Bibliothèque des histoires).
Coutinho, Eduardo (ed.) (1983): *Guimarães Rosa.* Rio de Janeiro: INL/Civilização Brasileira.
Cunha, Euclides da (2010): *Os sertões.* Rio de Janeiro: Centro Edelstein de Pesquisas Sociais http://www.doabooks.org/doab?func=fulltext&rid=16687 (accessed: 01/ 03/2022).
Cunha, Euclides da (1944): *Rebellion in the Backlands.* Translated and with an Introduction by Samuel Putnam. Chicago/London: The University of Chicago Press.
Depieri Amorim, Liana (2013): "A presença indígena na obra *Grande Sertão: Veredas*, de João Guimarães Rosa." In: *Nau literária* 9, 2, pp. 1–13.
Fabian, Johannes (1983): *Time and the other. How anthropology makes its object.* New York: Columbia Univ. Press.
Guimarães Rosa, João (1994 [1956]): *Grande Sertão: Veredas.* São Paulo: Nova Aguilar.
Guimarães Rosa, João (1963): *The Devil to Pay in The Backlands.* New York: Knopf.
Lay Brander, Miriam (2020): *Schreiben in Archipelen. Kleine Formen in post-kolonialen Kontexten.* Berlin/Boston: De Gruyter (Mimesis, Band 83). https://doi.org/10.1515/9783110639483.
McClintock, Anne (2015): *Imperial leather. Race, gender and sexuality in the colonial contest.* New York/London: Routledge.
Meyer-Clason, Curt (1984): "Der Sertão des Guimarães Rosa." In: Strausfeld, Mechtild (ed.) (1984): *Brasilianische Literatur.* Frankfurt am Main: Suhrkamp, pp. 249–272.
Nicolazzi, Fernando (2010): "O tempo do sertão, o sertão no tempo: antigos, modernos, selvagens. Leitura de Os sertões." In: *Anos 90* 17, 31, pp. 261–285. DOI: 10.22456/1983-201X.18945.
Nowotny, Helga (1990): *Eigenzeit. Entstehung und Strukturierung eines Zeitgefühls.* Frankfurt am Main: Suhrkamp.
Ricœur, Paul (1983): *Temps et récit.* Paris: Éditions du Seuil (Points essais, 227).
Santiago, Silviano (2019): "Silviano Santiago e a monstruosidade de 'Grande sertão: veredas.'" https://www.youtube.com/watch?v=ngKtlj5mZGw (accessed: 01/03/2022).
Saramago, Victoria (2020): "Birds, Rivers, Book." In: *Luso-Brazilian Rev.* 57, 1, pp. 125–149. DOI: 10.3368/lbr.57.1.125.
Saramago, Victoria (2021): *Fictional environments. Mimesis, deforestation, and development in Latin America.* Evanston, Illinois: Northwestern University Press (FlashPoints).
Scott, James C. (1998): *Seeing like a state. How certain schemes to improve the human condition have failed.* New Haven, Conn.: Yale University Press (The Yale ISPS series).

Teixeira Pereira, Anderson Luiz (2020): "O Sertão presente na palavra poética: tempo e linguagem em Grande Sertão: Veredas." In: *Macabéa – Revista Eletrônica do Netlli* 9, 3, pp. 335–352. DOI: 10.47295/mren.v9i3.2337.

Uriarte, Javier (2020): *The Desertmakers. Travel, War, and the State in Latin America*. New York/London: Routledge.

Ventura, Roberto (1998): "Visões do deserto: selva e sertão em Euclides da Cunha." In: *Hist. cienc. saude-Manguinhos* 5 (suppl), pp. 133–147. DOI: 10.1590/S0104-59701998000400008.

Jobst Welge
Tropical Temporalities: Literary Landscape and Multiple Times in Alejo Carpentier's *Los Pasos Perdidos*

For Aleida[1]

Alejo Carpentier's novel *Los pasos perdidos* (*The Lost Steps*, 1953) can be understood as a consolidation of a specifically Latin American subgenre of the novel, the so-called *novela de la selva* (novel of the jungle). This literary tradition, which dates back to José Eustasio Rivera's novel *La vorágine* (*The Vortex*, 1924), has recently experienced a series of re-readings (Wylie 2009; Rogers 2019). In fact, literary studies focused on Latin America, under the influence of ecocriticism and post-anthropocentric approaches, and after a certain dominance of the treatment of urban themes, are now increasingly (re)turning to the representation of natural spaces. However, as I here want to show, the *novela de la selva*'s representation of natural spaces cannot be disassociated from the condition of modernity.

Therefore, given the intense concern with temporality in Carpentier's novel, I want to explore how the perception of the Amazonian, tropical landscape and its association with "original" nature is in fact framed and configured from the perspective of modernity and how different temporalities are confronted with each other. In order to better understand how the trans-national Amazonian landscape has been prototypically conceived as antagonistic to modernity and progress at the beginning of the twentieth century, I will first begin with some observations on the Amazonian writings by Euclides da Cunha. As we will see, in contrast to da Cunha's writings, Carpentier's post-war novel is grounded in a disenchantment with modernity that first appears to value a "return" to nature, but then also denies the possibility of such a return. Furthermore, I will argue that the novel, although it appears to follow a linear quest towards origins, is in fact structured like a temporal palimpsest and as a literary landscape.

---

[1] The initial idea for this essay was developed in the context of an interdisciplinary workshop on historiography and temporality at Stockholm University ("About Time!," Institute for Culture and Aesthetics, April 2017) with Aleida Assmann. The essay is dedicated to her, one of my very first teachers.

Jobst Welge, Leipzig University

https://doi.org/10.1515/9783110762273-006

1 The Other Time of the Amazon

In a recent essay, Javier Uriarte has discussed the representation of natural spaces through the use of temporal notions in two canonical accounts of displacement in Brazil, Euclides da Cunha's *Os sertões* (*Rebellion in the Backlands*, 1902) and Claude Lévi-Strauss's *Tristes Tropiques* (1955). The essay examines the ways in which the narrators imagine the temporal status of the spaces they visit and the importance of time and memory in the construction of these books, the nostalgic tone used by both narrators to describe the spaces and the peoples they encounter, and the ambiguous relation they establish with the notions of progress and modernization. As both travelers discover realities that were previously unknown to them, they transform their vision of the ideological and cultural origin of their voyages (Uriarte 2016).

This concern with temporality and (a somewhat less ambiguous) modernity can also be found in da Cunha's Amazonian writings. Significantly, the English translation of da Cunha's collection of essays on this region, published posthumously in 1909, the year of the author's death, has been entitled *The Amazon. Land without History* (the original title was *À margem da história*, "At the margin of history"). The engineer and journalist da Cunha had participated in a joint Brazilian-Peruvian expedition into the Amazon (*Comissão Brasileira de Reconhecimento do Alto Purús*, 1904–1905) for reasons of land measurements, reasons both practical and political.[2] Therefore it is no surprise that da Cunha's writerly habit was intensely concerned with a "mapping" impulse. In these writings the Amazon is represented as a region that is located outside the sphere of modern history, outside of the dimension of time itself (Fabian 1983), in which the observing "national" subject "feels dislocated in space and in time; not outside his country but nonetheless estranged from human culture, lost in the hidden recesses of the forest and an obscure corner of history" (da Cunha 2006: 32).

In the articles resulting from this exploratory trip, da Cunha qualifies the Amazonian landscape in terms of its "unbearable monotony," where nature is "lacking in internal coherence." Furthermore, he notes that "humankind is still an impertinent interloper here. We have arrived uninvited and unprepared for, while nature was still in the process of setting up this vast, magnificent salon" (da Cunha 2006: 4). Like da Cunha's more famous description of the Northeastern region of the Brazilian *sertão* in *Os Sertões*, his Amazonian writings are just as representative for what Stefan Helgesson has aptly called "the entangled, disjunctive experiences of colonial time" (Helgesson 2014a: 265; cf. Helgesson

---

[2] On da Cunha, see also the contributions by Fonseca and Lay Brander in this volume.

2014b). Da Cunha's essays struggle with the question of how the frontier region of the Amazon may be brought within the sphere of modernity and the modern nation, even as the specificity of Amazonian nature represents a major cognitive obstacle. For da Cunha, the Amazon represents a rift between man and nature, nation and landscape. He presents the Amazon as a paradoxical space in need of modern exploration, but also as constitutionally resistant to attempts at scientific ordering and subjective apprehension. For da Cunha the Amazon region is not only objectively a "land without history," but it becomes devoid of temporal structuring also for the experience of the individual spectator, who, in contrast to cultivated landscapes, does not encounter here "an externalization of previously idealized forms" (da Cunha 2006: 32). Thus, in the essay entitled "This Accursed Climate," da Cunha describes the phenomenological experience of how an exile-traveler journeys up the course of the great river:

> And the days pass without definition before the strange motionlessness of a picture done in one single color, one single height, and one single model, to which is added the dread sensation that life has simply stopped. Every impression is inert, the concept of time is abolished, for the succession of uniform external phenomena does not disclose it. (Da Cunha 2006: 31–32)

Da Cunha also suggests here that landscape is perceived not directly, but that it is preconditioned by the conventions of landscape painting. Yet even scientific apprehension and its technical means to segment nature fail in the face of this natural vastness and only produce disconnected fragments. Da Cunha's verbal representations of the (a)temporal sensations of the traveling subject echo the frustrating visual experience, and for this reason he does not conjure up a visual picture of the landscape as such, or, for that matter, narrative units that would unfold in linear time. Da Cunha's writing style seeks to capture that which is supposedly situated outside of time and change, yet which is also "new," inasmuch as it is marked as a frontier space awaiting further exploration and description. The peculiar writing style of da Cunha's essay collection has been described as "baroque" by Mark Anderson, who detects in it, as well as in the book *Inferno verde* (1908) by the regionalist writer Alberto Rangel (for which da Cunha wrote the preface), or in Rivera's *La Vorágine* (1924), a characteristic folding of language, as the rhetorical equivalent for the challenges to cognition presented by the Amazonian landscape (Anderson 2014: 59).

The Amazon, then, becomes for da Cunha a region at the margins of representation, distinguished by a "tragic collision of temporalities" (Foot Hardman 2001: 53), a divorce between landscape and nation, nature and man. Walking through this landscape's flora, travelers have the "disquieting sense that they have returned to a much earlier time, as though they had invaded the recesses of one of those mute Carboniferous forests the existence of which is known to us through the retrospective gaze of the geologist" (da Cunha 2006: 4). This "sensation of extreme antiquity" (da Cunha 2006: 4), of a lost paradise, and at the same time of "perpetually beginning anew" (da Cunha 2006: 11) leads da Cunha to observe that "the Amazon region may well be the world's newest land" (da Cunha 2006: 5) and that the lack of historical continuity makes Brazilians feel here like foreigners within their own land.

The constant movement of the river with its "telluric migration" of sediments becomes a symbol for a country with an allegedly insufficient past and for the notion that Brazilians are therefore essentially exiled from the accelerated historical time associated with the progress of modernity. The defining condition of conflicting temporalities in the Amazon deprives the country of a proper sense of national identity as rooted in historical time: "The concept of time is abolished, for the succession of uniform external phenomena does not disclose it" (da Cunha 2006: 32). This discursive practice of (deficient) national self-imagination is thus characterized by a fundamental lack, a suspension of time – and the Amazon, as an internal frontier zone, is portrayed as either "utopia" or a "a setting to exploit," a "topos for development" (Rodríguez 2004: 24) to be enlisted for what David Harvey has called a "Spatio-Temporal Fix" (Harvey 2004: 35).[3]

Starting from da Cunha's ambivalent characterization of the Amazon as both deficient and visually excessive, one might distinguish between texts that straightforwardly justify its economic exploitation and development, and literary texts or novels that (partly) develop formal and rhetorical strategies to counter linear forms of representation, for instance, by means of a succession of visual tableaux (Jules Verne, *La Jangada*, 1881; cf. Welge 2022), or through the inclusion of myth (Mário de Andrade, *Macunaíma*, 1927). To some degree, all of these texts expressive of the Amazonian imagination stage a conflict between different temporalities, between nature and history. It is on this literary and discursive legacy that Carpentier builds to develop his own narrative of conflicting times in *Los pasos perdidos*.

---

[3] For the connection between travel writing and temporality generally: Henrikson/Kullberg (2020).

2 Modernity and the Desire for Nature

At the time when he was residing in Caracas, Alejo Carpentier wrote some short travel essays on the Gran Sabana (Great Savannah) in southeastern Venezuela, the Venezuelan part of Guiana. Carpentier had visited the Great Sabana during two journeys into the interior of Venezuela, the first one in 1947, flying with a plane over the Orinoco, the second one in 1948, traveling by bus, to the western region of the Amazon. Carpentier described these two voyages in a series of articles under the rubric "Visión de América" ("Vision of America"). These articles were first published during 1948 in *El Nacional* (Caracas) and in *Carteles* (La Habana) and were originally intended for a travel book, *El Libro de la Gran Sabana* (*The Book of the Great Savannah*), never to be realized. In these texts he has established certain associations that will become central points for the writing of *Los pasos perdidos*: like da Cunha he portrays the Amazon as lying outside of the realm of time and history, but now this is seen from a largely positive, idealizing perspective.

For instance, Carpentier describes the plateau of the Gran Sabana as a "geological world," a "lost world," and (in the title of the first article) as the "world of genesis" (Carpentier 1990: 274). Already this repeated equation of the concrete landscape with a "world," points to the potentially autonomous, encapsulated status of this landscape. Moreover, the phrase about the "lost world" is a clear allusion to Arthur Conan Doyle's adventure novel *The Lost World* (1912), which brings Victorian scientific explorers to the Venezuelan plateau of Mount Roraima. Furthermore, this landscape is said to have been associated with the mythical realm of El Dorado: "[. . .] se confundió durante siglos con El Dorado de la leyenda – ese fabuloso reino de Manoa, de imprecisa ubicación, que los hombres buscaron incansablemente, casi hasta los días de la Revolución francesa" (Carpentier 2009: 275).[4] This association, then, serves to emphasize the transhistorical desire projected upon this landscape, the textual traditions concerned with its transmission (Walter Raleigh, Voltaire), the coexistence of concrete geographical referentiality to be expected in a travel text *and* the notion of the non-place of legend ("imprecise location"). Of course, this transcendence of reality ("lo fantástico se hacía realidad"; Carpentier 1990: 285)[5] has been famously conceptualized by Carpentier as the very distinction of Latin American nature, as the *real maravilloso* ("real marvelous") in the "Prólogo" to his novel *El reino de este mundo* (1949).

---

4 "[This landscape] was confused for centuries with the El Dorado of legend-that fabulous kingdom of Manoa, of imprecise location, which men sought tirelessly, almost until the days of the French Revolution" (my transl.).
5 "The fantastic became reality" (my transl.).

Still more important, in light of the central subjective dilemma to be developed in *Los pasos perdidos*, is the passage in which Carpentier realizes that in spite of his valuation and awe in front of this mythic, primeval world he, in his capacity as an intellectual, is forever barred from gaining true access to it ("yo hombre encadenado a la letra impresa;" Carpentier 1990: 276).[6] Finally, Carpentier stresses here the topic of temporal alterity: ". . . el tiempo estaba detenido ahí, al pie de las rocas inmutables, desposeído de todo sentido ontológico para el frenético hombre del Occidente [. . .]. No era el tiempo que miden nuestros relojes ni nuestros calendarios. Era el tiempo de la Gran Sabana. El tiempo de la tierra en los días del Génesis" (Carpentier 1990: 292–293).[7] While the travel essays provide concrete information about the Venezuelan geography, the text of *Los pasos perdidos* has deliberately suppressed such information in favor of a generic Americanness; only a "Note" at the end of the book, signed by the author, keys the elements of the "prototypical" landscape to a real topography, as in the following: "El río descrito que, en lo anterior, pudo ser cualquier gran río de América, se torna, muy exactamente, el Orinoco en su curso superior" (Carpentier 2009: 455).[8]

In *Los pasos perdidos* we encounter a nameless narrator/protagonist, who inhabits a large North American metropolis, probably to be identified as New York City, which thus stands metonymically, precisely by way of its mostly generic traits, for a place of cosmopolitan, global modernity. The protagonist of the novel is an intellectual, who works both as a musicologist and as a composer. The biographical facts of this protagonist position him in multiple cultural relations: he is the son of a Swiss-German father and a Caribbean mother; he was born in Latin America, emigrated to the United States and resided for two periods in Europe. Thus, questions of conflicting identities, origins, and acculturations come to the fore. In its first chapters the novel shows how the protagonist's matrimony with the North American actress Ruth has led to habits of unsatisfactory routines in the areas of private life and work – he describes himself as a modern Sisyphos. Significantly, this alienated form of life is from the beginning associated with the artificiality of theater and the repetitiveness of its performances:

---

[6] "I, a man chained to the printed letter" (my transl.).

[7] "[. . .] time was stopped there, at the foot of the immutable rocks, deprived of any ontological sense for the frenetic man of the West. . . It was not the time measured by our clocks and calendars. It was the time of the Gran Sabana. The time of the earth in the days of Genesis" (my transl.).

[8] "The river described above, which could have been any large river in America, becomes, very precisely, the Orinoco in its upper course" (my transl.).

[. . .] me consternaba pensando en lo dura que se había vuelto, para Ruth, esta prisión de tablas de artificio, con sus puentes volantes, sus telarañas de cordel y árboles de mentira [. . .]. Ruth, que había comenzado a decir el texto a la edad de treinta años, se veía llegar a los treinta y cinco, repitiendo los mismos gestos, las mismas palabras, todas las noches de la semana, todas las tardes de domingos, sábados y días feriados – sin contar las actuaciones de las giras de estío. (Carpentier 2009: 175)[9]

The artificial trees of the stage setting point forward to later parts of the novel in which Amazonian nature – apparently set up as the very opposite of urban, alienated life – turns out to be a sort of artificial copy. Just as this ever-identical work is said to wear down on the actors, the protagonist likewise suffers from his own office job: "[. . .] mi esposa se dejaba llevar por el automatismo del trabajo impuesto, como yo me dejaba llevar por el automatismo de mi oficio;" Carpentier 2009: 176).[10] This constriction of bourgeois life readily explains why the protagonist agrees to take on the offer of an academic institution, to embark on a "scientific" voyage into the South American jungle in search of rare indigenous musical instruments. Together with his French mistress Mouche, the protagonist makes his way into a non-specified Latin American country, where he will later take up relations with an indigenous woman, Rosario, who, in the narrator's perception, appears as an embodiment of uncorrupted, Latin American nature.

Faced with such fantasies of a "return to nature," readers might ask to what extent the novel's starkly oppositional discourse (Western alienation vs. "primitive" authenticity) and the palpable misogynist cliches (in the less than complex female characters of Ruth, Mouche, and Rosario) are attributable to Carpentier himself, or are rather to be assigned to an unreliable narrator, as ironical, critical symptoms of the protagonist's male anxiety. In contrast to da Cunha's discourse of progress, the male narrator in Carpentier's novel is from early on propelled by a longing to go back to a time before modernity – even while this longing is already marked as futile ("yo [. . .] añoraba – como por haberlos conocido – ciertos modos de vivir que el hombre había perdido para siempre"; Carpentier: 2009, 207–208).[11]

---

[9] "[. . .] I realized with a shock how hard it must have become for Ruth to bear this prison of lumber and contrivance, with its air-swung bridges, its string cobwebs, its artificial trees [. . .]. Ruth, who had begun to say her lines when she was thirty, now found herself crowding thirty-five and repeating the same words, the same gestures, every night of the week, every Sunday, Saturday, and holiday afternoon, not to mention summer tours" (Carpentier 1967: 4–5).
[10] "[. . .] My wife had been caught in the automatism of her enforced work just as I had been caught in that of my job" (Carpentier 1967: 5).
[11] "I [. . .] longed for certain ways of life that man had lost forever" (Carpentier 1967: 36).

3 Temporal Layers, Time Travel

Once the protagonist travels together with Mouche to a nameless South American city, they witness the turmoil created there by a sort of civil war or revolution. This motif subtly recalls the earlier scene in which Ruth is said to suffer from the ever-repeated theater performance, which concerns a play about the 1861 American Civil War ("Guerra de Secesión," Carpentier 2009: 174). In other words, from its very beginning the novel cuts not only radically different spaces against each other, but also encourages the reader to compare different moments in space and in time, which may in fact bracket and interrogate the logic of temporal development and progress (Kaakinen 2017: 199). This is further emphasized by the protagonist's comment about the political motion, whose historical motives are opaque to him. The "revolution" appears not just as a sign of historical repetition or pre-political atavism, but rather as a manifestation of an *internal* non-synchronicity:

> Cuando me acercaba a lo que podía ser, [. . .] un conflicto político propio de la época, caía en algo que más se asemejaba a una guerra de religión. Las pugnas entre los que parecían representar la tendencia avanzada y la posición conservadora se me representaban, por el increíble desajuste cronológico de los criterios, como una especie de batalla Librada, por encima del *tiempo*, entre gentes que vivieran en siglos distintos. (Carpentier 2009: 223)[12]

This notion of juxtaposing different temporal layers may be a reflection of the fact that "post-colonial" countries in Latin America (or in the Caribbean, for that matter) are not fully synchronized with Western modernity, and are themselves distinguished by the co-presence of heterogeneous temporal layers.

In *Los pasos perdidos* the transition from an (North American) urban space of modernity into the deepest recesses of the South American tropical jungle is presented as a subjective quest, a movement backwards toward a "primitive" stage of civilization, a prior epoch of humankind. Specifically, the spatial transition from North to South America is experienced as a movement backwards in time: "[. . .] el tránsito de la capital a Los Altos había sido, para mí, una suerte de retroceso del tiempo a los años de mi infancia" (Carpentier: 2009, 252).[13] These memories of things and words from childhood are in turn described as a

---

[12] "When [. . .] I tried to figure out what would seem a typical political conflict of our epoch, I found that I was dealing with something more akin to a religious war. Because of an incredible chronological discrepancy of ideals, the conflict between those who seemed to represent the conservative and the progressivist tendencies gave me the impression of a kind of battle between people living in different centuries" (Carpentier 1967, 50–51; translation slightly modified; JW).
[13] "[. . .] the change from the capital to Los Altos had been for me a kind of return, [. . .] to the years of my childhood" (Carpentier 1967: 77).

"discovery," as the "affirmation of new proportions" ("afirmación de proporciones nuevas"; Carpentier 2009: 252). While the journey on the river deeper into the jungle is accompanied by markers of chronological time, the symbolic time travel takes the protagonist ever more backwards in historical-evolutional time periods. It is somewhat perplexing that this confrontation with different temporalities, with the radical Other of modernity, is rather neatly identified with, and categorized according to Western historical rubrics, such as the essentially European epochal concept of the Middle Ages:

> Y me percato ahora de esta verdad asombrosa: desde la tarde del Corpus en Santiago de los Aguinaldos, vivo en la temprana Edad Media. Puede pertenecer a otro calendario un objeto, una prenda de vestir, un remedio. Pero el ritmo de vida, los modos de navegación, el candil e la olla, el alargamiento de las horas, las funciones trascendentales del Caballo y del Perro, el modo de reverenciar a los Santos, son medievales [. . .]. (Carpentier 2009, 355)[14]

The protagonist thus sees himself as moving back to the time of the conquest, to the civilization of the Middle Ages, and finally even back to pre-historic, paleontological time:

> Lo que se abre ante nuestros ojos es el mundo anterior al hombre. Abajo, en los grandes ríos, quedaron los saurios monstruosos, las anacondas, los peces con tetas, los laulaus cabezones, los escualos de agua dulce, los gimnotos y lepidosirenas, que todavía cargan con su estampa de animales prehistóricos, legado de las dragonadas del Terciario. [. . .] Acaban de apartarse las aguas, aparecida es la Seca, hecha en la yerba verde, [. . .]. Estamos en el mundo del Génesis, al fin del Cuarto Día de la Creación. Si retrocediéramos un poco más, llegaríamos adonde comenzaba la terrible soledad del Creador –la tristeza sideral de los tiempos sin incienso y sin alabanzas, cuando la tierra era desordenada y vacía, y las tinieblas estaban sobre la haz del abismo. (Carpentier 2009: 363–364)[15]

---

14 "And the amazing truth suddenly came to me: since the afternoon of Corpus Christi in Santiago de los Aguinaldos, I had been living in the early Middle Ages. An object, a garment, a drug belonged to another calendar. But the rhythm of life, the methods of navigation, the oil lamp, the cooking-pots, the prolongation of the hours, the transcendental functions of Horse and Dog, the manner of worshipping the Saints, all were medieval" (Carpentier 1967: 178).
15 "What lay before our eyes was the world that existed before man. Below, in the great rivers, were the monstrous saurian, the anacondas, the fish with teats, the big-headed *laulau,* the fresh-water dogfish, the electric eels, the lepidosirens, which still bore the stamp of prehistoric animals, a legacy from the great reptiles of the Tertiary. [. . .]. The waters have just been divided, the Dry Land has appeared, [. . .]. We are in the world of Genesis, at the end of the Fourth Day of Creation. If we go back a little farther, we will come to the terrible loneliness of the Creator, the sideral sadness of the times without incense or songs of praise, when the word was without order and empty, and darkness was upon the face of the deep" (Carpentier 1967: 186–187).

The first part of this quotation (like other references to epochs such as the "Paleolithic Era"; Carpentier 2009: 356; 392) makes clear that the tropical region of the Amazon is associated with a geological archive that "preserves" as in a time capsule traces of pre-history into the present – for the description of such geological time travel Carpentier was very likely influenced by Conan Doyle's *The Lost World*, already mentioned above (Echevarría 1998: 105; Harney 2012; Welge 2022). Of course, during the early nineteenth century, geology, as developed by Georges Cuvier, was precisely the field that played a crucial role for the temporalization of natural history, by suggesting the notion of a "deep time" in both vertical and horizontal terms (Dünne 2016: 41). It is significant that Carpentier should invoke such references to geological deep time alongside references to Biblical, legendary, and mythical times. The second part of the quotation ("If we go back") shows that this is a travel in space as much as a hypothetical thought experiment.

The travel narrative, then, presents not only a voyage backwards in time, as keyed to a series of successive spatial boundaries, but it is marked by a palimpsest of temporal layers ("Zeitschichten," in the parlance of Reinhart Koselleck [2003]), concerning both the historical dimension and the individual life history of the (nameless) narrating protagonist, as well as different modalities of experiencing time. Thus, each of the locations traversed by the protagonist is shaped by different senses of time, marking different phases of Western social and economic history. However, the protagonist's spatial voyage backwards in time, as a sort of reversed natural history, should not be misunderstood as bringing him in contact with distinctly identifiable and circumscribed past life worlds (as in "conventional" time travel narratives). As González Echevarría writes, the protagonist's voyage backwards in time occurs "trough an imaginary museum or through a compendium of world history," including his own personal memories (González Echevarría 1977: 160). As these metaphors suggest, the imaginative association with past epochs is not realized as a voyage *into* single periods of the past, but rather is comparable to how we access various media of storage (museum, compendium, memory) that hold events of different periods available and make them co-present.

The novel as a whole is distinguished by a non-developmental, kairological sense of time reminiscent of myth, and it is told through "a present-day collage of historical phases, demonstrating that 'third world' synchronic realities are more complex than Western modernity accounts for" (Brough-Evans 2016: 66). On a general level, Carpentier might be said to adhere to the characteristically time-subverting poetics of the modernist novel (Kern 2011: 109–112). The reader is constantly challenged to establish connections between different historical periods and to confront a dense network of literary and cultural references, just as the narrator joins disparate elements and times through his "analogical eye" (Saramago 2021: 73–74). More specifically, this narrative principle of juxtaposition may well be due to Carpentier's debt to the avantgarde movement of Surrealism: "In surrealist poetics juxtaposition is often seen as a means to liberate readers' or viewers' imagination from conventional perspectives" (Kaakinen 2017: 22).[16]

The novel's journey, then, constantly contrasts the sentiment of historical time travel with other conceptions and measurements of time (including in the realm of music), which question the developmental logic underlying the paradigm of historical time. Traveling on a river toward the jungle, the protagonist remarks: "Aquí, los viajes del hombre se rigen por el Código de las Lluvias. Observo ahora que yo, maniático medidor del tiempo, atento al metrónomo por vocación y al cronógrafo por oficio, he dejado, desde hace días, de pensar en la hora, relacionando la altura del sol con el apetito o el sueño" (Carpentier 2009: 288).[17] We also find affirmations reminiscent of da Cunha's rhetoric of the absence of historical time: "Hace dos días que andamos sobre el armazón del planeta, olvidados de la Historia y hasta de las oscuras migraciones de las eras sin crónica" (Carpentier 2009: 362).[18]

Moreover, the idea of historical retrocession is overwritten by the legendary myth of El Dorado, which, as "wandering" signifier, imaginatively links the geographical areas of the Latin American Amazon region and of the Caribbean. While the desire for enrichment projected upon El Dorado has repeatedly led to very concrete and historically specific practices of violence and economic extractivism (Rogers 2019), Carpentier also suggests that the mythic signifier of El Dorado becomes identified with a (desired) place that transcends history. Accordingly, Timothy Reiss has situated Carpentier's work within a broader context of Caribbean figurations of El Dorado: "Greeks and Germans, Spaniards and Dutch join with indigenous Amerindians across time and place, taken over by jungle, river, and mountain, whose 'immutable rhythms' overwhelm the manic 'measuring of time' governing western thoughts of history" (Reiss 2002: 347).

In contrast to Euclides da Cunha's phrase about the absence of history in the Amazon, Carpentier's Amazon points not just to the absence of history but

---

16 On the surrealist technique of juxtaposition in Carpentier, see Rogers (2011).
17 "Here man's travels were governed by the Code of the Rains. I noticed that I, to whom the measuring of time was a mania, shackled to the metronome by vocation and to the clock by profession, had stopped thinking of the hour, gauging the height of the sun by hunger or sleep" (Carpentier 1967: 111).
18 "For two days we had been crawling along the skeleton of the planet, forgetting History and even the obscure migrations of the unrecorded ages" (Carpentier 1967: 185).

to the incorporation and co-presence of its various phases and manifestations, of stasis and development. As Jens Andermann observes with regard to the *novela de la selva* generally, this genre encompasses a concern with "ecology" on the one hand, and "history," on the other (Andermann 2018: 227). I also agree with Victoria Saramago's insight that the journey through different time periods does not fundamentally alter the fact that the natural space of the Amazon is essentially portrayed as the Other of modernity, as an immutable realm of "environmental stasis" (Saramago 2021: 63), yet my point here is that this discursive fashioning, the othering of the Amazon, occurs from within a position of self-alienated modernity.

Modern writings on the Amazon have insistently asked the question of how practices and discourses of modernity are being challenged in this frontier region, but also how the very distinction between modernity and savagery may collapse in a sort of dialectic of Enlightenment. For instance, in a remarkable passage in *Los pasos perdidos*, the narrator, reflecting on the (then relatively recent) experience of the Holocaust and Nazi terror in the center of Europe (Carpentier 2009: 266), and the concomitant collapse of humanist culture, as embodied by the world of his father, comes to question the habitual contrast between Europe and Latin America on an axis of modernization as progressive development of humanity.

Moreover, as Charlotte Rogers has recently shown, the quest narrative of *Los pasos perdidos* is beset by multiple ironies, such as the fact that the voyage to the region of archaic origins is effected by air travel, thus resonating with Carpentier's own voyage into the region of Venezuela and marking this as a clear sign of contemporary modernity, in turn connected with the contemporary boom in the Venezuelan oil industry: "Carpentier's deliberate foregrounding of the mode of transportation indicates the significance of commercial air travel in 1950, the year in which the action of the novel takes place" (Rogers 2019: 47; cf. 53). Toward the end of the novel, a short airplane voyage of three hours takes the protagonist back to the "civilized" world he had left, stressing the experiential difference of different regimes of temporality: "Mientras otros se alegran de llegar, yo me acerco con angustiosa aprehensión a este mundo que dejé hace mes y medio, según los calendarios en uso, cuando en realidad he vivido la pasmosa dilatación de seis inmensas semanas que escaparon a la cronología de este clima" (Carpentier 2009: 415).[19] This travelling between different regions of time highlights non-synchronized realities of a (postcolonial)

---

[19] "Some were happy to be arriving, whereas it was with disturbing apprehension that I approached this world I had left a month and a half before by calendar calculation – but the immensity of the six weeks I had lived was incommensurable by the chronology of that climate" (Carpentier 1967: 239).

world but also the fact that this difference is experienced from the perspective of a modern subject.

4 The Amazon as Literary Landscape

If Carpentier's novel enacts a (frustrated) search for cultural and biographical origins, it is also a highly intertextual novel, which thereby foregrounds the fact that the Amazon is also a *literary* landscape, in which this novel is self-consciously inscribed (Wylie 2009). This means that the quest for literary originality (and, by implication, the idea of Latin American identity and autonomy) is beset by the awareness to write in the trace of others who have come before. The ironies of this situation are fully exploited when, towards the end of the novel, the protagonist decides to write a report about his adventures in the jungle, responding to the spectacular expectations that the public in the Northern city has set in his case. Rather than telling the truth, he will shape his narrative along the lines of a pre-established model: "Tengo en mi maleta una novela famosa, de un escritor suramericano, en que se precisan los nombres de animales, de árboles, refiriéndose leyendas indígenas, sucedidos antiguos, y todo lo necesario para dar un giro de veracidad a mi relato" (Carpentier 2009: 419).[20]

As several critics have pointed out, this allusion to an unspecified novel most likely refers to one (or both) of the most paradigmatic novels of the genre *novela de la selva*, either José Eustacio Rivera's *La Vorágine* (1924) or *Canaima* (1935) by Romulo Gallegos (Jaramillo 2016: 90). Of course, the intent to thus model the text on a "famous" novel refers to the protagonist's report, not to *Los pasos perdidos*. Yet the ironic force of this comment reflects back on Carpentier's own text, reinforcing the connection between travel and narrative, and highlighting the fact that all texts about Amazonian travels inevitably follow in the steps of others. The fact that the protagonist's account is structured like a travel narrative and is densely saturated with a plethora of implicit and explicit references to the genre of (tropical) travel literature, including the traditional colonial chronicles of New World "discovery," turns the novel, in its capacity as an "archival fiction," into a sort of meta-commentary on this Western genre (González Echevarría 1998: 153; Fürst-Söllner 2010: 47).

---

[20] "I had in my suitcase a famous novel by a South American writer, giving the names of animals, trees, native legends, long-forgotten events, everything needed to lend a ring of authenticity to my narration" (Carpentier 1967: 243).

Moreover, the *real maravilloso* of New World nature is frequently made familiar by being compared or likened to instances of the Western cultural tradition. Thus, the Roraima plateau in the Upper Amazon is likened to examples from art history: "[. . .] tenía mi memoria que irse al mundo del Bosco, a las babeles imaginaries de los pintores de lo fantástico, de los más alucinados ilustradores de tentaciones de Santos, para hallar algo semejante a lo que estaba contemplando" (Carpentier 2009: 349).[21] This awareness of a palimpsest-like structure of literary and discursive representation coexists in the novel with a rhetoric of immediacy, portraying the Amazonian forest as a "prenatal world" (Carpentier 2009: 382), full of "forms of art, poetry and myth" that are more instructive than any knowledge from books (Carpentier 2009; 385). In fact, on the last pages of the novel the protagonist acknowledges that the very act of writing and his status as an artist and intellectual put him outside the "Valley of arrested time": "[. . .] porque la única raza que está impedida de desligarse de las fechas es la raza de quienes hacen arte, [. . .]. Hoy terminaron las vacaciones de Sísifo" (Carpentier 2009: 453).[22]

The novel thus presents the paradoxical insight that the search for a "natural" landscape of the Amazon is in fact only conceivable as a palimpsest-like layering of textual sources, echoes, and allusions, which uses metaphors to adapt the unfathomable nature to familiar (or often very learned) reference points of the Western tradition: "The intertextual relations of *Los pasos perdidos* lead to a major interpretative conclusion: the act of naming and writing about the jungle from a fresh or uncontaminated perspective is a failed attempt" (Jaramillo 2016: 93). Late in the novel, when the narrator is no longer hopeful to attain a state of unalienated nature, he suggests that the tropical forest is itself a sort of fiction: "La selva era el mundo de la mentira, de la trampa y del falso semblante; allí todo era disfraz, estrategema, juego de apariencias, metamorfosis. [. . .]" (Carpentier 2009: 343).[23] This quote establishes an ironic correspondence with the "artificial trees" in the theater decoration from the first chapter of the novel; of course, it is also reminiscent of the baroque poetics in Euclides da Cunha.

Yet any comparison between da Cunha and Carpentier has to take into account that their discourses on the Amazon are separated by a temporal distance

---

[21] "My memory had to recall the world of Bosch, the imaginary Babels of painters of the fantastic, the most hallucinated illustrators of the temptations of saints, to find anything like what I was seeing" (Carpentier 1967: 171).
[22] "[. . .] because the only human race to which it is forbidden to sever the bonds of time is the race of those who create art, [. . .]. Today Sisyphos' vacation came to an end" (Carpentier 1967: 278).
[23] "The jungle is the world of deceit, subterfuge, duplicity; everything there is disguise, stratagem, artifice, metamorphosis" (Carpentier 1967: 166).

of nearly fifty years and the catastrophes of the twentieth century. We might say that the two writers embody two historically distinct ways to envision modernity, as they have been distinguished by Aleida Assmann. While da Cunha's belief in progress and science makes him a (sometimes skeptical) exponent of the "theory of modernization," Carpentier would seem to exemplify a "theory of modernity" that resorts to "cultural critique," "arguments from depth psychology" as well as "non-Western cultures of time," to point to the ambiguities and contradictions of modernity (Assmann 2013: 90; 140).

Bibliography

Andermann, Jens (2018): *Tierras en trance. Arte y naturaleza después del paisaje*. Santiago de Chile: Metales Pesados.
Anderson, Mark (2014): "The natural Baroque: Opacity, Impenetrability, and Folding in Writing on Amazonia." In: *Hispanic Issues on Line*, 16, pp. 57–83.
Assmann, Aleida (2013): *Ist die Zeit aus den Fugen? Aufstieg und Fall des Zeitregimes der Moderne*. München: Hanser.
Blanco, María del Pilar (2012): *Ghost-Watching American Modernity: Haunting, Landscape, and the Hemispheric Imagination*. New York: Fordham University Press.
Brough-Evans, Vivienne (2016): "Postcolonial Dissident Surrealist Mediums: Geotemporal Conflations of the Isles of Paradise in Alejo Carpentier's *The Lost Steps*." In: *Sacred Surrealism, Dissidence and International Avantgarde Prose*. New York: Routledge, pp. 61–102.
Carpentier, Alejo (1967): *The Lost Steps*. Transl. Harriet de Onís. New York: A. Knopf.
Carpentier, Alejo (1990): *Visión de America*. In: *Obras Completas de Alejo Carpentier*, vol. 13, pp. 274–294. Mexico City: Siglo XXI.
Carpentier, Alejo (2009): *Los Pasos Perdidos*. Madrid: akal.
Cunha, Euclides da (2006): *The Amazon. Land without History*. Transl. Ronald Sousa. Oxford: Oxford University Press.
Dünne, Jörg (2016): *Die katastrophische Feerie. Geschichte, Geologie und Spektakel in der modernen französischen Literatur*. Konstanz: Konstanz University Press.
González Echevarría, Roberto (1977): *Alejo Carpentier: The Pilgrim at Home*. Ithaca/London: Cornell University Press.
González Echevarría, Roberto (1998): *Myth and Archive. A theory of Latin American narrative*. Durham/London: Duke University Press.
Fabian, Johannes (1983): *Time and the Other. How Anthropology makes its Object*. New York: Columbia University Press.
Foot Hardman, Francisco (2001): "A vigança da Hiléia: Os sertões amazônicos de Euclides." In: *Revista Tempo Brasileiro*, 144, pp. 5–30.
Fürst-Söllner, Ulrike (2010): *Das Schreiben des Abenteuers – das Abenteuer des Schreibens. Intermediale Ästhetik und Medienarchäologie in Alejo Carpentiers Roman "Los pasos Perdidos."* Bielefeld: transcript.
Harney, Lucy D. (2012): "*Los pasos perdidos* as Lost World Fiction." In: *Filología y Lingüística*, 38, 1, pp. 47–62.

Harvey, David (2004): *The New Imperialism*. Oxford: Oxford University Press.
Helgesson, Stefan (2014a): "Unsettling Fictions: Generic Instability and Colonial Time." In: Cullhed, Anders/Rydholm, Lena (eds.): *True Lies Worldwide: Fictionality in Global Contexts*. Berlin/Boston: De Gruyter, pp. 261–273.
Helgesson, Stefan (2014b): "Radicalizing Temporal Difference: Anthropology, Postcolonial Theory, and Literary Time." In: *History and Theory*, 53 (Forum: Multiple Temporalities), pp. 545–562.
Henrikson, Paula/ Kullberg, Christina (2020): "Introduction: Time, Temporality, and Travel Writing." In: Henrikson, Paula/Kullberg, Christina (eds.) (2020): *Time and Temporalities in European Travel Writing*. London: Routledge, pp. 1–24.
Jaramillo, Camilo (2016): *Amazonia: A Laboratory for Fiction*. Diss. UC Berkeley. https://escholarship.org/uc/item/5km6b493 (accessed: 29.05.2022).
Kaakinen, Kaisa (2017): *Comparative Literature and the Historical Imaginary. Reading Conrad, Weiss, Sebald*. London: Palgrave, 2017.
Kern, Stephen (2011): *The Modernist Novel: A Critical Introduction*. Cambridge: Cambridge University Press.
Koselleck, Reinhart (2003): *Zeitschichten*. Frankfurt am Main: Suhrkamp.
Reiss, Timothy J. (2002): *Against Autonomy. Global Dialectics of Cultural Exchange*. Stanford: Stanford University Press.
Rodriguez, Ileana (2004): *Transatlantic Topographies*. Minneapolis: University of Minnesota Press.
Rogers, Charlotte (2011): "Carpentier, Collecting, and *Lo Barroco Americano*." In: *Hispania*, 94, 2, pp. 240–251.
Rogers, Charlotte (2019): *Mourning El Dorado. Literature and Extractivism in the Contemporary American Tropics*. Charlottesville/London: University of Virginia Press, 2019.
Saramago, Victoria (2021): *Fictional Environments. Mimesis, Deforestation, and Development in Latin America*. Evanston, Illinois: Northwestern University Press.
Shaw, Donald L. (1985): *Alejo Carpentier*. Boston: Twayne.
Uriarte, Javier (2016): "*Fora da ordem*, or on Time and Travel in Cunha and Lévi-Strauss." In: Félix, Regina/Juall, Scott D. (eds.): *Cultural Exchanges between Brazil and France*. West Lafayette: Purdue University Press, pp. 100–116.
Welge, Jobst (2022): "The Transmission of Knowledge in European Adventure Fiction of the Amazon." In: Boulanger, Alison/McIntosh-Varjabédian, Fiona (eds.): *Comparing Literature: Aspects, Method, and Orientation. Proceedings of the 8th Congress of the European Society of Comparative Literature*. Stuttgart: Ibidem, pp. 135–148.
Wylie, Lesley (2009): *Colonial Tropes and Postcolonial Tricks. Rewriting the Tropics in the Novela de la Selva*. Liverpool: Liverpool University Press.

Jörg Dünne

The Whims of the Climate: Landscapes of Deep Time in Juan José Saer's *Las Nubes*

1 Landscapes and the Terrestrial

That time manifests itself in a "sedimented" way in space is a guiding metaphor of historiography and cultural theory at least since the beginning of the 20th century (see Koselleck 2000; De Landa 1997). Yet the recent debate about the Anthropocene in cultural studies (for an overview, see Horn/Bergthaller 2020) has shown that geological layering of time in space has to be understood not merely as a metaphor for cultural history. It also plays a part in reformulating the modern dichotomy of nature and culture precisely to the extent that stratigraphy reveals the historicity not only of culture, but also – returning to the original sense of the word – of nature. Although geological deep time and human history operate at different time scales, they interact in various ways. This debate also helps focus our attention on a new aspect of landscape that has been accorded little significance in traditional landscape theories, which are based upon a mainly visual paradigm encapsulated in the well-known definition of landscape as a "portion of land which the eye can comprehend at one glance" (Jackson 1984: 3; see also Collot 2015). This definition – which presupposes, on the one hand, a stable subject of contemplation and, on the other, an open space that appears as delimited by a horizon-like structure of human perception – can be challenged in a number of ways.

A prominent way of destabilizing and bringing a distanced subject's sublime point of view over a horizontal landscape "down to earth" is the "terrestrial," a concept introduced by Bruno Latour. In the opening paragraphs of his seventh "Gifford Lecture," delivered in Edinburgh in 2013 (Latour 2017: 220–223), Latour deconstructs the point of view of the landscape painter in remarking on a painting by Caspar David Friedrich titled *The Great Enclosure* (*Das große Gehege*). It is not insignificant here that this painting shows a waterscape, a feature to which I will return below in discussing Argentina and the Argentinean writer Juan José Saer. In contrast to the distanced observation of a landscape whose extension is only limited by the perceptual horizon of the spectator, Latour finds "stable ground" neither in Friedrich's waterscape, nor in the "impossible vantage point of the virtual spectator of the painting" (Latour 2017: 222) who is incapable of

Jörg Dünne, HU Berlin

https://doi.org/10.1515/9783110762273-007

combining two globe-like perspectives – the riverscape in the foreground and the sky in the background – to form a comprehensive totality. What Latour derives from the impossibility of a landscape that can be comprehended at one glance by a distanced spectator in Friedrich's painting is a reterritorialization of human agency. This implies a shift not only in spatial positioning, but also in dealing with geological temporality, generating an entanglement between nature and culture.

In both *Facing Gaia* (2017) and his subsequent essay *Down to Earth* (2018), Latour suggests a new frame of reference for thinking space-time that goes by the proper name of "Gaia." Gaia, or, the terrestrial, has to be considered as an actor or a "quasi-subject" that re-acts against or counter-acts human actions that have become so invasive that humankind in its totality has become a geophysical force. Geologists have been able to detect this force in the stratigraphy of the earth's crust at least since the middle of the 20th century, which has led them to propose the concept of the "Anthropocene."

Latour's conception of the terrestrial as an "attractor" for the assembly of the social implies that today's state of globalization can no longer be thought of in terms of spatial extension centered exclusively on human subjectivity – as a site where human operations take place as foundational acts on a passive, inert ground. Building upon this assumption, I would like to argue that "horizontal" cultural techniques, such as visual control over a horizon-shaped landscape are nowadays being progressively supplanted by the paradigm of the terrestrial, which reintroduces a certain type of verticality into the epistemology of space and privileges cultural techniques of scaping space and time in a way that differs from traditional understanding of landscape.[1] The terrestrial becomes the geological layer where the geohistorical dimension of the biosphere and the geopolitical dimension of the ever-increasing human impact on biospheric conditions interact. I would like to insist on the fact that what Bruno Latour calls the "terrestrial" is not only a matter of geology and stratigraphy but – and this is a crucial point for what follows – also of meteorology: in earth systems science, the thin layer composed of the uppermost part of the earth crust and the lowest part of the atmosphere that is responsible for the possibility of life, human and other than human, on the planet is called the "critical zone" (see Arènes/Latour/Gaillardet 2018).

As Jérôme Gaillardet has shown in his contribution to a catalogue of an exhibition at the Center for Art and Media in Karlsruhe (Gaillardet 2020: 120), the

---

[1] On "scapes" as a possible paradigm for spatial theory, see Dünne (2019); on the horizontal paradigm of geographic extension as being replaced by the "vertical" paradigm of geological superposition in terms of stratigraphy, see Dünne/Haase (forthcoming).

"critical zone" as a sensitive interface between meteorology and geology is closely related to the concept of biosphere introduced by the Russian geologist Vladimir Vernadsky. What I am particularly interested in here in terms of spatiality is the notion of "zone" in the context of the hypothesis I started with, which postulates that there is currently a shift from horizontal extension to vertical dynamization in terms of spatiotemporality. Living in the critical zone would thus mean no longer living *on* the earth as a surface but dwelling *in* a biospheric zone where human and nonhuman agencies interact.

"Zonal thinking" as a tool for linking together nature and culture is, of course, nothing new. We find it above all in climate theory since antiquity (see Ételain 2017). This may entail static, premodern climate zones with their determining influence on character and state formation, or zonal models such as the biosphere. But what all such models of thinking have in common is a conception of zones as a volume, not as a surface, and of "contact zones" as sites where cultural and natural history interact.[2] In the following, I will argue that literature – especially, but not exclusively in Latin America – provides us with a particular genealogy of zonal thinking in which geohistory and geopolitics co-emerge in a poetic way. In particular, I would like to show that, beyond Latour's understanding of the "critical zone," which relies exclusively on earth science, the worldmaking capacity of literary fiction can also contribute to making the contours of this zone of interaction between nature and culture emerge. Furthermore, I will retrace some elements of such a genealogy for the Argentinean literature of the recent past and also show that this analysis allows for a critical reexamination of familiar (post)colonial conceptions of territoriality in Latin America.

2 Rereading the History of Argentinean Literature from a Terrestrial Perspective

Argentina and Argentinean literature might be exemplary cases in point for illustrating the shift described above from the horizontal paradigm of extension to the paradigm of the terrestrial with its implied zonal conception of the earth's surface. The history of the Argentinean nation since the early 19th century is not only the history of an "imagined community" in the sense of Benedict Anderson

---

[2] This use of "contact zones" extends the scope of the concept originally introduced by Pratt (1991) to "naturecultures."

(1983), but also the history of an "imagined territory" that paradigmatically illustrates how reality is made "flat" (Latour 1990: 45) and land is transformed into a space of extension by specific cultural techniques such as cartography. The key operation for this flattening of Argentinean reality is the invention of a figure of spatiality that is much more than a mere natural given. This figure, as recent studies by Fermín Rodríguez (2010) and Javier Uriarte (2020) have shown in the context of nation-building, is the desert.

The desert is a configuration of the land that is produced in a joint geopolitical and geo-imaginative operation. "Desertmaking" is a figure for emptying the vast planes of the grasslands of the pampa, as well as the arid regions of Patagonia – not only in literary imagination but also militarily, as can be seen from the example of the so-called "conquista del desierto" in the second half of the 19th century in Argentina.³ The Argentinean pampa, which has been described as such a desert, seems – at least at first sight – to be a prototypical case for a horizontal space of extension. The model of the desert, which has become a topos for the description of the pampa since 19th-century romanticism, is deeply rooted in a literary tradition of the sublime and thus, according to Jens Andermann (2018a; see also Andermann 2018), in a certain tradition of landscape theory where the human subject finds itself confronted with an experience of an incommensurably open space.⁴

This horizontality linked to the visual experience of a sublime landscape can be questioned by conceiving the pampa not as a purely horizontal desert but rather as a zone of contact that is both biospheric and cultural. As already indicated above, the vertical, zonal dimension of spatial history is not only present in geology and stratigraphy, but also in the atmospheric "boundary layer" of the critical zone that is situated above the surface of the earth. I would like to shift the image of the pampa as a desert to something else that is precisely not a landscape in the horizontal sense Andermann understands it, and that is not determined by a paradigm of visual distance, but which manifests itself as a geologically layered landscape of space-time. Indeed, most parts of the Argentinean pampa are anything but uninhabited and desertic, as one might expect when speaking of a dry and stony desert as opposed to a lush and green land.

---

3 The literary invention of the desert in Argentina's 19th-century literature and in accounts from foreign travelers is thus closely related to the conquering of the desert and what has been described as the genocide of the indigenous population of these vast lands. See, apart from the two studies by Rodríguez and Uriarte already mentioned, Torre (2010), and Viñas (1982).
4 A prototypical description of the desert as an incommensurable open space in Argentinean literature can be found in the well-known first verses of Esteban Echeverría's 1837 long poem *La Cautiva* (Echeverría 2001: 125, V. 1–5).

Rather, huge parts of the Argentinean flatlands are part of what is known as the "pampa húmeda" (or "flooding pampa"), which appears less like a terrestrial landscape and more like a liquid "waterscape" (see Tvedt 2015: 1–18). This is the point that gives rise to my argument about possible contemporary uses of the concept of landscape as a part of a new environmental aesthetics.[5]

Looking at Argentina from the water is also part of a terrestrial approach in a larger sense: zonality is crucial here not only because of the meteorological and climatic dynamics generated by "hydrologic cycles" (Linton 2010: 105–125), but first and foremost because only slight changes in the waterline of the pampa due to heavy rainfall can lead to inundations that make certain parts of the flooding pampa appear as metabolic landscapes. In opposition to the imagination of the pampa as a desert, these metabolic fluvial landscapes present no affordance for being described as inert and passive spaces upon which a nation can be founded. Rather, they produce "unfounding fictions" (see Dünne 2020) that are open for the description of the intertwining of human and terrestrial agency in the critical zone of the biosphere.

This is what I aim to show in the following by analyzing Juan José Saer as a paradigmatic representative of fluvial literature in Argentina.

3 Delirious Landscapes in Juan José Saer

Since the end of the 20th century – the years of neoliberalism and rising neo-extractivism – important novels in Argentina have rewritten 19th-century figurations of the pampa as a desert.[6] Among the authors who have contributed to a shift from the commonplace of the desert to new perceptions of the pampa in terms of a complex waterscape is Juan José Saer.[7] Juan José Saer has become known as writer of the "zone," the imaginary geography of the shores of the Paraná River between Santa Fé and Buenos Aires that he first explored in a collection of short stories in 1960 (Saer 2003). This notion continues to influence all of Saer's later writings, which will be analyzed in the following as a particular

---

[5] This approach slightly modifies the position of Jens Andermann, who argues in favor of an environmental aesthetics *after* landscape, acknowledging, however, that there might be alternative ways of rethinking the notion of landscape through contemporary literature or cinema (see Andermann 2018a: 368–390).

[6] Well-known examples range from César Aira's *La liebre* (1991) to Gabriela Cabezón Cámara's *Las aventuras de la china Iron* (2017).

[7] I have explored some aspects of the following reflections on Saer's *Las nubes*, albeit without reference to landscape theory, in another article (Dünne 2022).

version of a "zonal" literary aesthetics (see Prieto 2006). His 1997 novel *Las nubes* (Saer 2002, English translation: *The Clouds*, Saer 2016), set in the flooding pampa near the shores of the vast riverscape of the Paraná River, may be regarded as paradigmatic in rewriting and unfounding, as it were, the 19th-century narrative of nation-building in the desert against the backdrop of Saer's particular zonal aesthetics.

The story takes place in the year 1804, in the last years of the colonial period at the moment of the founding of the oldest psychiatric institute in Latin America, named Las Tres Acacias, in the outskirts of Buenos Aires. This institute, which has never existed outside the fictional world, transfers fantasies of freedom from the French Revolution to South America, although and ironically only in the years that precede the foundation of the Argentinean nation, which the institute does not survive. Born in Argentina and educated in France, the narrator, Dr. Real, remembers a particular episode of the institute's history when he was a young physician. He receives the order from his master, Dr. Weiss, to deliver a group of five "enfermos mentales" (mentally sick persons) from Santa Fe to the institute near Buenos Aires. They include the quixotic self-proclaimed world-revolutionary Troncoso and the erotomaniac "sor Teresita," a parody of the Spanish mystic Teresa de Ávila, as well as their companions. The travelers comprise a cast of characters recalling not only canonical texts of world literature that reach back to Virgil's *Fourth Eclogue* and its description of a Golden Age, but also the thematically significant figures of the Argentinean pampa and of gaucho literature, which contribute to the particular aesthetics of the "zone" in Saer.

At the same time, Saer's historical novel can also be read as a counterfactual fiction about a possible turning point of the history of madness at the threshold between what Michel Foucault has described as "the great confinement" of the 18th century and the psychiatric treatment of madness in the 19th century (Foucault 1972: 50–76).[8] The young doctor Real and the older doctor Weiss might be considered in this respect as renegades of the school of Philippe Pinel, the father of modern psychiatry. In comparison to the institution Pinel has established in France, Las Tres Acacias is a remarkably open place where the patients spend most of their time outside in the fresh air. The fact that the proper story told in the novel is not about the institute itself but about the transport of five patients from Santa Fe to the institute in Buenos Aires reenforces the

---

[8] Because space is limited, I will not consider here the frame narrative set in the contemporary world of the 1990s where the narration of Dr. Real is presented as a found manuscript, and which revisits climatic conditions in terms of the contrast between summer in Paris and winter in Argentina.

contrast between the closed spaces of the clinic and the open land in which the protagonists of the novel dwell, as if we were still living in the early modern times of a "fool's ship" (see Foucault 1972: 15–49) sailing on the open seas of the pampa.[9]

The topic of madness cannot be detached from the topographical experience of the pampa in *Las nubes*. This becomes clear when the narrator explains the etymology of the word "delirio" (delirium) in a scene where one of the patients, the revolutionary Troncoso, loses control and sets out on a ride through the desert that lasts for several days, and during which he tries to convince the indigenous "cacique Josesito" to join his plans for a planetary revolution. According to the etymology, his *delirio* is not just a mental state, but precisely the material trace of Troncoso's riding through and acting out his plans in the desert, as the narrator comments in the following passage:

> Y como si no hubiese ignorado que, si nos remontamos a sus orígenes latinos, el verbo delirar significa 'salirse del surco o de la huella,' esa misma noche apoyándose en la molicie cómplice de el Ñato, Troncoso puso en práctica esa etimología. (Saer 2002: 153)[10]

Thus, *Las nubes* is about people on the move who literally trace their madness into the surprisingly populated desert as its surface of inscription. Far from being an inert ground or a passive surface of inscription, the pampa is a complex environment to which a proper agency is attributed, as can be seen from the *incipit* of the novel which is a prolepsis of the events to come:

> Ríos por demás crecidos, un verano inesperado y esa carga tan singular: así podrían resumirse, con la perspectiva del tiempo y de la distancia, para explicar la dificultad paradójica de avanzar en lo llano, nuestras cien leguas de vicisitudes. (Saer 2002: 17)[11]

From the beginning, Saer's narrative foregrounds the abnormal meteorological events taking place in the flatlands in relation to the human destinies implied in what is described here as a "most peculiar cargo": in August of 1804, during wintertime in Argentina, a "terrible helada," a sudden cold snap, occurs in the

---

9 On the use of the *topos* of the fools' ship in Saer, see Vezzetti 1997; on the tradition of comparing the plains of the pampa to the sea in *Las nubes*, see Sarlo (1997: 35) and for a more general overview, Silvestri (2008).
10 "And as [if] he was not unaware that the word delirium is derived from the Latin verb for to leave the groove or track, that same night, supported by El Ñato's conspiratorial coddling, Troncoso put that etymology into action" (Saer 2016: 126).
11 "Rivers swollen to excess, an unexpected summer, and that most peculiar cargo: With the perspective of time and distance, these three things could sum up our hundred leagues of troubles, explaining the paradoxical difficulty of crossing the flatlands" (Saer 2016: 9).

pampa. What begins with this unusual winter weather while Dr. Real is travelling to Santa Fe continues on his way back with the five patients, as an extreme flooding of the river landscape forces the travelers to travel to Buenos Aires by a devious route leading them far into the desert in order to escape from the floods. In doing so, they experience another form of agency which is more-than-human: "El río cuya compañía habíamos rechazado, saliendo de su lecho, vendría a buscarnos por propia iniciativa para imponernos sus leyes rigurosas" (Saer 2002: 78).[12]

The Paraná River is personified here as an active agent reducing the human travelers to passive-reactive beings subject to the sovereign rule of the waters. The passivity of the travelers becomes even more intense when the flood gives way to a no less brutal heat wave, which leads to fires in the pampa. The scenery is described in more and more apocalyptic terms when, towards the end of the novel, the travelers are trapped between the burning pampa on one side and the flooded grassland of the vast riverscape on the other. They construct an improvised fortress of wagons in shallow water for protection from the front of fire:

> A la madrugada, ese fuego nos alcanzó. [. . .] El incendio iluminaba todo el campo alrededor, que asumía el brillo excesivo de una fiesta un poco ostentosa, y como las llamas se duplicaban al reflejarse en la laguna, cuyas aguas se habían vuelto de un color naranja ondulante, los que estábamos adentro, metidos hasta el cuello en ese elemento llameante y rojizo, teníamos la impresión de estar atrapados en el núcleo mismo del infierno, sobre todo porque, a causa quizás de la tierra recalentada y de la interminable extensión de las llamas, nuestra piel podía percibir cómo la temperatura del agua iba aumentando, a tal punto que empezábamos a preguntarnos, en nuestro fuero interno desde luego, porque aparte de los hermanos Verde, que no había modo de hacer callar, nadie hablaba, si de un momento a otro no iba a hervir. El humo, que a la distancia parecía firme y duro como una muralla, era de cerca un fluido turbulento que se retorcía locamente [. . .]. (Saer 2002: 177/179)[13]

The pampa as solid ground and earth beneath the characters' feet is dissolved in the metabolic space of a great circulatory system of water. The whole scene

---

[12] "The river whose company we rejected would come for us, rising up of its own accord to impose its harsh rule" (Saer 2016: 57).

[13] "At daybreak, the fire reached us [. . .] The blaze lit up the entire countryside, which took on the excessive brightness of a rather flashy party, and the flames doubled when reflected in the lake, whose waters had turned an undulating orange, so we were within it, up to our necks in that reddened and flaming element, had the impression of being trapped in the very heart of the inferno, especially because, perhaps owing to the overheated earth and endless expanse of flames, our skin could detect the rise in water temperature to the point that we began to wonder – to ourselves, of course, for apart from the Verde brothers, who were impossible to silence, nobody spoke – whether it might begin to boil at any moment. The smoke, which at a distance appeared firm and sturdy as a wall, was a wildly writhing, turbulent fluid up close [. . .]" (Saer 2016: 157/158).

can be understood either as a metaphor for uterine regression or a representation of hell fire. But the passage goes beyond human representations of psychological or religious environments, giving way to a material, sensory experience of the physical world where the human body acts as a thermometer. At the same time, spoken language falls silent among the travelers, largely giving way to the intensely corporeal experience of a prelinguistic environment encompassing all the characters involved. At the end of the passage, even the distinction between smoke and water is dissolved when the latter is described as a "turbulent fluid." Thus, at the climax of the delirious deviation of the travelers from the beaten track of a regular journey from one place to another, cultural and natural order alike are dissolved into an elementary scene of primeval turbulence that takes the meteorological figure of the clouds as a paradigm for the dissolution and reconstitution of physical and social orders (see Serres 1980).

4 Literary Cosmogonies and Landscapes of Deep Time

How does this literary scenario of an aquatic scene of origins relate to the "terrestrial" and the "critical zone" with which my contribution started? I have tried to show that Saer's *Las nubes* exteriorizes the history of madness from a plot centered on the human psyche to a geohistorical dimension. What Saer's travelers through the pampa experience is the constitution of a turbulent fluvial microcosm where the physical state of exception of the climate corresponds to – or even actively contributes to shape – the mental state of exception in the travelers. Like several other of Saer's novels, *Las nubes* is a "literary cosmogony" that can be understood as the crucial element of Saer's entire literary aesthetics of the "zone." This becomes clear in a scene of creation in *Las nubes*, where the expression that prompted the title of this essay appears:

> El viaje, prolongándose más de lo habitual, nos había incitado, de modo imperceptible, a crear nuestras propias normas de vida, y los caprichos del clima, que hacían sucederse las estaciones inapropiadas con la rapidez con que se suceden los días y las horas, sumados a la composición singular de nuestra caravana, nos habían incitado a crear un universo exclusivo [. . .]. (Saer 2002: 169)[14]

---

[14] "The unusually prolonged trip had forced us, imperceptibly, to set our own standards of living, and the whims of the climate, which made the untimely seasons follow one another with the speed of days and hours, added to the singular composition of our caravan; we had had to create a peculiar universe [. . .]" (Saer 2016: 148).

It is probably not entirely accidental that the notion of "climate" appears precisely in this context of microcosmic creation: having been educated in France, the narrator Dr. Real must have been familiar with the climate theory of Enlightenment thinkers such as Montesquieu; and since he writes down his memories only 30 years after the event in 1834, he would have done so in the wake of the romantic transformations of this theory that followed Johann Gottfried Herder, in which rigid climate zones were superseded by ideas about acclimatation and the constitution of regional microclimates (see Horn/Schnyder 2016). Dr. Real's experience of climate is thus historically located between a traditional, static zonal model of climate as a determining factor for human behavior and modern theories of environment in which climatic conditions and human agency start to interact dynamically.

From the standpoint of environmental history, the "zone" in which Dr. Real and his patients in Saer's novel dwell is obviously not the same as the one Bruno Latour describes as "critical zone," and it goes without saying that the extreme weather event that Saer narrates cannot be understood in any way as a prefiguration of climate change. Nevertheless, Saer's conception of climate as an active, dynamic environment points to an important threshold in the conception of the relation between human culture and nature. The "peculiar universe" described in *Las nubes* in its effects upon the group of people dwelling in the ever-changing pampa might remind us of the premodern analogy between human micro- and macrocosm, but the fact that such a universe is "created" by the travelers themselves rather points to the modern paradigm of the environment conceived as a form of interaction between a living organism and its *Umwelt* (see Wessely/Huber 2015). For the protagonists of the novel, dwelling in a certain climate zone is thus no longer an experience of order and stability, but rather of variability that becomes visible not only in what human beings do in the land but in the transformation of land itself. And Saer's text, which rewrites the history of the pampa, appears at a turning point in landscape and environmental history where the long-lasting narrative of a horizontal extension in a desert landscape driven by human heroes is starting to be questioned, and where other, more complex types of interaction between humans and their environment appear.

The zonal dimension of Saer's novel is bound up with the temporality of these scapes, which are no longer just spatial configurations like landscapes that can be comprehended visually at one glance. Rather, similar to what the anthropologist Timothy Ingold has described in a seminal article on "The Temporality of the Landscape" (Ingold 1993), they are spatiotemporal "taskscapes" that are based on a set of human practices and thus comprise an "embodied" experience that is "immersive" rather than "contemplative" (in the sense of being based upon visual control).¹⁵ In contrast to Ingold, however, who explicitly notes that "the temporality of the taskscape is essentially social" (Ingold 1993: 158), the landscapes of time – or rather: the landscapes of *deep* time that I am interested in here – refer not only to the human practice of dwelling, as in Ingold's approach, but also to a geohistorical temporality reaching beyond any individually embodied human temporality.

The question, though, is how to get a grip on such a landscape of (deep) time if there is no longer any clear visual framing or horizon-like structure in terms of spatial extension, and if such a type of landscape cannot be reconstructed as the trace left by the "taskscape" of embodied human practices. Here, the poetological dimension of Saer's aesthetics of the "zone" comes into play, and here it becomes clear that the creation of a spatiotemporal environment, as the narrator claims it for the key scene analyzed above, is obviously also (and maybe even primarily) the task of the act of narrating and writing itself: the specificity of the literary configuration of landscapes of time in Saer's *Las nubes* and in other of his "cosmogonic" literary texts is the particular experience of spatiotemporality that goes beyond visual control "at one glance," and which is in search of an experience of temporality that unfolds at different scales at once, a human and a more-than human meteorological or geological scale.¹⁶ This later scale becomes perceptible in its proper agency only in those exceptional moments where human experience becomes synchronized with geohistory, as happens in the central scenes of *Las nubes* in the flooded and burning pampa, where the temporalities of human history and geohistory exceptionally correspond. In *Las nubes*, "madness" might ultimately be another word for this type of correspondence.

The art of the landscape writer might then consist in producing such a delirious spatiotemporal scenario by manipulating time scales in a way that enables a peculiar landscape of time to be produced in a momentaneous scene of correspondence between human and more-than-human temporality.¹⁷ Such a scene not only allows for an immersion into the primeval materiality of

---

15 I borrow the opposition of "immersive" vs. "contemplative" landscape from a study on filmic landscape by Martin Lefebvre (2011), who further develops Ingold's argument in relation to narrative cinema.
16 Comparable scenes of cosmogony can be found in *Nadie nada nunca* (1980, Saer 2004) and *El río sin orillas* (1991, Saer 2003a).
17 The correspondence between human "microcosm" and "macrocosm" is, of course, a premodern figure, but its experience in Saer is by no means based on some prestabilized harmony. Rather, it has to be actively produced and becomes perceptible only in exceptional moments.

terrestrial processes; it is also at the origin of possible alternative configurations of history, since it suggests the – ultimately Utopian – birth of the Argentinean nation out of a shared moment of geohistorical madness.[18]

Bibliography

Aira, César (1991): *La liebre*. Buenos Aires: Emecé.
Andermann, Jens (2018): "Introduction." In: Andermann, Jens/Blackmore, Lisa/Carrillo Morell, Dayron (eds.): *Natura: Environmental Aesthetics After Landscape*. Zurich: Diaphanes, pp. 1–16.
Andermann, Jens (2018a): *Tierras en trance: arte y naturaleza después del paisaje*. Santiago de Chile: Metales Pesados.
Anderson, Benedict (1983): *Imagined Communities: Reflections on the Origin and Spread of Nationalism*. London: Verso.
Arènes, Alexandra/ Latour, Bruno/ Gaillardet, Jérôme (2018): "Giving Depth to the Surface: An Exercise in the Gaia-Graphy of Critical Zones." In: *The Anthropocene Review*, 5, 2, pp. 120–135.
Cabezón Cámara, Gabriela (2017): *Las aventuras de la china Iron*. Buenos Aires: Random House.
Collot, Michel (2015): "Landschaft." In: Dünne, Jörg/Mahler, Andreas (eds.): *Handbuch Literatur & Raum*. Berlin/Boston: De Gruyter, pp. 151–159.
De Landa, Manuel (1997): *A Thousand Years of Nonlinear History*. New York: Swerve Editions.
Dünne, Jörg (2019): "Von spaces zu scapes. Alternative Konzeptionen von Räumlichkeit in den Literatur- und Kulturwissenschaften." In: *Archiv für das Studium der neueren Sprachen und Literaturen*, 256, 2, pp. 371–384.
Dünne, Jörg (2020): "Cultural Techniques and Founding Fictions." In: Dünne, Jörg/Fehringer, Kathrin/Kuhn, Kristina/Struck, Wolfgang (eds.): *Cultural Techniques. Assembling Spaces, Texts & Collectives*. Berlin/Boston: De Gruyter, pp. 47–60.
Dünne, Jörg (2022): "Lines of Flight and Aquatic Environments. The Pampa as Experimental Space of the Aesthetic in the Novels of César Aira und Juan José Saer." In: *Iberoromania*, 95, 1, pp. 1–16.
Dünne, Jörg/ Haase, Jenny (forthcoming): "Introducción." In: Dünne, Jörg/Haase, Jenny (eds.): *Pensar y escribir la tierra*. Frankfurt am Main/Madrid: Vervuert/Iberoamericana.
Echeverría, Esteban (2001 [1837]): *La cautiva*. Madrid: Cátedra.
Ételain, Jeanne (2017): "Qu'appelle-t-on zone? À la recherche d'un concept manqué." In: *Les Temps modernes*, 692, pp. 113–135.
Foucault, Michel (1972): *Madness and Civilization: A History of Insanity in the Age of Reason*. Alexandria: Alexander Street Press.
Gaillardet, Jérôme (2020): "The Critical Zone, a Buffer Zone, The Human Habitat." In: Latour, Bruno/Weibel, Peter (eds.) (2020): *Critical Zones: The Science and Politics of Landing on Earth*. Karlsruhe: ZKM, pp. 120–127.

---

[18] On madness as an alternative founding scenario of Argentinean history in *Las nubes*, see Rojas (2015); however, her interesting reflections do not take into account the "deep" historicity of this scenario.

Horn, Eva/Bergthaller, Hannes (2020): *The Anthropocene: Key Issues for the Humanities.* London/New York: Routledge.
Horn, Eva/ Schnyder, Peter (2016): "Romantische Klimatologie. Einleitung." In: *Zeitschrift für Kulturwissenschaften*, 1, pp. 9–18.
Ingold, Tim (1993): "The Temporality of the Landscape." In: *World Archaeology*, 25, 2, pp. 152–174.
Ingold, Tim (2017): "Taking Taskscape to Task." In: Rajala, Ulla/Mills, Philip (eds): *Forms of Dwelling: 20 Years of Taskscapes in Archaeology.* Oxford: Oxbow Books, pp. 16–27.
Jackson, John Brinckerhoff (1984): *Discovering the Vernacular Landscape.* New Haven/London: Yale University Press.
Koselleck, Reinhart (2000): *Zeitschichten.* Frankfurt a.M: Suhrkamp.
Latour, Bruno (1990): "Drawing Things Together." In: Lynch, Michael/Woolgar, Steve (eds.): *Representation in Scientific Practice.* Cambridge/London: MIT Press, pp. 19–68.
Latour, Bruno (2017): *Facing Gaia: Eight Lectures on the New Climatic Regime.* Cambridge: Polity Press.
Latour, Bruno (2018): *Down to Earth: Politics in the New Climatic Regime.* Cambridge: Polity Press.
Lefebvre, Martin (2011): "On Landscape in Narrative Cinema." In: *Revue Canadienne d'Études cinématographiques/Canadian Journal of Film Studies*, 20, 1, pp. 61–78.
Linton, Jamie (2010): *What is Water? The History of a Modern Abstraction.* Vancouver/Toronto: VBC Press.
Pratt, Mary Louise (1991): "Arts of the Contact Zone." In: *Profession*, 91, pp. 33–40.
Prieto, Martín (2006): "Escrituras de la 'zona.'" In: Jitrik, Noé (ed.): *Historia crítica de la literatura argentina*, vol. 10. Buenos Aires: Emecé, pp. 343–357.
Rodríguez, Fermín (2010): *Un desierto para la nación.* Buenos Aires: Eterna Cadencia.
Rojas, Eunice (2015): "The Asylum as Juan José Saer's Argentine Founding Myth." In: *Spaces of Madness: Insane Asylums in Argentine Narrative.* Lanham: Lexington Books, pp. 161–177
Saer, Juan José (2002 [1997]): *Las nubes.* Barcelona: Muchnik.
Saer, Juan José (2003 [1960]): *En la zona.* Buenos Aires: Seix Barral.
Saer, Juan José (2003a [1991]): *El río sin orillas: tratado imaginario.* Buenos Aires: Seix Barral.
Saer, Juan José (2004 [1980]): *Nadie nada nunca.* Buenos Aires: Seix Barral.
Saer, Juan José (2016 [1997]): *The Clouds.* Trans. Hilary Vaughn Dobel. Rochester: Open Letter.
Sarlo, Beatriz (1997): "Aventuras de un médico filósofo. Sobre *Las nubes* de Juan José Saer." In: *Punto de Vista*, 59, pp. 35–38.
Serres, Michel (1980): "Solides, fluides, flammes." In: *Hermès V. Le Passage du Nord-Ouest.* Paris: Minuit, pp. 40–66.
Silvestri, Graciela (2008): "La Pampa como el mar." In: *La Biblioteca*, 7, pp. 54–71.
Torre, Claudia (2010): *Literatura en tránsito: la narrativa expedicionaria de la conquista del desierto.* Buenos Aires: Prometeo.
Tvedt, Terje (2015): *Water and Society. Changing Perceptions of Societal and Historical Development.* London/New York: Tauris.
Uriarte, Javier (2020): *The Desertmakers: Travel, War, and the State in Latin America.* New York: Routledge.
Vezzetti, Hugo (1997): "La nave de los locos de Juan José Saer." In: *Punto de Vista*, 59, pp. 39–41.
Viñas, David (1982): *Indios, ejército y frontera.* Ciudad de México: Siglo XXI.
Wessely, Christina/ Huber, Florian (eds.) (2015): *Milieu. Umgebungen des Lebendigen in der Moderne.* Paderborn: Fink.

III **Specters, Ruins, Catastrophes**

Carlos Fonseca
The Landscape in Ruins

1 Geohistory, Catastrophe, and the Archaeology of the Modern Nation-State

> We must not lose sight of one notable geological agent, however – man. In fact, he most usually has had a brutal effect upon the land and, if we might say so, has famously assumed along the whole path of history the role of a terrible maker of deserts.
>
> Euclides da Cunha, *Backlands*

A terrible maker of deserts: so designates Euclides da Cunha the ecological role of the human in his 1902 classic *Os sertões*, in words that inevitably resound with contemporary debates concerning the Anthropocene. Written as part of his account of the infamous Canudos campaign, the phrase also bring to mind the ways through which the newly established Brazilian Republic sought to supress the historical reality of the *sertão*. To make a desert meant, first of all, to erase. To turn the *sertão*, envisioned as space of barbarism and underdevelopment, into a *tabula rasa* where the dreams of modernity of the emerging nation-state could be projected against a natural space devoid of proper history. To make a desert meant, in this sense, to landscape. If the nation-state's political project was to produce a political imaginary that included all of its citizens within its process of modernization, then the first step was to envision a representative apparatus through which this inclusion could happen. Landscape emerged in that socio-political context, alongside maps, museums and foundational romances, as a way of figuring this nascent imagined community and its modern pretensions (Andermann 2007: 12).

The young civil engineer who in 1897 received the invitation of *O Estado de São Paulo* to join the fourth expedition of the Canudos Campaign must have gladly accepted, considering it his task to participate in this project of modernization. As an ardent Republican and fervent positivist who had been taught by followers of Auguste Comte, Euclides da Cunha must have seen the invitation as an opportunity to corroborate the theories of social Darwinism and environmental determinism that first influenced him via his readings of authors such as Herbert Spencer and Henry Thomas Buckle (Stavans 2010: xv). The story must have also seemed intriguing: in the northeastern state of Bahia, amidst

Carlos Fonseca, University of Cambridge

the arid backlands of the *sertão*, an army of outlaws led by a pro-monarchical messianic leader known as Antônio Conselheiro had declared war on the Republican army. By the time da Cunha's invitation arrived, three failed military campaigns had attempted to conquer Belo Monte, as the inhabitants called the settlement, and thousands of soldiers had died, including the famous Colonel Antônio Moreira César. The thought of joining the fourth expedition, albeit fear-provoking, must have been exciting: the backlands of Canudos represented, at the end of the day, the frontier battleground where the civilizing stakes of modernity and the fate of the nascent Republic were being played out.

It is not surprising that *Os sertões*, published in 1902, five years after the fourth expedition that brought the final destruction of Canudos, reads like a product of its time. At first sight, da Cunha's history of the terrible conflict seems to partake in many of the positivist ideologies through which the *sertão* was actively produced within the modern imaginary as space of alterity: in its act of landscaping, the prose envisions the backlands as a natural remnant outside of history, characterized by racial degeneration and environmental determinism. The *sertão* remains, within that first reading, the barbaric and ahistorical tabula rasa against which the modern nation-state can posit its civilizing history of modernity. Nature appears as the primitive remnant that must be domesticated and subsumed by the scientific eye of the reporter if it wishes to be part of the modern imaginary. Inverted image of a nascent modernity, Canudos comes to signify in the pages of da Cunha's book the barbaric residue that must be eradicated in the name of progress. *Ordem e Progresso*: the Comtean phrase inscribed within the Brazilian flag that the soldiers carried into battle was already the first sign of what was at stake in Bahia. For what was at stake was the taming of the natural: nature had to be landscaped and suppressed if it wished to belong to the progressivist modern imaginary proposed by the state.

However, like many nineteenth century foundational texts, what makes *Os sertões* such a fascinating read is the capacity to sustain readings against the grain. The book's pretensions of positivism and progressivism are quickly undone by a subterranean current that is quick to critically disassemble its original ambitions. This is not a mere accident but rather a product of the complex double bind by which modernity was staged, at least in Latin America, through the mirroring fantasy of its outside: barbarism (Taussig 1987: 127). Two sides of the same coin, the polar opposites previously sketched by Domingo Sarmiento, civilization and barbarism, seem to only exist as mirror opposites of each other, with the same phantasmagorical ontology with which culture defines itself via its contrasting relationship to nature. *Os sertões*, like Sarmiento's *Facundo* before it, situates itself at the crux of this double knot underlying the modern fantasy, allowing the readers to position themselves against the grain of its original intentions. This critical stance, which is the one I wish to explore, sketches a counter-hegemonic stance that shows the limitations and prejudices of the nation-state's representational apparatus.

"The troops were attacking the very bedrock of our race. Dynamite was the only suitable weapon," da Cunha would famously write towards the end of the book, while describing the final battle and the way the bombing brutally reduced Canudos to ruins (da Cunha 2010: 454). By then his enthusiasm had waned: he had realised that the campaign was barbaric in itself, a violent imposition that he would later call a crime against humanity. In its attempt to sketch the *tabula rasa* upon which it could later project its dreams of modernity, the nation-state had paradoxically ended up conjuring a landscape of ruins. In what follows, I wish to explore the idea that it was this attention to the figure of the ruin, the rubble and the remnant, mediated by a geohistorical discourse of catastrophe, what allowed da Cunha to sketch, against the grain proposed by the landscaping eye of the state, a counter-discourse that returned both to nature and to the outlaws of Canudos their respective historicity.

2 A Geological Counter-Modernity: The Desert as Land-Archive

> Its function as a geological agent is revolutionary. . .
> Euclides da Cunha, *Backlands*

In the game of mirrors that produced the modern political imaginary throughout Latin America, the desert was strategically seen as the outside of civilization and therefore as the outside of history (Lienhard 1992: 80). Through their multiple campaigns to "conquer the desert," the modern Republics attempted to erase the historicity of the indigenous inhabitants of the backlands, mapping their lands as empty pages that could then be filled by the state's imaginary (Garramuño 2012: 19). The *sertão* was no different, as da Cunha is quick to notice in the first pages of *Os sertões*: "Our best maps, based on scanty reports, have a blank there, a hiatus. Terra incognita. . ." (da Cunha 2010: 13). Hypothetically, the young engineer's job was precisely that: to fill the void by projecting upon it the landscaping dreams of the modern nation-state. To imagine this space as a natural dominion outside of history and outside of culture. *Os sertões*, however, works around this imaginary, by proposing a geohistorical discourse of catastrophe that reimagines nature as a revolutionary space traversed by what, following James Hutton, we could call deep history. Countering the idea of the ahistorical tabula rasa, da Cunha's gesture is to turn the *sertão* into a geological archive, within which the figure of Antônio Conselheiro emerges as fossil:

> It was not surprising that our deep ethnic strata pushed up the extraordinary figure of Antônio Conselheiro, "the Counselor." He is like a fossil. Just as the geologist can reconstruct the inclinations and orientation of very old formations from truncated strata and build models of ancient mountains, so can the historian deduce something about the society that produced this man, who himself is of little worth. (Da Cunha 2010: 124)

Showing the backlands to be a space traversed by time and history, the fossil analogy grounds da Cunha's account against the geohistorical discourses that were beginning to emerge throughout the late eighteenth century. Within this discourse, where nature was understood to be a revolutionary agent rather than a mere passive background, fossils were seen as the archival remnants of past catastrophes. Working in the aftermath of the French Revolution, geohistorians like George Cuvier and Horace Bénédict de Saussure began to speak of "nature's archives" as a testament to earth's epochs and revolutions (Rudwick 2005: 2). For them, catastrophism was a way of thinking historically and even revolutionarily about nature: a way of portraying it as a violent space of eventuality.

Da Cunha's *Os sertões* inherits from the founders of geohistory this notion of deep time, visualizing the *sertão* as a catastrophic and revolutionary space that refuses to be fully tamed by the landscaping eye of the journalist. Against the linear and horizontal temporality of the nation-state's progressivist modernity, the backlands open up to a vertical temporality that stops the progress of time. It is within this space that the fossil figure of Antônio Conselheiro emerges, as the geological remnant incommensurable with modernity. Metonym for the more than twenty thousand *jagunços*, landless farmers, outlaw bandits, former slaves and indigenous people that conformed his improvised army, the fossil figure of Antônio Conselheiro stands for the "eruption of the past into the present" (da Cunha 2010: 281). A pre-modern remnant that refuses to be smoothly subsumed within the state's representative apparatus and which instead forces the chronicler to adopt the stance of an archaeologist:

> Canudos was a miserable hole in the desert, not even a dot on our maps, as remote and indecipherable as a page torn from an old book. The only comparison that comes to mind is that of geologic strata, which when disturbed or inverted reveal a modern formation below an ancient one [. . .]. Canudos was, more than anything else, a lesson that should have awakened curiosity similar to that aroused in an archaeologist when he discovers a prehistoric village under the foundations of a modern Swiss city. (Da Cunha 2010: 24)

Like an earthquake disturbing the stability of the state's territory, bringing forth the spectres of forgotten pasts, Canudos traces, against the *sertão*'s blank page, the figure of an archaeological ruin. "He will feel that he is treading the ruins from an earthquake as he climbs up the hills closest to the Canudos," da Cunha writes in the first pages of the book, foreshadowing the catastrophist discourse through which he will seek to understand Brazil's stratified modernity (da Cunha 2010: 24). Reminiscent of Sarmiento's comparison of Argentina to a "nameless, subaltern volcano," this emphasis on catastrophe points to the fundamental incommensurability between Canudos and the enlightened political categories through which positivist historiography wished to tell its story (Sarmiento 1998: 75). Refusing to be tamed by the ideology of progress, behaving as a fossil found in the middle of the desert, Canudos forces the young engineer to stop the clock of modernity and to look at the past with the eyes of an archaeologist.

What then, appears, once one adopts this archaeological stance? What view, or counter-view, of Brazilian modernity becomes visible once the positivist landscaping eye awakens to the catastrophic history of the *sertão*? These are some of the questions that allow us to read *Os sertões* against the grain of its modernizing intentions and its racist prejudices, as a book that restores, via a catastrophe, a historicity to the outcast nature and pariah peoples of the *sertão*. Like Walter Benjamin's angel of history, whose criticism of modernity stems from his capacity to see history *as* catastrophe, as a "heap of rubble" rather than as an arrow pointing to the horizon of an open future, da Cunha's archaeological stance awakens us to the violence inherent in the process of modernization. "The concept of progress must be grounded in the idea of catastrophe," Benjamin would later go on to state, in words that remind us of how catastrophe becomes, within his philosophy of history, the flipside of progressive modernity (Benjamin 2002: 473). Da Cunha's feat was to remain attentive to the two sides of this historical process, opening for us readers a critical space from which to access this campaign which he himself would describe, in the book's preliminary note, as a crime.

From this archaeological stance, the *sertão* becomes visible in front of us, not as the blank page or terra incognita the state wished it to be, but rather as an archive of catastrophes. "It is something like the rubble left over from the eternal conflict between land and sea," states da Cunha in the first page of the book, in words that resound with the messianic imaginary proposed by the Counsellor's most famous prophecy: "The backlands will become the sea, and the sea the backlands" (da Cunha 2010: 250). Against the landscaping eye that wished to portray the backlands as a barbaric space outside of history, the archaeological stance shows the *sertão* to be a space traversed by a history that refuses to be tamed. Marked by its deep temporality, nature becomes an archive, a palimpsest where history is violently erased and rewritten. Against the ahistoricity of the *sertão* understood as desert landscape, what emerges is the possibility of seeing it as a geohistorical *land-archive* bearing the traces of the past struggles between human and nature. Undoing the acts of that terrible maker of deserts, man, this counter-reading allows us to critically read nature against the modernizing optics of the nation-state.

If the nation-state's relationship to nature had been mediated by what we could call a landscape contract – namely, the fact that nature could only be incorporated into the civilizing project of the state under the domesticating and ahistorical frame of landscape – then what the archaeological stance unearths is the revolutionary historicity of nature. Cuvier often spoke of fossils as archival documents bearing witness to nature's revolutions. His catastrophism was a way of thinking of nature as a revolutionary and historical agent, capable of "bursting the limits of time" (Rudwick 2005: 2). Adopting a similar vision, da Cunha's *sertão* bursts through the domesticating frame of landscape, pointing to the failure of the state's representative apparatus. "In a latter case the traveller has at least the relief of a broad horizon and the perspective of open plains. Here the *caatinga* brushland engulfs him. It cuts off his field of vision. It attacks and stupefies him. It tangles him up in its thorny scheme of things" (da Cunha 2010: 35). No longer the master of nature, the human finds that the backland nature defeats his representational capabilities, entangling him in a world that is always excessive and catastrophic:

> The structural makeup of the land has been coupled with a great upheaval of external agents in the design of stupendous reliefs. A torrential period of excessive weather will suddenly appear after long infusions of sun, and as it hits the slopes it leaves exposed parts that decay over a long period of time. (Da Cunha 2010: 17)

Excessive and merciless, nature overwhelms the human, not even granting the journalist the perverse pleasure of a sublime landscape. Representation enters into crisis in this world, in ways that resonate with the incapacity to represent the Counsellor himself as anything but monstrous: "In Bahia a dour hermit appeared with hair to his shoulders, a long matted beard hiding an emaciated face – a monstrous figure with piercing eyes, wearing a blue homespun robe . . ." (da Cunha 2010: 134). Nature's extremeness, its capacity to burst through the frame of landscape, is mirrored here in the state's incapacity to envision the Counsellor – and alongside him any of the thousands of *jagunços* that accompanied him in Canudos – as anything more than a monster, an excessive multitude that had no space within the imagined community of the nascent republic. It is this confluence between issues of natural representation and issue of political representation, between questions of ecology and issues of citizenship, which makes *Os sertões* such a fascinating text for exploring the limitations of the modern nation-state.

3 Too Much or Too Little: Incommensurability in *Os Sertões*

> Human existence comes to depend on the painful cycle of drought and flooding of the great rivers of the region.
> Euclides da Cunha, *Backlands*

Civilization, we know, is often defined in terms of measure and form. The modernizing project of the nation-state was no exception: in the name of civilization it wished to formally tame excess in all its modes. Everything that fitted within the contours of its frontiers had to be accounted for within the multiple representational apparatuses the modern republics had set for themselves: maps, identity cards, museums, landscapes. Landscapes, in particular, made the idea of measure particularly palpable: within its frame, nature behaved properly, domesticated by the eye of the artist. As Gabriela Nouzeilles puts it: ". . . landscape refers to a Western mode of perceiving space and imagining a relationship to nature as one with a scene located at a certain distance from the observer, as if it was a painting" (Nouzeilles 2002: 21). Within this world, nothing was supposed to be outside the representational frames of the nation-state. It is this idea of constraint via representation what is constantly questioned throughout da Cunha's *Os sertões*. Breaking loose of the framing measures of landscape, nature posits itself as the incommensurable excess that refuses to be represented. Either too little or too much, either as absolute lack or as complete excess, the nature of the backlands defies the landscaping measures of State.

Insightfully, da Cunha finds in the dialectic between droughts and floods that cyclically strike the *sertão* a way of speaking about this fundamental incommensurability at the heart of Brazilian national identity. The *sertão* never "fits" nicely within the landscape frame because it fluctuates between the nothingness characteristic of the drought and the extravagance of the flood, as part of a cyclical history of catastrophes that ends up violently inscribing itself within the land-archive:

> The forces that work on the land attack it, in its deepest parts and on its surface, with no let-up in their destructive action, each taking over in an invariable intercedence during the only two seasons the region has. They break it during the scorching summers and they break it during the torrential winters. (Da Cunha 2010: 18)

This passage from "extreme aridity to extreme exuberance," from desert to sea, helps da Cunha figure the backland's nature as a historical agent producing a landscape of ruins: an excessive space within the frontiers of the nation-state where the representational apparatus of the modern Republic enters into crisis. We must not forget that Monte Santo had been formed around an exclusion:

the more than ten thousand members that composed the Conselheiro's *jagunço* army consisted precisely of those excluded from the Republic's modernizing project. The bandits, landless farmers, former slaves, religious and indigenous people, which bravely fought and defeated three expeditionary army forces sent by the Brazilian government, saw themselves as outcasts. Pariahs forgotten by the representative democracy that had emerged in 1889 after the monarchy was overthrown. Their political stance then was to remain stubborn in their excessiveness. To become a symptom of a deeper crisis crossing the Republican model as a whole: the failure to truly achieve the utopia of full representation that the nation-state promised its citizens (Garramuño 2012: 19). Either invisible or monstrous, defined either by lack or by excess, the *jagunços* were the incommensurable remnant that had been left behind by the secular modern imposition of order and progress.

What da Cunha was beginning to encounter *through* his writing were the limits of the aesthetic and political models through which nature had been until then represented within modernity. Envisioned either as garden or as sublime landscape, nature had remained until then tamed by what, following Timothy Morton, we could call the Romantic act of aesthetic enframing. Paradoxically, in their anti-Enlightenment attempt to return to nature, the Romantics had ended up detaching themselves from the very nature they claimed to revere: "Putting something called nature on a pedestal and admiring it from afar does for the environment what patriarchy does for the figure of Woman" (Morton 2007: 5). This representational positioning of the Romantic gaze, which Morton calls the beautiful soul syndrome, was a way of distancing the subject's position from what was perceived as the object of desire: nature. Against this model, Morton's dark ecology has highlighted the necessity to go beyond this aesthetic enframing, daring to enter into dialogue with an ecology that breaks the frames that wish to imprison it. It is this double gesture of trying, on the one hand, to fit nature within the aesthetic frame of the Romantic gaze and, on the other, failing to do so, what marks the critical rhythm of da Cunha's text. If he admits feeling vertigo when confronted with what seem to be sublime scenes, this vertigo is quickly eclipsed by the overwhelming feeling of being trapped inside an environment that is as oppressive as it is brutal. Nature is never the beautiful "out there" but rather the overwhelming environment that reduces man to the unbearable sweaty present. "It tangles him up in its thorny scheme of things," as we read in a passage that suggests how, bursting free of the landscape frames that wished to encapsulate it within the regime of State-sponsored symbolic representations, nature proves to be the thorny thing that resists symbolization (da Cunha 2010: 35).

Working against the grain of the text's original ideological intentions, this reading would suggest a second undercurrent working below the environmental determinism that underlies the book's tripartite structure, with its three subdivisions entitled "The Land," "Man" and "The Struggle," suggesting that it has been the brutal and inhospitable environment of the backlands what has produced the fanatical, barbaric and ungovernable body of the backlander. If, as Mark Anderson has noted, da Cunha had portrayed the *sertanejo* as the barbaric sociological fossil inevitably produced by such a crude environment, this gesture simultaneously opens up the possibility of a critical space where nature, by acting catastrophically, shows itself to be incommensurable with the symbolic frames through which western subjectivity desired to view the world. Either too much or too little, nature refuses to be an object simply given to representation. Instead, it opens a cyclical temporality that ends up thwarting another one of the sacred bastions of modernity:

> The strong storms that quench the dull fire of the droughts, in spite of the rebirth they bring along with them, set up the region for greater troubles. They harshly denude it, leaving it more and more unprotected from summers to come [. . .]. The region goes through a deplorable interlude that resembles a vicious cycle of catastrophes. (Da Cunha 2010: 54)

This cycle of catastrophes works against the teleological temporality that the state wishes to impose upon the history of the nation. Against the Benjaminian storm of progress that wishes to propel the nation and its citizens into an empty future without caring for the catastrophic ruins it leaves behind, da Cunha's catastrophic nature stands stubborn against this teleological imaginary. If the Counsellor emerges then within this world as sociological fossil, it is not only as symptom of the inhospitable environment that envelops him, but as a ruin that forces us to stop for once to see the deserts man has created.

Defined by either lack or by excess, nature in *Os sertões* can never be here seized in its totality as landscape. Instead, the reader feels that what is left to grasp is nothing but the ruins of landscape, the ruins left behind by the violent landscaping attempts enforced by the hegemonic eye of the state. "The new town arose in a few weeks, a city of ruins. It was born old. Seen from a distance, spread out over the hills over an enormous area, split by ravines and rugged slopes, it has the appearance of a city that has been shaken and thrown by an earthquake," (da Cunha 2010: 151) we read as we enter the last part of the book, in words that suggest that Canudos emerged from the ruins left behind by a merciless modernizing project that in the name of progress had forgotten about the needs of a great part of its people. A city built like a ruin that would finally be reduced to ruin when, in the early days of October 1897, the remaining survivors of Canudos witnessed how the troops of General Arthur Oscar de Andrade Guimarães marched into Belo Monte, and proceeded to destroy the city. Having won the war, the Republican army seemed obstinate in erasing from history the memory of Canudos: the city was bombarded, the houses were burnt and the survivors were murdered, in an act of madness that according to the story told in *Os sertões* ended up with the last four remaining members of Belo Monte – an old man, two full grown men, and a child – facing an army of five thousand soldiers. Whereas this is probably an exaggeration by da Cunha, who was not present to see the events themselves, the atrocities committed by the army during those final days were so traumatic that they forced the journalist to relinquish description:

> We will forgo describing the final moments. They are impossible to describe. The story we are telling was a deeply moving and tragic one to the very end. We must finish it hesitantly and with humility. We feel like someone who has climbed a very high mountain. On the summit, new vistas unfold before us, and with that greater perspective comes vertigo. (Da Cunha 2010: 463)

Os sertões therefore ends by both suggesting and veiling the view of a landscape so traumatic that it resists positivist description. A landscape of ruins and suffering that, precisely in being marked by the negativity of death and destruction, defies in its excesses the realm of representation. In the name of progress, a utopia had been reduced to a heap of rubble.

4 After Catastrophe: Nature after the Ruin of Landscape

> [R]ubble may signal the start of a collective regeneration
> that points not toward the past but toward the future.
> Gastón Gordillo, *Rubble*

What happens, then, to nature after the ruin of landscape? What new ecology emerges after the enlightened ideal of the landscaped garden fails? The closing pages of *Os sertões* are illuminating in this regards, for they highlight the final incapacity of the Republican army to fully erase the traces of what had once been a utopic city. "Let this simple statement be read in the bright light of the future," da Cunha states in a passage that denounces the government's barbaric crimes against its own population, opening the possibility of future justice within a text that until then had looked only at the past (da Cunha 2010: 435). This opening of the text to the future finds in the ruin, the rubble and the remnant, its preferred seating. There, in that particular midpoint between nature and culture that is the ruin, da Cunha finds the site where the subaltern voices of Canudos await a spectral redemption. Against the power of a State that wished to turn the *sertão* into a *tabula rasa*, the rubble of Canudos stands as the incommensurable remnant that opens up politics as the passionate struggle to redeem what the modern Republic, in its representative and landscaping mission, could only see as excess: the voices of those thousands of outlaw bandits, *jagunços*, landless farmers, former slaves and indigenous people that on the 4th of October of 1897 saw their dreams toppled by the merciless power of dynamite.

The history of Canudos is then the history of the State's attempts to landscape it and of the capacity of both nature and culture to escape the regimes of political and ecological representation that the government had espoused. Most famously, in 1966 the government attempted to supress the memory of Canudos by building the *Cocorobó Dam* precisely in the grounds where once stood Belo Monte, submerging its ruins below the waters. Paradoxically realising one of Antônio Conselheiro's famous prophecies – "The backlands will become the sea and the sea will become the backlands" – the State wished to erase the spectres of a history that refused to settle. Even then, in the months of drought, the ruins of the old church became visible as a call for justice reminiscent of da Cunha's words when describing the final battle: "The *janguços* were coming back from the dead, as always" (da Cunha 2010: 451). The image of the ghostly ruins of the Counsellor's church coming out from the waters bore witness to that deep history that the government had unsuccessfully tried to bury behind the glossy surface of maps and of landscapes. Canudos would always be more than a mere desert.

"The terrible things that followed are buried for all time," we read as we enter da Cunha's tale of the final days of the battle, a phrase that reminds us of the logic of burial and unearthing that runs throughout the text delimiting what I have called the archaeological stance of the reader (da Cunha 2010: 463). It remains for the reader to excavate the text in search for the fossil counter-modernity that remains buried within the deserts of the modern-nation state. This project, however, is not limited to the Brazilian case here studied, but rather extends to what we could call the Latin American ecological imaginary. In his 1975 essay "The Baroque and the Marvellous Real," Alejo Carpentier sketches a possible way of thinking through this counter-hegemonic imaginary in terms of a radical nature that refuses to be tamed or domesticated:

> Our world is baroque because of its architecture – this goes without saying – the unruly complexities of its nature and vegetation, the many colours that surround us, the telluric pulse of the phenomena that we still feel. There is a famous letter written by Goethe in his old age in which he describes the place near Weimar where he plans to build a house, saying: "Such joy to live where nature has already been tamed forever." He couldn't have written that in America, where our nature is untamed, as is our history, a history of both the marvellous real and the strange in America. . . (Carpentier 2005: 105)

Against the gardens imagined by Goethe, Carpentier's Latin American nature would then be characterized by its counter-enlightened radicality: by its refusal to be tamed by the landscaping frames of enlightened modernity. The important thing here is to see that this ecological radicalism is then mirrored, according to the Cuban writer, upon its history, the baroque history of a continent that remains faithful to the "telluric pulse" that envelops it. Catastrophe would emerge then, within this imaginary, as a geohistorical way of thinking through the eventuality of nature, its radical historicity and insubordination. As a way of moving from landscape to land-archive and finding there, buried below the history of modernity, the fossils of counter-modernity that await the light of day.

Bibliography

Andermann, Jens (2007): *The Optic of the State. Visuality and Power in Argentina and Brazil*. Pittsburgh: University of Pittsburgh Press.
Andermann, Jens (2018): *Tierras en Trance*. Santiago: Metales Pesados.
Anderson, Mark (2014): "National Nature and Ecologies of Abjection in Brazilian Literature at the Turn of the Twentieth Century." In: Kane, Adrian Taylor (ed.) (2014): *The Natural World in Latin American Literatures: Ecocritical Essays on Twentieth Century Writings*. Jefferson, NC: McFarland & Co., pp. 208–32.
Benjamin, Walter (2002): *The Arcades Project*. Edited by Rolf Tiedemann. Translated by Eiland, Howard and McLaughlin, Kevin. Cambridge, Massachusetts: Harvard University Press.
Carpentier, Alejo (2005): "The Baroque and the Marvelous Real." In: Parkinson Zamora, Lois (ed.) (2005): *Magical Realism: Theory, History, Community*. Durham: Duke University Press, pp 89–107.
Cunha, Euclides da/Translated by Elizabeth Lowe (2010): *Backlands: The Canudos Campaign*. New York: Penguin Classics.
Garramuño, Florencia (2012): "Pueblo sin estado: Los sertones y el imaginario moderno." In: da Cunha, Euclides da (2012): *Los sertones: Campaña de Canudos*. Buenos Aires: Fondo de Cultura Económica, pp. 7–20.
Gordillo, Gastón (2014): *Rubble: The Afterlife of Destruction*. Durham: Duke University Press.
Lienhard, Martin (1992): "Writing and Power in the Conquest of America." In: *Latin American Perspectives*, 19, 3, pp. 79–85.
Morton, Timothy (2007): *Ecology Without Nature: Rethinking Environmental Aesthetics*. Cambridge, Massachusetts: Harvard University Press.
Nouzeilles, Gabriela (ed.) (2002): *La naturaleza en disputa: Retóricas del cuerpo y del paisaje en América Latina*. Buenos Aires: Paidós.
Pratt, Mary Louise (2007): *Imperial Eyes: Travel Writing and Transculturation*. London: Routledge.
Rodríguez, Fermín (2010): *Un desierto para la nación*. Buenos Aires: Eterna Cadencia.
Rudwick, Martin J.S. (2005): *Bursting the Limits of Time: The Reconstruction of Geohistory in the Age of Revolution*. London: University of Chicago Press.
Stavans, Ilan (2010): "Introduction." In: Cunha, Euclides da (2010): *Backlands: The Canudos Campaign*. New York: Penguin Classics.
Taussig, Michael (1987): *Shamanism, Colonialism and the Wild Man*. London: Chicago University Press.

Anna Jörngården
Presencing Absence: Ruin as Counter-Monument in Caribbean Literature

"Where are your monuments, your battles, martyrs? / Where is your tribal memory?" (Walcott 1979: 25). In his poem "The Sea is History" (1979), Derek Walcott makes reference to the colonialist perception of the Caribbean as a historically empty area. On these so-called sugar islands, as the area has often been reductively referred to, nothing had happened before the European landfall, and precious little after that, except the production of tropical consumer goods which brought wealth to the metropoles but left no cultural or material traces of any consequence on the islands themselves. As Frantz Fanon describes this colonialist mindset in *Les damnés de la terre* (1961): "The settler makes history; his life is an epoch, an Odyssey. He is the absolute beginning: 'This land was created by us'; he is its unceasing cause" (Fanon 2001: 39–40). Hand in hand with this belief is the conviction that the land would decay and revert to its previous immobility if colonialism would come to an end: "'If we leave, all is lost, and the country will go back to the Middle Ages'" (Fanon 2001: 40). In a striking image, Fanon describes this simultaneous erasure of the settled land's own history and inscription of that of the imperialists as crystallized in the symbolic oppression of monuments. The "colonial world" is "a world of statues: the statue of the general who carried out the conquest, the statue of the engineer who built the bridge; a world which is sure of itself, which crushes with its stones the backs flayed by whips."

As Fanon's statement conveys, the monument in its traditional form is an expression of power. It attempts to naturalize the foundational myths of a certain dominant group, by materializing a particular version of history in the landscape. Built in durable materials, the monument is made to remain in the same form in the same place, projecting its world order into eternity. Hence, it "makes a claim to immortality, to an eternal present and an unceasing state of becoming," as in the Austrian art historian Alois Riegl's definition (1982: 38), a grandiose temporality that reveals the affinity between the colonial worldview and the monumental form.

Anna Jörngården, Stockholm University

https://doi.org/10.1515/9783110762273-009

While Fanon wrote his interrogation of colonialism and anti-colonial struggle in *Les damnés de la terre* in light of his experiences in Algeria, he may well have had in mind the statues of his native Martinique and the wider Caribbean region. In *Peau noire, masques blancs* (1952), he comments scathingly on the problematics of a particular category of monuments, namely those commemorating the abolition of slavery, or, as he writes, "the impressive number of statues throughout France and the colonies representing the white figure of France caressing the frizzy hair of the docile black man whose chains have just been broken" (Fanon 2008: 195).

While probably thinking of the statue of Victor Schœlcher in Cayenne, sculpted by Louis-Ernest Barrias in 1896, or the one of the same abolitionist politician in Fort-de-France, sculpted by Marquet de Vasselot and inaugurated in 1904, Fanon describes a broader, transnational blueprint of how emancipation has been visualized by the states formerly engaged in colonial slavery. Both of these statues depict Schœlcher holding a protective arm around the shoulders of a reverential former slave, the other arm extended in a grandiose gesture towards the freedom that is now theirs. The sky is the limit, it seems. In Cayenne, the newly freed subject is a lithe young man, naked except for a loin-cloth, whose whole attitude is one of admiration and gratitude. In Fort-de-France it is a child; a little girl holding her hand over her mouth in awe, looking up into the benefactor's determined face. In *The Horrible Gift of Freedom* (2010), Marcus Wood shows how this iconography rests on an emancipation myth that annihilates the memory of slavery: "Suddenly slavery has gone, and the memory of slavery has been replaced in a flash by a space of celebration and thanks that insists on the fiction of an enforced equality of black and white" (Wood 2010: 27). In one stroke, the master has been transformed into a magnanimous moral example, the agency of the enslaved in their own fight for freedom has been negated, and the continued inequalities that are the legacy of the system of slavery have been obscured.

While erasure of history and memory, then, is an inevitable consequence of all colonial projects, the Caribbean case is particularly extreme. As the "oldest theatre of overseas European expansion," to use Stephan Palmié and Francisco Scarano's expression, the Caribbean was entirely reshaped by modern mercantilism and capitalism and thrown into what Sidney Mintz has called a "precocious modernity," centred on the plantation system (Palmié/Scarano 2011: 7; Mintz 1996: 2, 289–311, 295). Hence, the Caribbean epitomizes Walter Mignolo's compound term "modernity/coloniality," which emphasizes the mutual interdependence of these forces (Mignolo 2000: 22). The near-complete destruction of the Amerindian civilizations followed by the violent repopulation of the archipelago with enslaved Africans, and later, with indentured Indian and Chinese labourers, meant that displacement and discontinuity with the past effectively came to define the Caribbean experience. "Everybody there came from somewhere else," Stuart Hall writes, making the Caribbean "the first, the original, and the purest diaspora" (Hall 1995: 6). In an early essay, Derek Walcott describes the sense of lacking roots in the soil as the feeling that "we have not wholly sunk into our own landscapes," to the extent that "one gets the feeling at funerals that our bodies make only light, unlasting impressions on our earth," a compelling image of lack of historical depth (Walcott 1970; in: Walcott 1998: 18). Similarly, Édouard Glissant claims that in the Caribbean, unlike in Europe, "historical consciousness could not be deposited gradually and continuously, like sediment as it were" (Glissant 1989: 62). Instead, such consciousness "came together in the context of shock, contraction, painful negation and explosive forces," creating rather the experience of a "nonhistory."

This radical erasure and oblivion, combined with the imposition of a colonialist version of history on the landscape, has meant that the Caribbean material culture of memory has become perceived as a situation of at once too little and too much. This dilemma is legible already in one of the first modern classics of Caribbean literature: Aimé Césaire's *Cahier d'un retour au pays natal* (1939). On the one hand, the return home in this poem means coming to terms with a lack of inscription. In Césaire's iconic image of Caribbean pastlessness, the place is experienced as "these countries without stela, these paths without memories, these winds without tablets" (1995: 93). On the other hand, the markers of memory that *are* erected in the landscape are even more telling of the alienation of its inhabitants. In his poem, Césaire lists three monuments in Fort-de-France that make up a decidedly colonial world of statues. One of "Empress Joséphine of the French dreaming high, high above negridom," one of the "conquistador" – Pierre Belain d'Esnambuc, the founder of the first permanent French colony on Martinique – and the one previously mentioned of Schœlcher, or "the liberator rigidified in its liberation of whitened stone" (Césaire 1995: 75).

As of 2020, none of these statues are left standing. In the wake of the Black Lives Matter movement, which originated in the US but inspired a wave of monument contestation world-wide, these statues were toppled and smashed to pieces. In many parts of the world, the BLM-inspired questioning of the power structures governing the material culture of commemoration brought critical attention to previously ignored or taken for granted monumental spaces. In the Caribbean, however, and particularly in Caribbean literature, this debate has a long prehistory. This tradition reveals the necessity to not only address the often problematic colonialist memorializations of the past, but also to direct attention to that which is *not there*: the silences, absences and lacunae that sometimes speak louder than any monument, at least to those who are prepared to listen.

In this chapter, I explore some examples of how Caribbean literature enlists *ruins* and their counter-monumental potential to uncover an unmarked, fragmented and half-buried past and to challenge the historiographical processes that obscured it behind the monumental history of the colonizer. The texts I consider are *Guyane: Traces-mémoires du bagne* (1994) by Patrick Chamoiseau, *After the Dance* (2002) by Edwidge Danticat and *The Chosen Place, The Timeless People* (1969) by Paule Marshall (Chamoiseau, with photographs by Rodolphe Hammadi 1994; Danticat 2002; Marshall 1969). *Guyane* is an essay about the ruins of the penal colony in French Guiana, with photographs by Rodolphe Hammadi. *After the Dance* likewise describes the author's visit to an actual, existing ruin, but this time related to the sugar industry outside the city of Jacmel in Haiti. By contrast, Paule Marshall writes about a fictional ruin landscape in her novel *The Chosen Place, The Timeless People* (1969), a book Simon Gikandi calls "one of the monumental texts on modernization and colonial historiography in the Caribbean" (Gikandi 1992: 175). First, however, a few preliminaries on the relationship between ruins, monuments and counter-monuments.

1 Ruins, Monuments, Counter-Monuments

While ruins and monuments each function to convey messages from the past into the present, and some ruins can be said to have turned into monuments and vice versa, the ruinous and the monumental are in a phenomenological sense two categories in fundamental conflict, because of the disparate ways that they relate to the passage of time. To parse the relationship between ruins and monuments, it is again useful to turn to Alois Riegl's essay "The Modern Cult of Monuments" (1903). Underlining the desire for fixity and the attempt to suspend time as intrinsic to the monumental, Riegl points out that the same claim to permanence applies also to historical structures and objects that were not built for commemorative purposes in their own time, but have by subsequent generations been ascribed value, and hence become what he calls "unintentional monuments" (Riegl 1982: 23). While the historical significance of such objects rests on the recognition that time has indeed passed, all signs of the continuousness of this process are suppressed as soon as a structure is perceived as a monument. "[H]istorical value singles out one moment in the developmental continuum of the past and places it before our eyes as if it belonged to the present," Riegl writes; "it aims above all at the most complete conservation of the monument in its present state, and this requires that the natural course of decay be stayed as much as is humanly possible" (Riegl 1982: 38).

For ruins, however, the opposite is the case. It is the decay that has seized the object that makes it interesting to the observer. In Riegl's vocabulary, the attraction that ruins exert falls in the category of "age-value," which manifests itself "in the corrosion of surfaces, in their patina, in the wear and tear of buildings and objects," displaying the "slow and inevitable disintegration of nature" (Riegl 1982: 32). Such crumbling objects, he stresses, appeal "directly to our emotions," eliciting an affective response that has its source in the awareness of vanishing that condition all aspects of human existence (Riegl 1982: 33).

Writing from the perspective of the turn of the twentieth century, Riegl sees "age-value" as a "new" commemorative value "whose ultimate consequences cannot yet be assessed" (Riegl 1982: 24). But this ambivalent fascination with "the cycle of becoming and passing away" has been at the very core of ruin aesthetics at least since late-eighteenth century Romanticism (Riegl 1982: 32). As such, it is deeply connected to the experience of modernity with its heightened awareness of transitoriness and transformation, and, indeed, discontinuity and destruction. As singularly affective objects, ruins evoke emotional responses that range from mildly melancholic but at the same time pleasurable – awe-filled states connected to the pull of history, the brevity of existence and the unstoppability of time – to more acute and uncanny experiences of coming in contact with lingering trauma and pain caused by a past that refuses to entirely disappear and instead returns according to the logic of haunting.

While sometimes dismissed as simply a kind of sentimental voyeurism, attention to ruins can level a pervasive critique of the core tenets of modernity, and, indeed coloniality. As Andreas Huyssen describes it in a discussion of eighteenth-century ruin imagery, "the ruin as a product of modernity" communicates "the transitoriness of all greatness and power, the warning of imperial hubris, and the remembrance of nature in all culture" (Huyssen 2010: 21). In this vein, Percy Bysshe Shelley's sonnet "Ozymandias" (1818) offers an enduring image of how the ruin's critical message is directly aimed at the monument's claim to everlasting authority. While it might be going too far to read his poem as an outright critique of colonialism, it cannot be understood without being considered in light of the contemporary expansionism of the British empire. In "Ozymandias," a traveller recounts his discovery of a crumbled antique statue in the middle of the desert. Two "trunkless legs" are the only parts still standing (Bysshe Shelley 1994: 589). The head is lying below, half-covered by the sand, but the "shattered visage" still reflects an attitude of arrogance and despotism, communicated also by the inscription of the pedestal: "My name is Ozymandias, king of kings: / Look on my works, ye Mighty, and despair!" But there is nothing left to see except the expansive desert, an at once poignant and ironic message about the futility of the imperialist fantasies of eternal rule.

Indeed, "time mocks the rigidity of monuments," as James E. Young writes, a scholar who for several decades has specialized in the processes of memorial art, in particular as it revolves around pain, loss and trauma (1996: 247). In studying Germany's attempts to publicly remember its own crimes during the Nazi era, Young coined the term "counter-monument" in 1992 to account for the new type of state-sponsored monuments that came out of this process of national self-indictment, and which departed from the traditional monumental form. According to Young, the aim of the counter-monument is

> not to remain fixed but to change; not to be everlasting but to disappear; not to be ignored by its passersby but to demand interaction; not to remain pristine but to invite its own violation and desecration; not to accept graciously the burden of memory but to throw it back at the town's feet. (Young 1996: 277)

In as much as Young theorizes an antithesis to conventional monuments, it might as well be a ruin he is describing. The counter-monument's way of escaping the totalizing claims of the monumental is to cross the line towards the ruinous, to open itself to the forces of destruction.

While aesthetic norms as well as ruinscapes have changed since modern ruin discourse began to be formulated in the eighteenth century, ruin aesthetics continue to revolve around the same ambivalent tension between presence and absence. Being material traces of the history of a particular place, ruins offer a situated and embodied contact with that past. But at the same time, they embody their own vanishing and turn attention to processes of destruction and forgetting. As spectral presences, no longer serving any practical function but nevertheless *still there*, they communicate messages about that which is left behind as times move forward. Since, as in Walter Benjamin's famous words, modern progress has been increasingly perceived as a storm that piles "wreckage upon wreckage" until the "debris" reaches the sky, it is no wonder that the interest in the critical testimonies of ruins has not abated during the twentieth and twenty-first centuries (Benjamin 1969: 257–258).

For ruins to be able to do this critical work, however, their ruination needs to be an ongoing process. If ruins cease to express their own vanishing, they lose their aesthetic-emotional mode of voicing dissidence. This means that if monuments are threatened by decay, the threat to ruins by contrast comes from conservation and restoration, which transform ruins into monuments. In Michael Roth's words, "ruins resist because they persist, but not too well" (1997: 2). At the same time, the consequence of interminable decay is that the ruin will eventually completely cease to exist, which also means an end to its ability both to evoke emotions and to voice critique. The dilemma of ruin gazing, then, is that both caring too much and not caring at all will eventually lead to the destruction of ruin value. Can there be a productive response to this impasse? If we would believe Huyssen, such a ruin response is a thing of the past. Objects and structures are no longer left to age, he claims, but are either done away with or done up. "Authentic ruins, at least as they existed in the eighteenth and nineteenth centuries, seem to have no place in late capitalism's culture of commodity and memory," he argues (2010: 19). Even if Huyssen's reasoning in this respect seems a bit too categorical, and maybe too centred on the European situation, he nevertheless addresses a fundamental tension that all ruin discourse must take into consideration and that preoccupies each of the three authors that I will now turn to consider.

Each of the following sections – on Chamoiseau, Danticat, and Marshall respectively – focuses on the author's engagement with a key counter-monumental function that ruin imagery can perform. Thus, in the section on Chamoiseau, I focus on *suffering*, or how ruins can communicate the traumas of history. In Danticat's text, I read the ruin as representation of *demodernization*, or, the Caribbean's paradoxical relationship to modernity which reverses the relationship between the modern and the outmoded. In Marshall's novel, I focus on the ruin as a symbol of *resistance*, or as a counter-monument to visual representations of the abolition narrative.

2 Ruins of Suffering: Chamoiseau

"Our Monuments remain like suffering. / They bear witness to suffering. / They preserve suffering."[1] Opening his essay on the ruins of the French penal colony in Guiana with these words, Chamoiseau addresses a tension already activated by the publication context of this slim volume. It was first published in 1994 by *Caisse nationale des monuments historiques et des sites*, a French government body founded in 1914 with the aim to acquire, protect and conserve historically valuable sites. In 2000, this institution changed its name to *Centre des monuments nationaux*, and today it manages the upkeep and public accessibility of almost 100 monuments in France, ranging from prehistoric monoliths to modernist architecture. "Ces monuments sont porteurs de la mémoire de la Nation," its president stated in 2014, echoing Pierre Nora's *Les lieux de mémoire*.[2] With *Guyane: Traces-*

---

[1] Chamoiseau (2020: 5).
[2] https://francearchives.fr/fr/pages_histoire/39475: "These monuments are carriers of the memory of the Nation."

mémoires du bagne, Chamoiseau not only intervenes by invoking memories that do not rest easily within this national narrative, but also explicitly critiques this kind of national heritage production and its underlying values.[3] Initially it is this critique, rather than the *bagne* itself, that takes centre stage.

After the epigraph, Chamoiseau ceases to use the term "monument" to refer to material objects that can offer contact with Caribbean history. Instead, much like Fanon employs the image of the colonial world of statues, Chamoiseau refers to monuments as materializations of "History with a capital 'h'" or the "colonial Chronicle," which exalts the acts of European domination at the same time as it actively silences the narratives of the peoples who were the victims of these acts, resisted them, and against all odds found "a way to survive, then to live together, and eventually to produce an original culture and identity" (Chamoiseau 2020: 5–6). Hence, Caribbean "monuments [. . .] bear witness to colonials, to the dominant power, to the colonial act with its genocides, enslavements, and assassinations of the Other;" and "[s]tatues and marble plaques celebrate explorers and conquistadores, governors and elite administrators" (Chamoiseau 2020: 6). In contrast to this celebratory materiality, the history of these Others is expressed only in terms of absence. Echoing Césaire's images of a land without memorial markers, Chamoiseau describes this history as being "without stelai, without statues, without monuments, without documents" (Chamoiseau 2020: 5).

As a result of monument culture's complicity in a continued colonial oppression perpetuated through its symbols, the statues that are there fail to offer much meaning to the people of the Antilles, Chamoiseau claims; "these structures don't inspire much affective response" (Chamoiseau 2020: 5). Or if they do, such affect itself becomes a cause of alienation: "When they turn to face the Monuments that define their spaces, they don't find themselves there. Or, through venerating these structures, they become enslaved by colonial Memory and History" (Chamoiseau 2020: 6).

---

3 This is central to all previous studies, which however read this critique in other contexts than the material memory culture of the transnational Caribbean region. In *The Holocaust and Colonialism in French and Francophone Fiction and Film* (2015) and "Memory Traces: Patrick Chamoiseau and Rodolphe Hammadi's *Guyane: Traces-mémoires du bagne*" (2010). Max Silverman reads *Guyane* in relation to representations of Nazi concentration camps. In "Postcolonializing the *Bagne*" (2018), Charles Forsdick studies it in the context of a body of texts about French overseas penal colonies. Imprisonment is also the focus of Sophie Fuggle's recent article, which studies carceral spaces across Chamoiseau's writing, see "Reimagining the ruins of the penalscape: Patrick Chamoiseau's carceral ruinology" (2020). Andy Stafford analyzes *Guyane* as a postcolonial photo-text in *Photo-Text: Contemporary French Writing of the Photographic Image* (2010: 140–155).

While various decolonization processes in the Caribbean archipelago have contributed, in part, to the creation of new memorial landscapes, for example through the erection of statues of maroons and leaders of slave rebellions (or at least of what they might have looked like, since historical information is scant), Chamoiseau is after something else. The kind of memory that offers real resistance "cannot be made manifest by a monument, by stelai, by statues," he states (Chamoiseau 2020: 7). Instead, he calls for a radical intervention to transform material memory culture and challenge the way history is conceptualized: "it is necessary to reinvent the notion of the monument, to deconstruct the notion of heritage [patrimoine]" (Chamoiseau 2020: 6). This reinvention is to be achieved by ignoring the self-aggrandizing materiality of conventional monuments, and instead seeking other histories through attention to what he calls *Traces-mémoires*, or "memory traces." That is: decidedly counter-monumental, fragmented, half-forgotten and unassuming vestiges of the lives and deaths of those who have not been deemed worthy of commemoration.

While Chamoiseau's *Traces-mémoires* can also be more intangible than a physical ruin, the concept continues to be firmly rooted within the tradition of ruin aesthetics. To begin with, a process of becoming-ruin is necessary for memory traces to emerge. This process involves the original structure, object or phenomenon being forgotten, or perhaps repressed from memory, and thereby submitted to the ravages of time. The decay and destruction that results from such neglect, however, is not interpreted as loss, but rather as an opening up for other hidden, subterranean memories to surface; the return of the repressed. In a central formulation, "the ruin becomes open memories" – *mémoires-ouvertes* – since the process of ruination involves an ongoing accumulation of memories that turns the ruined structure into a multilayered space in which disintegration is also a process of becoming (Chamoiseau 2020: 13). This openness and ability to acquire new meanings places ruinous memory traces in explicit opposition to the monumental. While the monument means "a dead crystallization," the memory trace "is a frisson of life" (Chamoiseau 2020: 8). While the monument is static and "has only one signification that most often fades in one or two generations" the memory trace is plural and dynamic; its meanings "are constantly evolving." This emphasis on the productiveness of decay in contrast to the suffocation of permanence is reminiscent of Young's conceptualization of the counter-monument.

In the particular case of the structures of the *bagne*, they have become a *Traces-mémoires*

> because for many years they were abandoned to a solitary confrontation with vegetal fury, coiling roots, and suffocating branches. The walls had to fight with the tortured tree life rising from their hearts; tree stumps unearthed enormous rocks one by one. Rain,

insects, and humidity petrified the wood, wore down iron, stone, grilles, and broke into holds and buildings. People came, rampaged, pillaged, and lived in the desolation. (Chamoiseau 2020: 11)

This process of destruction only intensifies the possibility for the place to communicate the memory of the unremembered: "But the memory of the men who had been there, who had suffered there, was mysteriously still alive. From the wear and tear of this confrontation were borne the most stunning of human patrimonies: the Memory traces of the penal colony of French Guiana" (Chamoiseau 2020: 11).

In fact, the ruination that ensued as soon as the structure was abandoned is essentially a continuation of the process that charged the place with the lives of those incarcerated there in the first place. "The rubbing confrontation of human and stone, human and steel," has produced messages that can be discerned by observers who are receptive to the "specific patina that bears witness to an everyday gesture," visible in the "black that congeals next to the openings," or in the rust having been "fed by sweat" (Chamoiseau 2020: 16, 19). The friction of bodies and erosion of nature makes the ruin itself appear human-like. The scarred and mossy walls give the impression of "facing skin itself" (Chamoiseau 2020: 14). But most importantly, the continued embodied contact between man and stone has turned "the materials into receptacles of emotion": "these interminable sorrows, these suffocating disappointments, these stupors, these fleeting moments of happiness, this life of emergency, began to penetrate the material world" (Chamoiseau 2020: 13–14).

Later, as the structures begin to disintegrate, this emotional intensity seeps out, and the vegetation contributes an almost gothic charge to the ruination process. The roots of the trees that invade the place pull "inconceivable lifeblood from stones and cement," the ruinous remnants expel a "mysterious energy that the plant life absorbs" (Chamoiseau 2020: 24). This description is one of the few of Chamoiseau's passages that Rodolphe Hammadi – whose photographs comprise the second half of the book, as a related but independent essay in images – will explicitly illustrate. Chamoiseau's words return within quotation marks in Hammadi's narration in images as a caption to a picture of a powerful ceiba tree, which coils through the door of a cell like a giant, primaeval serpent and crushes the grille ceiling as it reaches for the sky (Figure 1). In Caribbean lore, the ceiba or silk-cotton tree is often associated with the spirits of the dead and thus traditionally both feared and revered. As Hammadi connects the image of the tree's destruction of the prison structure to Chamoiseau's words on vegetation feeding on the suffering of the long-dead *bagnards*, the result is an emotionally powerful message from a past that refuses to be put to rest. Chamoiseau extends this Caribbean vision across the hemisphere to the American South, linking the two geographies through the plantation system

Figure 1: A ceiba tree breaking in and out of a prison cell on Île Saint-Joseph. Patrick Chamoiseau/Rodolphe Hammadi (1994): *Guyane: Traces-mémoires du bagne*. Paris: Caisse nationale des monuments historiques et des sites, p. 111. © Rodolphe Hammadi.

and a shared history of suffering: "I saw the same in Louisiana. Plantation owners had thrown the corpses of spent slaves into the middle of a vast field. Over the course of time, trees with twisted branches grew in this crude cemetery, which seemed to moan during the harvests."

Knowing this buried history entails making oneself able to hear the moans that emanate from all kinds of crumbling structures belonging to the Caribbean ruin archive; "the slave holds, the sugar mills, the sugar plantation lodgings" (Chamoiseau 2020: 15). As with romanticism's poetic ruin practices, this involves adopting an embodied, emotionally hypersensitive approach, which attempts to establish contact with the "unfathomable," "beneath," or "beyond" (Chamoiseau 2020: 8, 11, 12). Chamoiseau comes to the *bagne* as a "wanderer," he insists, not as a "visitor" (Chamoiseau 2020: 27). Rather than following any set tour or paying attention to recorded information, facts and figures, he turns himself into a sensitive instrument and tunes into the place emotionally and physically. "[C]ircling through detours," the "divagations of my steps and spirit" perform "a sort of unraveling." "I am ready to feel," as he writes: "Je suis disponible pour les sensations" (Chamoiseau 1994: 44). In *Guyane*, these ruin emotions effectively deconstruct colonial monumental history and intuit another, decolonized narrative emerging from the cracks.

3 Ruins of Demodernization: Danticat

While Chamoiseau's ruin aesthetics gives voice to the dead, Edwidge Danticat's ruins mediate also the stories of those whose lives today are still entirely conditioned by the colonialism by which the Caribbean both anticipated and enabled Europe's modern industrial development. Danticat writes about Haiti, where as early as the 1790s accounts of the deforestation and land destruction attested to the intense monoculture of the semi-industrial sugar production (Benson 2005: 100). In Danticat's text, the ruins of this early industrial moment are followed by even more ruins, not the byproduct of unrelenting progress, as in the dominant narrative of modernity, but by modernization suddenly coming to a halt. "The 'modernization' stopped," writes Sidney Mintz, "as the Caribbean's definition as a key world economic region declined, and what had once seemed modern soon seemed archaic" (Mintz 1996: 296).

In *After the Dance*, the Caribbean's paradoxical relationship to modernity is communicated by a ruin. Central to the narrative is that the ruin can only perform this work as long as it is allowed to continue its existence as a *ruin*, rather than being turned into a historically valuable monument. Part travelogue and part essay contemplating Haiti's history, culture and contemporary society, *After the Dance* revolves around the author's visit to Jacmel in 2001 to experience the city's legendary carnival. During the visit, she leaves the town with a friend on a quest to find a "symbol of nineteenth-century industrial Jacmel": "Our destination is an abandoned steam engine scattered in two very large pieces across a grassy plain that was once the site of a thriving sugar plantation called Habitation Price" (Danticat 2002: 53). As she learnt on a previous guided visit to the spot, the steam engine is considered an important industrial heritage object. "Among the first patented by the Scottish engineer James Watt, it was brought to Haiti in the early 1800s by a former British military man named Price," and it is now "one of a handful of Watts engines left in the world" (Danticat 2002: 53–54) This makes it "such a valuable relic that the Smithsonian archaeological society is said to have offered to remove it from its outdoor location in Jacmel to one of its museums in the United States" (Danticat 2002: 54).

Even so, the engine turns out to be hard to find, as are all other traces of this area once having been in the vanguard of the industrial revolution. Walking through banana fields, the author observes men working the land with pickaxes and hoes, a stark image of demodernization. One of these men, Ovid, eventually points them in the right direction, but not before taking them to visit his little house and telling them the story of his life, which like that of his parents has taken place entirely in the vicinity of the ruined engine. A farmer since boyhood, he has never gone to school, and the one-room house he shares with his wife lacks electricity. The visitors end up spending a long time "listening to their stories but mostly their complaints: about the lack of opportunities, the bad roads, the need for a widespread irrigation system to water their crops" (Danticat 2002: 60). Reminding Danticat of her relatives, Ovid and his wife become in her narrative representatives of Haiti's poor rural people and their entirely disenfranchised lives.

After taking leave of Ovid and his wife, Danticat finally approaches the long defunct engine. Her first impression is being "startled" by the fact that there is a donkey tied to a part of the structure, which has sunken deep into the soil (Danticat 2002: 61). "The flywheel is some ways off in the distance, near a harvested cornfield," her description continues. "Still standing upright, the wheel looks like a small shipwreck, part of some strange vessel that has washed ashore."

After first being almost impossible to find, and then serving as a tethering pole for a donkey, the crumbling machine could not be further from being treated as the relic it is in the eyes of the Smithsonian archeologists. The same tension between monument and ruin conditions Danticat's way of relating to the object on this second visit, compared to the first time she was there. During the previous guided tour, "these two large chunks had seemed almost grand to me, constant and durable in spite of the century-old layers of rust covering them. I had thought them as symbols of Haiti – I was always looking for such symbols – weathered and depreciated, but still robust at the core" (Danticat 2002: 61). On this later visit, however, she understands the artifact as something far less grandiose and far more ambiguous she is approaching, which allows for a more textured response:

> This time, however, I am thinking that perhaps the "beauty" of this engine lies in the tales that it does not tell. The fact that there are no signs indicating its locale, no cards explaining its importance, no admission fee for the privilege of gawking at it forces its rusty fragments to be its only testimony.
>
> I prefer looking at it this way, without a guide encouraging me to admire or appreciate it. I like the blank slate, the silence, which allows for ambiguity. I can love it, despise it, be indifferent to it, or all three. There is neither forced celebration nor a condemnation in the moment. It is simply a flash of an era frozen in time. (Danticat 2002: 62)

While the rust on the first visit was something she saw *through*, in an attempt to decipher an uncorroded core, rust is now the object's main mode of signification. Left to itself, the machine has become an authentic ruin; neither disposed of, nor preserved. As Danticat shows, the machine's uninterrupted becoming-ruin allows it to offer a multilayered history of Caribbean modernity, which would be stripped of its complexity and ambivalence if it were to be monumentalized as a museum piece. The dilapidated steam engine tells the story both of how Haiti became the wealthiest colony in the Americas, and how it is now one of the poorest countries in the world, and most importantly, it stresses the connection between these historical extremes. The exploitation of people and nature that made the Caribbean colonies "the principle cause of the rapid motion which now agitates the universe," as the French Enlightenment writer Guillaume Thomas Raynal phrased it in 1776, is not simply a thing of the past, but still a reality conditioning the lives of Haiti's poor majority (Raynal 1965: 107). Silently rusting away, the ruin from colonialism's sugar boom accumulates also Ovid's story; becoming a *mémoire-ouverte* of the afterlives of colonial modernization as well as demodernization.

4 Ruin of Resistance: Marshall

Danticat's Ovid is a real-life character, who, as is only reasonable, simply desires a better life – more modernity, if you will. The fictional Caribbeans in Paule Marshall's *The Chosen Place, The Timeless People,* however, remain in ruination by choice, by consciously resisting modern development. The novel takes place in Bournehills, an impoversihed district of the fictive Bourne Island, a former British colony in the Caribbean archipelago. In sharp contrast to the green, smiling part of the island, home to the neo-colonial elite and luxurious hotel complexes catering to the tourist industry, Bournehills is a ruin, or at least a "near-ruin" (Marshall 1973: 101). First coming into view from an airplane, Bournehills "resembled a ruined amphitheatre whose other half had crumbled away and fallen into the sea" (Marshall 1969: 14). The same association with crumbling antique structures recurs when the main characters approach the district by car. The hills look "like the crude seats of some half-ruined coliseum, where an ancient tragedy was still performed" (Marshall 1969: 99). Bearing the scars of colonial exploitation made manifest in exhausted soil and land erosion, Bournehills is made up of "shabby woebegone hills and spent land" (Marshall 1969: 402); it is "wrecked," "scarred" and "ravaged" by centuries of misuse and monoculture (Marshall 1969: 21; 99; 402).

The people travelling to this place belong to a small American research team carrying out an anthropological survey, the findings of which will inform the design of a multimillion-dollar development scheme to lift the people of Bournehills out of poverty. All the many previous efforts to this end have failed, and the newcomers are determined not to repeat their mistakes but instead reach a thorough understanding of the district before attempting to bring on change.

Soon, however, they come to realize that the Bournehills' resistance to progress defies reason. There is also "something other, and deeper" that impels them (Marshall 1969: 216). This intangible something has its roots in the place's function as a memory space, as the title indicates, which communicates through its ruins. In opposition to the willed amnesia of the island's well-to-do middle classes, the ruined landscape functions as a reminder of a past that has not been marked by any monument. It is a "memorial – crude in the extreme when you considered those ravaged hills and the blight visible everywhere, but no other existed, they had not been thought worthy of one" (Marshall 1969: 402). Opening the ruinous realm of the uncanny, in Bournehills another time makes itself felt as "a palpable presence beneath the everyday reality," a sense of haunting that also forces several of the characters to return to and relive traumatic, repressed events in their own past.

Living in a ruin increasingly appears as a deliberate choice for the Bournehills people, in which the keeping alive of a painful memory functions as a form of resistance. No surprise, then, that however well-meaning, all attempts from outsiders to improve the situation for the impoverished district end in failure. In fact, as the leader of the American research team comes to realize, his work is "indirectly serving their ends," since the changes he tries to effect leave intact the capitalist world order which caused the inequalities in the first place (Marshall 1969: 226). His reforms exist "within the old framework," thus maybe even hindering real change, by "helping to keep the lid on things." Is there then no way forward, the reader might ask, can there be no alternative to the poverty and lack of opportunities of the Bournehills people?

It is another ruin, "the blackened ruin of Pyre Hill," a piece of elevated land destroyed by fire and a reminder of the island's most successful slave revolt, which provides the answer (Marshall 1969: 410). A grand estate house once stood on top of the hill. During the time of slavery, the master of this house also owned the entire Bournehills area and its inhabitants, until one night, the enslaved people led by a man called Cuffee Ned killed the owner and set fire to the house and the cane fields. They managed to live for a period of two years as a free, self-governing people. "It's the only bit of history we have worth mentioning on Bourne Island," as a representative of its inhabitants states, and the hill functions as an unofficial memorial to this one event Bournehills is proud of: "It's something to see, yes" (Marshall 1969: 101–2).

Pyre Hill, then, functions as a counter-monument, which tells a radically different version of history than the ubiquitous monuments celebrating abolition discussed in the introduction. Rather than representing freedom as a gift – magnanimously offered by the previous oppressor, by this act transformed into a beacon of moral enlightenment – the ruin of Pyre Hill restores the agency of the enslaved people. It makes visible how slavery was never a stable system, being instead continuously contested and destabilized from within and under constant threat to break down at any time, as the enslaved ceaselessly chipped away at the cracks that were there already from the beginning. The ruin of Pyre Hill also affirms that, contrary to the abolition narrative, nothing is over. Comprising "an awesome sight, which held the eye even when you tried looking away," the hill appears as if the fire that razed it "might have only just stopped burning," to the extent that the hill might still be emanating smoke and heat (Marshall 1969: 101). In the same way, Marshall's novel insists, the inequalities of the past are by no means erased, on the contrary, they continue to define the lives of generation after generation. And as long as there is no *real* change, in the sense of a complete overthrow of global power hierarchies, any cosmetic or surface reforms are only detrimental to the cause.

In a conclusion that resounds of Fanon's ideas of the redemptive potential of violence as part of a complete decolonization process, Marshall's ruin imagery ultimately bears a message about the need for a revolutionary consciousness: "Only an act on the scale of Cuffee's would redeem them. And only then would Bournehills itself, its mission fulfilled, perhaps forgo that wounding past and take on the present, the future" (Marshall 1969: 402). In an essay about her own writing from 1973, Marshall describes her commitment to this belief, thus reaching beyond the fictional universe of the novel. This vision involves

> the rise through revolutionary struggle of the darker peoples of the world and, as a necessary corollary, the decline and eclipse of America and the West. The two phenomena, the emergence of the oppressed and the fall of the powerful, I mention together because to my mind one is not really possible without the other. (Marshall 1973: 107)

In the meantime, while waiting for this revolutionary spark, the most productive thing to do is to devote oneself to keeping alive the officially uncelebrated history of resistance. In *The Chosen Place, the Timeless People*, this act of remembrance is centred on the ruin of Pyre Hill. During the island's annual carnival, the Bournehills people perform the same pageant each year. In defiance of a rule that stipulates innovation, they continue to reenact Cuffee Ned's revolt, complete with a replica of Pyre Hill on a float. In fact, similar performative ruin celebrations recur in Marshall's novels, for example providing the redemptive crescendo also in *Praisesong for the Widow* (1984). To be able to move forward, we must carry the past with us, Marshall stresses; its presences, its absences, and most important of all, its resistances.

5 Presencing Absence

As monuments have fallen in the name of the Black Lives Matter movement in recent years, it has become increasingly clear that these acts of destruction or removal do not have the kind of finality they might initially have appeared to offer. The now empty sites continue to engage, sparking seemingly endless debates about what should happen to them now, what a counter-monument could look like and how to address the legacy of oppression that has not disappeared along with its material manifestations. As Victor Buchli and Gavin Lucas remind us: "It is not just that memorials commemorate and iconoclasm causes forgetfulness; the relation between remembrance and forgetfulness is not a linear process, but a struggle, a tension – in every memorial, something has been left out or forgotten, in every removal, something is left behind, remembered" (Buchli/Lucas 2001: 80). The ruin writing of Patrick Chamoiseau, Edwidge Danticat and Paule Marshall focus the attention precisely on these absences, on that which has fallen in-between the remembered and the forgotten, to represent a historical consciousness that can do justice to the complexities of the Caribbean. In doing so, they deconstruct the colonial world of statues, as Fanon called it, as effectively as any wave of iconoclasm could do. At the same time, they gather the fragments of these laden objects and allow them to tell their untold histories. Presencing absence, they show how ruin aesthetics is radicalized in a transnational exchange and developed into a critique that reaches far beyond its original scope as a product of European romanticism.

Bibliography

Benjamin, Walter (1969): "Theses on the Philosophy of History." In: *Illuminations*. New York: Schocken Books, pp. 253–264.
Benson, LeGrace (2005): "A Long Bilingual Conversation Concerning Paradise Lost: Landscapes in Haitian Art." In: DeLouhrey, Elizabeth M./Gosson, Renée K./Handley, George (eds.) (2005): *Caribbean Literature and the Environment: Between Nature and Culture*. Charlottesville: University of Virginia Press, pp. 99–109.

Buchli, Victor/Lucas, Gavin (2001): "Between Remembering and Forgetting." In: Buchli, Victor/Lucas, Gavin (eds.) (2001). *Archaeologies of the Contemporary Past*. New York: Routledge, p. 80.

Bysshe Shelley, Percy (1994): *The Complete Poems of Percy Bysshe Shelley*. With notes by Mary Shelley. New York: Random House.

Césaire, Aimé (1995): *Notebook of a Return to My Native Land/Cahier d'un retour au pays natal*. Eastburn: Bloodaxe Books.

Chamoiseau, Patrick/Hammadi, Rodolphe (1994): *Guyane: Traces-mémoires du bagne*. Paris: Caisse nationale des monuments historiques et des sites.

Chamoiseau, Patrick/Hammadi, Rodolphe (2020): *French Guiana: Memory Traces of the Penal Colony*. Middletown, CT: Wesleyan University Press.

Danticat, Edwidge (2002): *After the Dance: A Walk Through Carnival in Jacmel, Haiti*. London: Vintage.

Fanon, Frantz (2001): *The Wretched of the Earth*. London: Penguin Books.

Fanon, Frantz (2008): *Black Skin, White Masks*. New York: Grove Press.

Forsdick, Charles (2018): "Postcolonializing the Bagne." In: *French Studies*, 2, pp. 237–255.

Fuggle, Sophie (2020): "Reimagining the ruins of the penalscape: Patrick Chamoiseau's carceral ruinology." In: *Social Identities*, 26, pp. 811–828.

Gikandi, Simon (1992): *Writing in Limbo: Modernism and Caribbean Literature*. Ithaca, NY: Cornell University Press.

Glissant, Édouard (1989): *Caribbean Discourse*. Charlottesville: University Press of Virginia.

Hall, Stuart (1995): "Negotiating Caribbean Identities." In: *New Left Review*, 209, pp. 3–14.

Huyssen, Andreas (2010): "Authentic Ruins: Products of Modernity." In: Hell, Julia/Schönle, Andreas (eds.): *Ruins of Modernity*. Durham: Duke University Press.

Marshall, Paule (1969): *The Chosen Place, The Timeless People*. New York: Harcourt, Brace & World.

Marshall, Paule (1973): "Shaping the World of My Art." In: *New Letters*, 40 (Oct), pp. 97–112.

Mignolo, Walter D. (2000): *Local Histories/Global Designs: Coloniality, Subalterns Knowledges and Border Thinking*. Princeton, NJ: Princeton University Press.

Mintz, Sidney (1996): "Enduring Substances, Trying Theories: The Caribbean Region as Oikoumenê." In: *Journal of the Royal Anthropological Institute*, 2, pp. 289–311.

Palmié, Stephan/Scarano, Francisco A. (2007): "Introduction: Caribbean Counterpoints." In: Palmié, Stephan/Scarano, Francisco A. (eds.): *The Caribbean: A History of the Region and Its Peoples*. Chicago: University of Chicago Press.

Raynal, Guillaume Thomas (1965): *A Philosophical and Political History of the Settlements and Trade of the Europeans in the East and West Indies*. Vol. 5. New York: Negro Universities Press.

Riegl, Alois (1982): "The Modern Cult of Monuments: Its Character and Its Origin." In: *Oppositions*, 25, pp. 21–51.

Roth, Michael S. (1997): "Irresistible Decay: Ruins Reclaimed." In: Roth, Michael S./Lyons, Claire/Merewether, Charles (eds.) (1997): *Irresistible Decay: Ruins Reclaimed*. Los Angeles, CA: Getty Research Institute, pp. 1–20.

Silverman, Max (2010): "Memory Traces: Patrick Chamoiseau and Rodolphe Hammadi's Guyane: Traces-mémoires du bagne." In: *Yale French Studies*, 118/119, pp. 225–238.

Silverman, Max (2013): *The Holocaust and Colonialism in French and Francophone Fiction and Film*. New York/Oxford: Berghahn Books.

Stafford, Andy (2010): *Photo-Text: Contemporary French Writing of the Photographic Image*. Liverpool: Liverpool University Press.
Walcott, Derek (1979): *The Star-Apple Kingdom*. New York: Farrar, Straus and Giroux.
Walcott, Derek (1998 [1970]): "What the Twilight Says." In: *What the Twilight Says: Essays*. New York: Farrar, Straus and Giroux, pp. 3–35.
Wood, Marcus (2010): *The Horrible Gift of Freedom: Atlantic Slavery and the Representation of Emancipation*. Athens: The University of Georgia Press.
Young, James E. (1992): "The Counter-Monument: Memory against Itself in Germany Today." In: *Critical Inquiry*, 18, 2, pp 267–296.
Young, James E. (1996): "Memory/Monument." In: Nelson, Robert S./Shiff, Richard (eds.) (1996): *Critical Terms for Art History*. Chicago: The University of Chicago Press, pp. 234–249.

Juliane Tauchnitz
Prisons, Ruins, Bodies, and the Extension of Space and Time in Patrick Chamoiseau's *Un dimanche au cachot*

Decolonizing Bodies

At the 1988 *Festival caraïbe de la Seine Saint-Denis*, Jean Bernabé, Patrick Chamoiseau and Raphaël Confiant praised for the first time their own creoleness in public. Even before its official publication at Gallimard one year later, their text had started to circulate and opened up a fundamental process of cultural rethinking in the Franco-Caribbean space that can be described in terms of detecting its traumatic history, language, and plural society – in terms of the search for its own identity. However, initial resonance to the text had been very restrained and nearly discouraging[1] and, over time, the critical voices became more strident, accusing the concept of *Créolité* as being essentialist, and eurocentric, even messianist, and reproaching the authors for their "masculinist rhetoric"[2] that would reduce women to stereotypical objects or even draw them in a completely "defeminized role" (Arnold 1995: 38), as can be seen by the incarnation of the *femme-matador* type, a female character with physically and psychologically masculinized features (Arnold 1995: 23 ff.).

The restricted frame of my contribution allows no clarification of whether these severe judgements had a direct impact on the textual production of the *Créolité* writers or of what concrete form a possible reaction to the critics could have taken. Nevertheless, in recent years, the number of novels that put female characters in another light[3] or even focus completely on them and their femininity has increased.

In this line of Franco-Caribbean novels, the fictional text that I will discuss here – *Un dimanche au cachot* by Patrick Chamoiseau (*A Sunday in the Dungeon*, 2007b) – exactly takes into account the feminine perspective on the complexity of colonial violence, both in the historical context of the plantation system and

---
1 See Taylor/Chamoiseau/Confiant/Bernabé (1997: 133).
2 Suk (2001: 151); see also Corzani/Hoffmann/Piccione (1998); Collier/Fleischmann (2003); Tauchnitz (2014: chapter 3.2.3).
3 For example Pépin (2010).

Juliane Tauchnitz, Institut Français Leipzig

in the actual time frame of the novel, which shows a strong decolonial impetus. The resulting perspective is no longer equated with a passive observation but turns into an active interventional possibility. This change is realized not simply by restaging (or *re*presenting) the female suffering body as an object but by presenting it as a subversive *agens*. And this acting of the female is directly generated by and correlated with a particular space and a particular temporal constellation, as we will see.

Everything begins on an ordinary rainy Sunday morning: the narrator, homonym of the author Patrick Chamoiseau, is working on a new book when all of a sudden his friend Sylvain calls to ask for help; Sylvain is the head of an organization – *La Sainte Famille* – that takes care of orphans and children who show signs of behavioral disorder. These children live at the so-called *Habitation Gaschette* in the east of Martinique, which once was a sugar plantation. It is certainly from those times that a small, unremarkable stone construction originates, a place to where a little girl named Caroline has now crawled away. The narrator is asked to help to haul the child out of this hole. But at the moment in which he first sees this stone pile, he knows immediately that it is a *cachot*, a dungeon, where slaves had once been tortured and imprisoned. He positions himself next to the girl that ended up at the *habitation* because she had been mistreated by her parents, and he starts telling her a story. The story of *L'Oubliée* – the forgotten one – who was a slave and had been locked up in this jail. A story on an ordinary rainy Sunday morning.

In the following, I analyze the function and role of this specific spatial situation – of the prison as the space that initiates simultaneously oblivion and memory – and I connect this analysis with the question of the meaning attributed to the body/bodies of those two prisoners within this process of memorizing and – even more decisively – which meaning is generated by the body itself. Thus, this focal point is based on the comprehension of the body as a *signifier*. Such an understanding presumes that the view, as Walter Mignolo formulated, is turning away from the "aboutness of our discourses" (Mignolo 2014: 24), that is, away from a thinking conceived as an entity independent or separated from the subject (Mignolo 2014: 24). Instead, the body needs to be recognized in its entirety as something "that 'embodies' knowledge through the senses in its structural coupling with the world: we *wear* knowledge" (Mignolo 2014: 24).[4]

---

4 This point had already been alluded to by Gloria Anzaldúa in 1987 (as referred to by Mignolo) when she opposed the hegemonic (neo)colonial discourse by presenting her concept of the *new mestiza*, who "rose" to speak out of a consciousness of the *borderlands* (*rose* in the meaning of Aimé Césaire's *s'emparer* – to seize –, a notion that is reminiscent of his

Remembering the Space of the Body

Shortly after the publication of his novel, Patrick Chamoiseau was invited to a book-signing in Guadeloupe. At that occasion, he said about his text that "[. . .] paradoxalement, l'oubli c'est un souvenir."[5] Of course, this is an exaggerated equation which, formulated in this way, is far-reaching, but it brings us back to Mieke Bal's statement that: "[. . .] forgetting is an act as much as remembering."[6] For the cultural theorist, this expression places the performativity[7] of both concepts at the centre and thereby underlines the idea that past "truth" cannot (and is not supposed to) be simply 'brought' to surface. She rather emphasises that "the memory is condemned to anachronism" as "memory [. . .] [cannot] transport its time frame" (Bal 2002: 274).

This idea is exactly what is elaborated in *Un dimanche au cachot*. The frame story and the embedded narrative of the novel – more precisely the story of the girl Caroline in the present and the events around *L'Oubliée* during past colonial times – initially seem to coincide in one and the same space, namely a narrow masonry, a *cachot*. Additionally, both plots take place on a single day, Sunday. Yet, the story exceeds the simple overlapping of space and time: the *cachot* is a space where (and through which) the temporality of the novel slips away, where the chronology of time is completely abolished.

It is this problem of a-temporality that will be pursued in the following part. On the level of the *histoire*, the two female characters show that an overlay of temporal levels takes place. And that is why the narrator, at a given moment, reveals his difficulty to distinguish them: "Je m'efforçais pour que L'Oubliée et Caroline ne se confondent pas. Mais, souvent, je ne savais plus laquelle se voyait évoquée" (Chamoiseau 2007b: 100).[8] This method of overlapping levels, by alluding to their different time levels by alluding their (con)fusion) is subsequently reflected upon, also thanks to a structure that becomes more

---

paradigmatic essay "*Nègreries, jeunesse noire et assimilation,*" published in 1935 in *L'Étudiant noir*). Thus, *borderland*, among others, refers to the space of the body – which becomes visible when Anzaldúa explains that: "[. . .] la mestiza undergoes a struggle of flesh, a struggle of borders, an inner war" (1987: 78) – the body both *is* the border and breaks it and becomes itself a border*land*.

5 "[. . .] the oblivion is a memory."
6 Bal (2002: 291); see also Assmann (⁴2009 [1999], especially: 53–55).
7 Performativity is read here in the sense of Butler: "Performativity must be understood not as a singular or deliberate 'act', but, rather, as the reiterative and citational practice by which discourse produces the effects that it names" (Butler 1993: 2).
8 "I endeavoured so that *L'Oubliée* and Caroline would not be confounded. But often, I didn't know anymore which one was brought up."

and more complicated because, at that point, a narrative voice that until then had been hidden is introduced and starts elucidating in a metafictional way on the 'other' narrator: "Mais, en projetant L'Oubliée sur Caroline, l'écrivain entêté lui offrait du présent: il élevait cette mémoire impossible au rang de témoignage" (Chamoiseau 2007b: 100).[9] This "impossible memory" is exactly the "monstrosity of the immemorial" that the Moroccan philosopher Abdelkebir Khatibi refers to in his essay "De la décolonisation" ("Of decolonisation") and in which context he exposes history itself as discontinuous, as a disorder, finally, as an optical illusion.[10] This kind of illusion is expressed in *Un dimanche au cachot*; Chamoiseau shows that the past is overlaid onto the present – which, in turn, transforms the former: the past itself becomes present and hence is not memorised but 'present.'

Such a bulge of the temporal is epitomized on the *discours* level: the novel is a celebration of slowness. On more than 300 pages, the reader seems to be confronted with the sole description of two times one single day. But this anisochronous temporal reduction turns out to be a delusion. While *L'Oubliée* is cowering in her prison, condemned to wait passively, many subplots are opened up to evoke the problems of colonial times – the claim of sexual possession of the plantation owners towards female slaves, the striving for reforms of this system, rebellions, the attempted escape of a slave (*marronage*), etc. This last case seizes on the narration *L'esclave vieil homme et le molosse* (*The Old Slave and the Mastiff*, 1997) and thus expands the textual universe Chamoiseau is creating. All these scarcely sketched episodes – that happen on the outside of this narrow prison – ambiguously give the novel a certain degree of rapidity. At the same time though, they contribute to slowing down the story of the forgotten slave, which here leads to the paradox that speed causes retardation.

This progress and the simultaneous standstill are unified in that one space that produces an ambivalence full of tension: the *cachot* which, following the terminology of Édouard Glissant, could be named a *space-time* (*espace-temps*)[11] – a space that *is* space and time but that also generates space and time. Again, it is helpful to reflect on a quotation by Abdelkebir Khatibi to better comprehend the

---

9 "But by projecting L'Oubliée on Caroline, the stubborn writer gave it the present time: he raised this impossible memory up to the rank of a testimony."
10 "Dans cette violence de l'être (historique), il y a toujours une perte, un non-retour. Et c'est cette perte, cette monstruosité de l'immémorial qui cachent, en l'appelant, notre accès à le pensée historiale" (Khatibi 1983: 32).
11 See note 5; see Glissant (1981: chapter 20).

pluridimensionality of this jail: "Non seulement la mémoire est en devenir, mais l'espace aussi" (Khatibi 1993: 51).[12]

The dungeon in Chamoiseau's novel, which is a witness of the past, dissolves any solidity in space and time and therefore becomes an impossible space. For the *cachot* is a black hole; it stands for the oblivion of those slaves who had been locked in and who, at that moment and due to this fact, lost their place within the working system and within their living world. Accordingly, the name of the main character – *L'Oubliée* – seems to conform like a logical consequence to this conception of forgetting.

For the world outside, this room simply does not exist – neither in the frame nor in the embedded narrative: "Car L'Oubliée comme Caroline, et moi-même, vivions un impossible; il n'y avait rien à passer, à dépasser, ni marche ni démarche, ni déplacement, ni remplacement: juste un impossible cheminement. . . dans l'impossible" (Chamoiseau 2007b: 102).[13]

The *cachot* is also impossible because it is never *now* – at any time it refers to another space and through this, becomes a *trace*. In her narrow prison, *L'Oubliée* touches its walls, these sometimes silent stones (see Chamoiseau 2007b: 102), and feels their past. And Caroline, through the story that the character Chamoiseau is inventing, starts becoming aware not of her own prison but of this presence-absence: *L'Oubliée* (see on this topic Tauchnitz 2010).

This brings us back to the initial quotation by Mieke Bal that forgetting is an act – as much as remembering. Forgotten by the exterior world, *L'Oubliée* tries to leave behind her past pain – such as being the progeny of a violation, that she herself was abused and that the pregnancy that resulted from that rape was ended by force. In this conscious process of forgetting, the memory forges ahead, and so *L'Oubliée* starts remembering, remembering her time, her place.

But all of this becomes blurred; the readers do not know anymore if they are looking inside the memory of *L'Oubliée*, if this is happening through the eyes of the girl Caroline or if it rather is an oneiric state, a state of trance as Bachelard described it, thanks to the notion of meditation:

---

[12] "Not only the memory is becoming, but the space, too." Khatibi obviously resorts here to the concept of *en devenir* (becoming) by Gilles Deleuze and Felix Guattari to which also Édouard Glissant refers repeatedly (f.e. 1981).
[13] "Because L'Oubliée as much as Caroline, and I myself, were living an impossibility; there was nothing to pass, to exceed, neither stair nor step, nor moving, nor replacement: just an impossible marching. . . into the impossible."

> Mais s'agit-il vraiment alors d'un souvenir? L'imagination, à elle seule, ne peut-elle pas grandir sans limite les images de l'immensité? L'imagination n'est-elle pas déjà active dès la première contemplation? [. . .]. [La rêverie] fuit l'objet proche et tout de suite elle est loin, ailleurs, dans l'espace de *l'ailleurs*. (Bachelard 2008 [1957]: 168; Italics in the original)[14]

The constitutive complexity by which the author Chamoiseau approaches topics related to the past, how he does no longer position memory and oblivion as if they were antipodal – all this prohibits any reduction of this state full of tension he is creating. The very idea that the girl Caroline is experiencing – in the sense of living – a purely invented history shows that *fictum* and *factum* are superposed.

This is all augmented at the end of the novel when the reader gets to know that the narrator was mistaken, for the little stone building never had been used as a prison (see Chamoiseau 2007b: 318 ff.). The central point appears to be that the character Chamoiseau is convinced that this "truth" has no meaning or does not effect any changes.

Presenting the Body as Space

So far, I directed attention especially to the space that produces the impossible memory: the *cachot*, which presents itself as a sort of narrative, spatial and time frame. But there is another space that functions as an agency of memory: the body. The narrator Chamoiseau moves from one to the other by the way he draws the *cachot* – as a narrow zone without light where there is nothing but the body of the person who is locked in what, though, causes the prisoner to be perpetually drawn back to herself. Thus, *L'Oubliée* wakes up that specific Sunday morning and hears the signal horn that announces the new day, yet she is still surrounded by darkness (Chamoiseau 2007b: 17). In this way, Chamoiseau prepares a first step, heading from the outer space, the *cachot*, to the inner one, the body: "Cette jeune femme, que j'appelle L'Oubliée, s'éveille mais rien n'est clair dans son esprit."[15] The awakening, hence, is not a real one, it only marks the passage from one inconcrete, oneiric state to another. The obscurity of the *cachot* determines the preoccupation of the slave with herself: "Le noir trop

---

14 "But is this really memory? Isn't imagination alone able to enlarge indefinitely the images of immensity? In point of fact, daydreaming, from the very first second, is an entirely constituted state. [. . .]. [. . .] it flees the object nearby and right away it is far off, elsewhere, in the space of *elsewhere*" (Bachelard ^{9}2008 [1957]: 168).
15 "This young woman that I call L'Oubliée, wakes up but nothing is clear in her spirit" (Chamoiseau 2007b: 42).

dense ouvrit l'espace en elle."¹⁶ The only thing the slave initially could actively do in her prison was to touch its walls. She does not see it, she does not recognize it, she only can experience it through the physical contact with the stones, and by this she does "[. . .] vérifier qu'elle était bien au-dedans de la chose et non enterrée vive derrière la bananière."¹⁷

The body of *L'Oubliée*, then, stands *pro toto* for the lived suffering of all (female) slaves. That is also reflected in the writing of her name – *L'Oubliée*, the forgotten one – which, in turn, is the absence of a name. In this absence, which shows its ontological status (see Eco 1996 [1993]), the *forgotten slave* literally corresponds to the figure of Friday in *Robinson Crusoe* who is 'named' and thus *made* by his master although the name he receives is none. This act manifests the colonizer's domination and power as much as is the case in Chamoiseau's novel where a slave would be forgotten because of the lack of a voice and a human value.¹⁸ The *forgotten slave* – *L'Oubliée* – becomes a depersonified totality for all slaves. Her mistreated, violated, scared body turns into a "field of appropriation," into the "territory" of the master, the body becomes "available," following Kossek's terminology (1993: 26). Thereby, 'body' functions here in a traditional sense as a representation, as a transmitter of signification (see Toro 2005: 13–41). In similar fashion, the *cachot* points to a "terrible palimpsest" (Chamoiseau 2007b: 30), when the narrator describes the scratches and traces at the walls so the body of the slave is (brand) marked in the same way.

Yet the novel does not stick to this representational level. The bodies of both *L'Oubliée* and of Caroline become *presentationality*: the body is not anymore a symbol that stands for anything else, for anything beyond, but it is the 'stage-setting' of itself (Toro 2005). This comes to light especially in the subchapter *Dénaissance* – non-birth – when *L'Oubliée* is in labour. The text describes contractions, but she delivers – nothing:

> Son corps se tend comme un bambou brûlé tandis que son ventre se contracte sur une masse qui s'en va et la délivre d'un coup. Elle hurle: rien ne lui est sorti du ventre. Ses jambes battent, ses cuisses tremblent. Elle tombe en hurlant dans ce vide qui aspire son nombril. (Chamoiseau 2007b: 219)¹⁹

---

16 "The dark that was too dense opened up the space inside her" (Chamoiseau 2007b: 92).
17 "[. . .] verify that she was still inside that thing and not buried alive under the banana tree" (Chamoiseau 2007b: 91).
18 By the way, Chamoiseau got back to the Robinsonade sub-genre in 2012 when he published *L'empreinte à Crusoé*.
19 "Her body tightens like a bamboo while her stomach contracts over a mass that is going and delivers her at one blow. She yells: nothing came out of her stomach. Her legs struggle, her thighs tremble. She falls down, howling into the void that inhales her navel."

This non-mimetic non-birthing expresses the performativity of that act – in accordance with how it was understood by Judith Butler (1993) and later specified by Dieter Mersch: "The term of the performative emphasizes especially the moment of its realization, the fact that an action must be instantiated so that it intervenes as an act into a world" (Mersch 2003: 70). Thus, the body of the *forgotten slave* transforms into a kind of producer of 'nothing' and signalizes in that way the active sabotage of the slavery system. Here, the process of that ambiguous mimicry takes place, which Bhabha formulated (based on the conception of Lacan 1973 [1964]: 85–96) as where "mimicry *repeats* rather than *re-presents* [. . .]" (Bhabha ^{9}2003 [1994]: 88). Mimicry hence is "at once resemblance and menace" (Bhabha ^{9}2003 [1994]: 86).

This example shows how, in this novel, the operating mode, history, and the capacity to remember are extended: it is not anymore about the reduction to the cognitive, based on principles of the 18th century, but rather – as formulated by Victor Turner (2009 [1982]: 144) – it is augmented by emotions and wishes that constitute a human being. The body does not remember the atrocities of the colonial system but rather becomes itself that memory, becomes a productive machine of knowledge and, by this, its realization. The body becomes the actualization of the lived experience.

Finally, we can emphasize that the *cachot* as a space of memory coincides with the body as a space for the act of remembering: the first one is the precondition for the latter, the latter de- and transforms the latter de- and transforms the first one. And so, close to the end of the novel the narration resumes exactly this superposition *and* interconnection of the two spaces that are the dungeon and the *forgotten slave's* body: "L'Oubliée ne comprend rien à ce qu'elle était, ni dans quoi elle était, ni ce qu'elle est maintenant. Juste quelques impossibles qu'elle sent maintenant reliés entre eux et qui l'ont transformée. . ."[20] Herein lies the impossible memory that nonetheless becomes manifest in the body. The spatiality of the body and the *cachot* as space *for* the body are two entangled and thus inseparable means that at the same time become fluid and solid in Chamoiseau's narrative.

---

[20] "L'Oubliée doesn't understand anything neither of what she has been, nor where she has been, nor what she is now. Just some impossibilities that she now feels being linked among each other and which have transformed her. . ." (Chamoiseau 2007b: 297).

Bibliography

Anzaldúa, Gloria (1987): *Borderlands. La Frontera. The New Mestiza*. San Francisco: Spinsters/ Aunt Lute.
Arnold, James (1995): "The gendering of *créolité. The erotics of colonialism*." In: Condé, Maryse/Cottenet-Hage, Madeleine (eds.) (1995): *Penser la créolité*. Paris: Karthala, pp. 21–40.
Assmann, Aleida (2009 [1999]): *Erinnerungsräume. Formen und Wandlungen des kulturellen Gedächtnisses*. München: C.H.Beck.
Bachelard, Gaston (⁹2008 [1957]): *La poétique de l'espace*. Paris: Presses Universitaires de France.
Bal, Mieke (2002): "Erinnerungsakte. *Performance der Subjektivität*." In: Bal, Mieke: *Kulturanalyse*. Frankfurt am Main: Suhrkamp, pp. 263–294.
Bhabha, Homi K. (⁹2003 [1994]): *The location of culture*. London/New York: Routledge.
Butler, Judith (1993): *Bodies that matter. On the discursive limits of "sex."* New York/London: Routledge.
Chamoiseau, Patrick (2007a): "Entretien avec Patrick Chamoiseau. Le Petit Lexique Colonial." http://www.potomitan.info/chamoiseau/entretien.php (accessed: 12/ 08/2009).
Chamoiseau, Patrick (2007b): *Un dimanche au cachot*. Paris: Gallimard.
Collier, Gordon/ Fleischmann, Ulrich (eds.) (2003): *A Pepper-Pot of Cultures. Aspects of Creolization in the Caribbean*. Amsterdam/New York: Rodopi.
Confiant, Raphaël (1996 [1993]): *Aimé Césaire. Une traversée paradoxale du siècle*. Paris: Écriture.
Corzani, Jack/ Hoffmann, Léon-Francois/Piccione, Marie-Lyne (1998): *Littératures francophones. II. Les Amériques. Haiti, Antilles-Guyane, Québec*. Paris: Belin.
Deleuze, Gilles (1993): *Critique et clinique*. Paris: Minuit.
Deleuze, Gilles (1997): *Essays Critical and Clinical*. Minneapolis: University of Minnesota Press.
Eco, Umberto (1996 [1993]): *La ricerca della lingua perfetta nella cultura europea*. Rome: Laterza.
Glissant, Édouard (1981): *Le Discours antillais*. Paris: Seuil.
Khatibi, Abdelkebir. (1983): *Maghreb pluriel*. Rabat: SMER.
Khatibi, Abdelkebir (1993): *Penser le Maghreb*. Rabat: Smer.
Kossek, Brigitte (1993): "Women slaves and rebels in Grenada." In: Bremer, Thomas/ Fleischmann, Ulrich (eds.) (1993): *Alternative Cultures in the Caribbean. First International Conference of the Society of Caribbean Research. Berlin 1988*. Frankfurt am Main: Vervuert, pp. 21–39.
Lacan, Jacques (1973 [1964]): "La ligne et la lumière." In: Lacan, Jacques (1973): *Le seminaire de Jacques Lacan*. Paris: Seuil, pp. 85–96.
Mersch, Dieter (2003): "Ereignis und Respons. Elemente einer Theorie des Performativen." In: Kertscher, Jens/Mersch, Dieter (eds.) (2003): *Performativität und Praxis*. München: Wilhelm Fink, pp. 69–94.
Mignolo, Walter D. (2014): "Further Thoughts on (De)Coloniality." In: Broeck, Sabine/Junker, Carsten (eds.) (2014): *Postcoloniality – Decoloniality – Black Critique. Joints and Fissures*. Frankfurt am Main/New York: Campus, pp. 21–51.
Pépin, Ernest (2010): *Toxic Island*. Paris: Desnel.

Suk, Jeannie (2001): *Postcolonial Paradoxes in French Caribbean Writing. Césaire, Glissant, Condé*. Oxford: Clarendon.

Tauchnitz, Juliane (2010): "Analogien der Gewalt. Die Problematik des Raumes in Raphaël Confiants *Case à Chine* und Patrick Chamoiseaus *Un dimanche au cachot*." In: Becker, Lidia/Demeulenaere, Alex/Fehlbeck, Christine (eds.) (2010): *Grenzgänger & Exzentriker*. München: Meidenbauer, pp. 435–449.

Tauchnitz, Juliane (2014): *La* Créolité *dans le contexte international et postcolonial du métissage et de l'hybridité. De la mangrove au rhizome*. Paris: L'Harmattan.

Taylor, Lucien/Chamoiseau, Patrick/Confiant, Raphaël/Bernabé, Jean (1997): "Créolité bites. A conversation with Patrick Chamoiseau, Raphaël Confiant, and Jean Bernabé." In: *Transition*, 74, pp. 124–161.

Toro, Alfonso de (2005): "Periférico de Objetos. Topografías de la hibridez: cuerpo y medialidad," In: *Gestos* 40, pp. 13–41.

Turner, Victor (2009 [1982]): *Vom Ritual zum Theater. Der Ernst des menschlichen Spiels*. Frankfurt/New York: Campus.

Christina Kullberg
Whirlwinds of Sounds: Rethinking Hurricane Temporalities through Contemporary Poetry from the Lesser Antilles

Recent years' natural catastrophes in the Caribbean have spurred intense creativity. Following the earthquake that hit Haiti in 2010 and hurricanes Irma and Maria in 2017, Caribbean poets in particular have responded to the hard-felt effects of what Rob Nixon (2013) famously identified as "slow violence." James Noël (Haiti) has reacted to the earthquake in *La Migration des murs* and through his editorial work with the journal *Intranqu'îllités*; Ana Portnoy Brimmer (Puerto Rico/New York) has written and performed several poems about hurricane Maria (Bonilla/LeBrón 2019), which resulted in her first collection of poetry, *To Love an Island* (2021). More literature from Puerto Rico about the storm was published in *Mi María: Surviving the Storm*, edited by Ricia Anne Chansky and Marci Denesiuk (2021). The Lesser Antilles have seen a similar wave of publications over the last few years: Fabian Adekunle Badejo (St. Martin) came out with *SOS: Season of Storms* in 2021; Celia A. Sorhaindo (Dominica) published the collection of poetry *Guabancex* in 2020; Lasana M. Sekou (St. Martin) wrote about the storms in *Hurricane Protocol* (2019); and Richard Georges (Virgin Islands) addressed the subject in *Epiphaneia* (2019).[1] To these works, we could add a number of artists, performers, and musicians who have reacted in various ways to the disasters. Musician and writer Anthony Joseph, for instance, states forcefully on the track "Language (Poem for Anthony McNeill)": "I seen what hurricanes can do to islands."

But what do they do to time? The question seems urgent in a region haunted by centuries of violent memories, silent archives, persistent inequalities, and biological transformation and exploitation due to colonial capitalism (Campbell/Niblett 2017; Grove 1995; Watts 1987). This chapter is an attempt to rethink the

---

[1] I discovered this immense field of creativity thanks to the Boca Litfestival, notably a round table with Georges, Sekou, and Sorhaindo, moderated by Folami Imoja, Naila (2021): "The Strength of Islands." In: <https://www.youtube.com/watch?v=IT6Q5Udg3Mg> (accessed 24/5/2021). This article is a continuation of a previous work (Kullberg 2022).

Christina Kullberg, Uppsala University

https://doi.org/10.1515/9783110762273-011

temporal predicament of hurricanes in the poetic works by Georges, Sekou, and Sorhaindo from the Lesser Antilles in light of Martinican poet and thinker Édouard Glissant's notion of the *tourbillon* or whirlwind. Looking at their poems from the point of view of Glissantian unsettling of temporalities allows for tracing a significant shift in the representation of natural catastrophes in the archipelagic space. Rather than thinking of hurricanes in terms of events, creating radical new beginnings, these poets seek to relate to them. They try to make sense of the devastated landscape by teasing out intimate connections in the present and in the past. I see a refusal to relate to a larger symbolic frame and a desire to *respond* to the hurricane. This response, as we shall see in the readings that follow, entails a different exploration of time.

1 Hurricane Continuum

Natural catastrophes are indeed powerful cultural signifiers. In the Caribbean context, hurricanes, especially, are charged with meaning because of the extraordinary force with which they hit the islands and the devastating impact they have on already precarious societies, and because of their longstanding presence in Caribbean imaginary. The word hurricane, as is often recalled in research dealing with the phenomena in literature, derives from indigenous language, and thus marks one of few direct, palpable manifestations of a lingering indigenous presence. This is of cultural significance since native populations were almost entirely expulsed from the archipelago during the early colonial era. There is also an aesthetic dimension to hurricanes linked to the articulation of a proper Caribbean poetics. "The hurricane does not roar in pentameters," Edward Kamau Brathwaite famously wrote, asking, how "you get a rhythm which approximates the *natural* experience, the *environmental* experience?" (1984: 10). The Caribbean "nation language," as it were, is an English shaped by hurricanes; a "dialect of mad cyclones" and a "patois of furious rains" to speak with Haitian poet Franketienne (2014: 8). At the same time, the strength of tempests also speaks to the European imaginary. The idea of a completely new landscape as a result of raving hurricanes resonates with the modern European image of the island as *terra nullius*, where the European man can recreate himself; a starting point for experimenting with the formation of society (Lestringant/Tarrête 2017; Lestringant 2002). Moreover, natural catastrophes have propelled thinkers and writers to establish correspondence between the force of nature and societal upheavals, notably in the wake of the era of revolutions (Fonseca 2021; Kappeler 2018; Munro 2015; Rudwick 2005).

Indeed, as convincingly shown by Sharae Deckard (2017: 27), storms have become an "overdetermined" figure for social unsettling throughout the history of Caribbean writing. It is a profoundly carnivalesque trope, she argues, even if it has been used differently depending on the perspective:

> If storms served throughout the imperialist imaginary as an intertextual, transhistorical metaphorics for rebellion, mutiny, and colonial insurgency, then in the postcolonial imaginary tempests, cyclones, hurricanes, and typhoons have been linked to insurrection, slave rebellions, labour unrest, general strikes, anti-colonial liberation movements, nationalist movements, and socialist revolution. (Deckard 2017: 26)

In a broader sense, the figure of the storm has contained two, if not three, contradictory yet interlinked imaginaries within Caribbean literary history. First, it has served as an expression of anxiety from the perspective of the colonizers. Storms represent the threat of revolt, the fear that the brutally repressed will rise and crush the system of slavery on which colonial society built. Second, from the perspective of the people, precisely the possibility of that revolt, unleashed by the uncontrollable powers of the hurricane, brings hope. Only – and this is where the third imaginary comes in – the transformative power of the hurricane can be recuperated by authoritarian regimes to create a narrative of a new community under one leader, as was the case when the category four hurricane San Zenón hit the Dominican Republic in 1930 and the newly elect leader Rafael Trujillo quickly used the event for propaganda purposes. Keeping all these societal irruptions in mind, the very word hurricane, as Deckard pointedly argues, is indeed a "palimpsest of the eruptive history of multiple colonizations, dispossessions, and exterminations in the Caribbean, preserving the trace of Amerindian cultures, and recording the continuity of extreme weather conditions as they marked multiple cultures throughout the *longue durée*" (2017: 27). To this palimpsest we can add the effects of the contemporary global climate crises, reinforcing and intensifying the hurricane season and making the islands even more vulnerable.

In line with Deckard's observation, hurricanes seem to incite Georges, Sekou, and Sorhaindo to explore time. Already the titles of their collections suggest a desire to think through natural catastrophes by weaving together disparate temporalities as if searching for a moment where times and places converge. Sorhaindo's *Guabancex* invokes the name of the native Caribbean word for the supreme female deity associated with all natural destructive forces. Sekou's poems might be designated as protocols – a dry registration of what has taken place – yet the book turns to the longer sacral history of the region: the poems are accompanied with drawings copied from the Dresden Maya Codex as a tribute to the indigenous cultures of the region. The presence of an indigenous archive in a central European city with only indirect connections with the Americas testifies to the layers and displacements of Caribbean memory and history. A similar spatially relational deep-time breaks through the title of Georges' book. The Greek word – *Epiphanea* – could be placed within Derek Walcott's conceptualization of the Caribbean as a New World Mediterranean, where antique sources echo and are transformed. Time draws lines of horizontality, connecting places and in so doing silently recalling the violence committed to peoples on the islands.

Clearly, the writings of Georges, Sekou, and Sorhaindo express a raised consciousness of the multiple temporalities of Caribbeanness emerging out of the storm. Yet they do not, in my view, engage in those revolutionary temporalities that have permeated representations of storms in the region. What we have is rather an engagement with direct experience: bodies struggling to resist the strong winds, people cleaning up, looking for things. It is more of a hurricane *praxis*, to use Sorhaindo's words, explored aesthetically. This turning away from the explicit political articulation of hurricanes or of contemporary climate crises more generally, follows what Chris Campbell and Michael Niblett (2017) see as an attempt by postcolonial authors to rethink and recreate a world ravaged by global warming. They convincingly argue for reconsidering Caribbean artistic responses to natural catastrophes through the lens of aesthetic practice (Cambell/Niblett 2017: 11). Aesthetics is here conceptualized as a "modality of worked matter" that contributes to remaking reality by producing it as an object of perception and understanding (2017: 5). Such materialist conception of aesthetics chimes with the idea captured in Sorhaindo's term of praxis. Yet the poems by Georges, Sekou, and Sorhaindo are also drawn in by the hurricane – in the direct experience of it and in the praxis when responding to it. They are expressions of immersion, where the storms are not just constructed as objects, but turn into agents, with which the poems engage. The experience of immersion followed by the concrete yet intimate practice of responding open up for a different conceptualization of time and temporalities. Take Sekou for instance, known for being overtly political in his writing. He notes in the preface to his book that the hurricane imposed a different, more intimate, poetics. Facing a completely reshaped island space, he says his writing became "personal," conveying experiences that he was in fact reluctant to write about. Similarly, the opening lines of Sorhaindo's *Guabancex* trace a negative movement as she states the impossibility of expressing verbally the experience of the hurricane: "words will never carry you to what / its like actually lets just leave it like that words cannot ever take you there at all. . . / go out and experience it for your self / metaphor the world however you want" (Sorhaindo 2020: 1). Initially, then, Sorhaindo negates the very act of writing because it cannot capture and much less transpose the experience of the catastrophe to an outside audience. What seems to be an obstacle of representation is in fact a temporal problem: the hurricane cannot be narrated since it cannot be reduced to linearity; it has no chronotope in the Bakhtinian sense since it lacks unifying time. It seems like the poetry coming out of the hurricanes explores connections between intimate experiences of time and a larger timeframe that would be questioning rather than adapting revolutionary temporality.

This intricate exploration of time that I detect in their poetry resonates with Glissant's conceptualization of time in our current globalized world. He speaks of time in terms of a *trou-bouillon* or *tourbillon*, the French word for whirlwind, which is at once enclosed (the whirlwind is shaped like a circle) and open (it spirals and moves), repetitive, cyclic, and chaotic. As always in Glissant's thinking there is no coherent development or theorization of the notion *tourbillon*. Rather it comes from the imaginative and cultural experience of living in an interconnected world, which he calls *tout-monde* or *mondialité* in opposition to economic globalization (*mondialisation* in French). Tellingly, this particular concept is best expressed by a fictional character from the 1993 novel, *Tout-Monde*. The protagonist Mathieu embarks on an adventure throughout the *tout-monde* and tries to conceptualize his experience by dialoguing with Papa Longoué, an old man with special powers. The topic of the conversation where the notion of *tourbillon* occurs is the relationship between the local place and the global space. Longoué suggests that Mathieu is inhabited by a particular place – the hills around Bezaudin and the descent towards Lamentin in Martinique (the place where the author himself grew up) – that he will use when he explores the world. Mathieu on the other hand is skeptical: it seems contradictory that he would travel the world only to put faraway places in relation to the tiny island space of his childhood. Longoué then answers:

> Qu'est-ce qui vous dit que le temps passe? Et si moi je crie que le temps est trou-bouillon? Qu'il tourne en rond comme citron? Et si moi je dis que vous allez passer votre temps à tourner en rond dans le tourbillon du vent sur combien de pays au loin? Car ce voyage là que vous avez fait de Bezaudin au Lamentin [. . .] vous le porterez partout dans votre déambulation, car ce que vous cherchez [. . .] c'est quelqu'un, est-ce une femme est-ce un homme un vieux corps un enfant, qui raccorde le pays de mer et le pays de terre, et qui est partagé partout dans le tout-monde [. . .]. (Glissant 1993: 207–8)[2]

---

2 "What tells you that time passes? And if I, I cry out that the time is a stew-hole? That turns in rounds like lemon? And if I, I say that you will spend your time turning in rounds in the whirlwind of the wind in how many faraway countries? Because this voyage here that you have made from Bezaudin to Lamentin [. . .] you will carry it with you everywhere in your wanderings, because that which you are looking for [. . .] it is somebody, is it a woman is it a

Starting from the word *tout* (all), Papa Longoué operates through a poetics of expansion and inversion. *Tout* becomes *trou* (hole), the *r* inserting a fold in the word, which turns it inwards. It thus works against the all-encompassing movement suggested by *tout* as all. Then it takes yet another turn, expanding again to *tourbillon* (whirlwind), which comprises the lexicon *tour*, a tour or a round, which carries both the idea of expansion and limitation (you tour a specific area). Such directional tensions are fundamental for many Glissantian concepts. Here too his poetics typically slice up the term, making it proliferate and take on new meanings; it has several articulations in one. What is crucial for the argument in this chapter is the idea that a person is connected to a certain place that she will carry with her and which will be mediated and expressed through different forms and senses. I argue that this idea implies a notion of time that is non-linear: through the mediation of a place that we carry with us, the past exists within us and can be actualized at any moment. Past, present, and future coexist in this way of experiencing the world and they do so by means of relation; that we relate to other places through the senses.

The *tourbillon* is thus a temporal concept that captures heterochrony, where natural and cultural times are intertwined. It expresses time in historicized spaces, in landscapes perceived as memory, as marked by culture. In later writings, Glissant will develop the concrete association with hurricanes and link the tourbillon to oceanic space (2006: 14). In a similar vein but without using the Glissantian notion of tourbillon, Elisabeth DeLoughrey claims that because hurricanes are sea phenomena they can operate as a point of departure for thinking beyond the region and move toward an "ocean imaginary" (2018: 94). Also writing in the aftermaths of Maria and Irma, but from a distance, DeLoughrey instead draws on Kamau Brathwaite's notion of tidalectics, i.e. a Caribbean dialectics modelled after the constant turbulent movements of the ocean, refusing separations between land and sea, proposing a chaotic yet unified notion of both time and space (see Brathwaite cited in Mackey 1995). Glissant's thinking is indeed closely related to Brathwaite's and readers of the two poets know that they often quote one another and share the emphasis on thinking horizontally (Reckin 2003). In tidalectics as in *tourbillon* we find similar spatio-temporal undulations between contraction and expansion. However, the notion of the *tourbillon* seems to depart from Glissant's (and Brathwaite's) concern with reconfiguring dialectics. Instead, it is a concept to rethink chaos and fragmentation, which is why it

---

man an old body a child, who put the ocean country together with the earth country, and is shared everywhere in the all-world. . ." (Glissant 1993: 207–8; my translation).

seems particularly prone to analyze time in relation to poems written in the aftermaths of hurricanes. The *tourbillon* is a rift in time and yet a continuation.

For in fact, Glissant combines the idea of a rift (*trou*) with movement. Contradictory, multilayered, and above all anti-linear – as a way to think the continuum not as a succession of time, but as a temporal simultaneity. What we have is a non-linear continuity, where times are superimposed onto one another which I think will be productive for reading temporalities in poetry coming out of the hurricanes. Continuum stems from Latin *continuare*, i.e. to plunge in space to form a whole, to make sequences follow upon one another in time (*faire succéder dans le temps*). In other words, the notion of continuum contains a spatial formation that is at once enclosed and extended, in conjunction with an enlarged notion of time, of duration. Surely, continuum could be posited as the opposite of the chaotic, fragmentary temporal concepts proposed by Brathwaite and Glissant. Yet note that the definition of continuum as forming a whole also implies fragments and builds on dynamic differences, which is precisely what Glissantian temporality tries to capture. It seems to me that Georges, Sekou, and Sorhaindo work with differences and fragments in a similar way. Writing after the hurricane, they operate with that which is left rather than with the idea of a radical new beginning. They seem to relate to the words like debris, and poetry links to practical ways to recreate the present landscape while restoring that sense of multiple space-times that is characteristic of the Caribbean diasporic cultural expressions.

2 Sounding Out Hurricane Temporalities

The question of time literally encircles Sekou's collection of poetry. Covering the period spanning over September 8, 2017, to November 30, 2017, when the hurricane season end, followed by a string of poems under the section "Back matter[s]" that functions as material and poetic afterlives, the protocol draws up lines, weighs out time. Hurricane protocol 9.22.17, notes, "'the sun crossed the line'//as today//so tonight//it is still//September//*Fuck!*" A moment in time is here punctuated by celestial phenomena, which are explained on the bottom of the page. Sekou uses a vernacular expression – "the sun crossed the line" – to designate the end of the hurricane season for the islands and in 2017, "the autumn date on which the sun crossed the celestial equator was September 22," as he explains at the bottom of the page (2019: 22). The poem signals transgression in the midst of the on-going turbulence. Within the protocol there is another time-frame that serves as a measure, relying on ancient, local knowledge.

Another transgression then occurs to close the protocol series on November 30, 2017. Here the vernacular returns to stop the series: "lead ben'//season en'" (Sekou 2019: 31). The expression, Sekou explains at the bottom of the page, signals the end of a St. Martin folktale (lead ben', story en'), here transposed to the universe of natural catastrophe as the Atlantic hurricane season ends on that very date.

The meticulous marking of the days surrounding the hurricanes encircles the catastrophe, singling out these hurricanes, the extraordinary devastation they brought along and the impact this had on peoples and islands. There is then a tension between the sequential structure, according to which the days are following one upon another, and the sense of a completely upheaved temporality, as in Hurricane protocol 9.14.17:

> it may come to this
> such an aftermath of time
> of nameless, hourlessfullonging days after
> and longing way
> after what appears to be no end to a day
> that you will see
> roofless remains
> of windowless panes
> of unhinged doorlessness
> of what was once upon a moment ago, known
> as closed.belongings of unknown neighbors
> now screen the leafless hillsides, broken
> branches&bared roots
> and all about us
> a breaching silence enters the thresholds
> breaching the cleavage,
> the hallowed tender reach
> the hollow you thought was fleshed full a'ready
> already baring to the brim
> brimming with the family and friends
> you had once upon a moment ago known
> but now it's a breastbone pressed to open
> a valley to rest bare belongings of the unknown
>
>   you see nothing
>   you hear nothing
>   you speak nothing
> nothing in the repeating pings of it all
>   you smell nothing
>   you sense nothing
>   you will
> nothing (Sekou 2019: 21–13)

The opening line expresses uncertainty in the discrete insertion of the word "may." The hurricane aftermaths are unsure even as one observes their effects, the material damage, the communitarian life smashed to pieces. The poem works with temporal juxtapositions that are evocative rather than stated, breaking with causality yet making room for observation: what was "once upon a moment ago" is no more. Time is thus still measured in sequences (before, now, what may come), but is turned into an incomprehensible present where the senses are numbed and language ceases to function.

A similar sentiment can be traced in Sorhaindo and Georges. A poem by Sorhaindo entitled "Horology – TimeXemiT(ion)" evokes the loss of a watch given to the lyrical *I* by her father. Whereas the ". . . timepiece had survived Maria [. . .]" the hurricane has thrown the people into another temporality: "This time after the storm, I can't work out/exactly what month, day, hour my life so frantically inhabits" (2020: 13). *Guabancex* further describes how the devastated landscape changes peoples' perspectives, a shift tied to their experience of time right after the hurricane. The persons inhabiting Sorhaindo's poems do not look at the sky; standing in water they "look down, then out" (7). This gives movement to the hurricane experience: there is no transcendence, but a wave-like fluctuation inwards and outwards. This motion is paired with an acute sense of the present: "Past and future do not yet exist [. . .]" (7). Sorhaindo writes: "In this now morning / after, this brutal wake-up silence, this downside-tippedup / outsidenowin we are deciphering, thank you thank you: if / only for these two words we all still easily re-call for now. / Listen---" (7). The dash ending the stanza opens the poem rather than closes it, inviting the reader to listen as it paradoxically ends. Words are no more. Instead, the poem expands infinitely into space and time where an unusual silence prevails.

Georges places the experience of time losing all measures in a larger cosmic frame:

> [. . .] When the unmaking is stilled, the land
> A negative space, there are still ghosts outside,
> Unstilled. There are still so many winds still
> To come. That blue porcelain will not remain
> Long above us so plainly, so unremarkable. (Georges 2019: 37)

We recognize the imagery of the island becoming *terra nullius* as a consequence of the storm. It is a "negative space," but in Georges' poetic universe this negativity is not an origin: the hurricane has done a work of *unmaking* the landscape, constructions and nature alike. And it will happen again. The poem lands in this knowledge of a cyclic time of repetition, which is what ultimately becomes the temporal measure after the hurricane. Other poems by Georges also open up to the larger universe, both spatially and temporally, taking Elizabeth DeLoughrey's notion of an oceanic imaginary even further. Georges turns to the seas and captures the hurricane as an oceanic phenomenon that he then connects to geological deep-times with mythological overtones, as in the poem entitled "Origins." The last lines evoke the creation of the world, connected to the constructive power of language, and conclude with an address to the reader: "Did you not question did you not wonder why / This world always begin and end with ocean?" (46). The hurricane is the destructive force of an element that gives life.

Yet this cosmic expansion is intimately tied to the islands. Georges' poems are locally anchored and it is from here that they expand spatially and temporally as if putting into practice a poetics of relation, to use Glissant's term (1997), by opening the island space to the vast ocean. "Listening" sounds out to Africa and the Mediterranean and then connects to personal, detailed observations of the hurricane aftermaths, as in these lines:

[. . .]
If there were still leaves in this naked place

they would be still too, or at least listening
for the sighing tides of the Atlantic
for the shuddering clouds' fearsome report,

for the cyclic storms of trauma tracing
the exhausted courses of our ancestors,
for the chanting sky's low hollow sound. (Georges 2019: 42)

The "sighing tides" echo the Middle Passage, as the hurricane approaches from the Atlantic. Working to include the singular event into a continuum of Caribbean aesthetics and experience, Georges alludes to a long traumatic, cyclic history of soundings, linked to the un-representable. The poem is filled with motion, zooming in and out, expanding and closing in, resonating with Brathwaitian tidalectics. As argued by Stephanie Hessler, tidalectics tries to capture time in terms of continuous change. It "assumes the shape of an unresolved cycle rather than a forward-directed argument or progression" (2018: 33). In Georges' poem temporal linearity is suspended in favor of co-existence. Times and places are actualized simultaneously on one plane. So time is not suspended but is articulated in the movements, circular and expanding: the poem operates horizontally by connecting lines between a before, in, and after the hurricane, bridges of sound to histories of survival and death, resilience and transformed nature, violence, resistance, and subjugation.

In different ways, Georges, Sekou, and Sorhaindo continue the work of making the present moment resonate with a longer history of pain and survival. In this context, the eruptive and violent manifestations of nature are considered as an integrated part of the cycle of life (Deckard 2017, Kullberg 2022, Niblett 2009). The arrival of hurricanes is shocking, devastating, and irruptive on a material, cultural, and societal level,[3] but they come with regularity; they cannot be defeated, you have to live with them. Mark D. Anderson writes that disasters are the "culmination of historical processes that have resulted in certain populations living in a state of heightened vulnerability" (2011: 21). A similar argument is advanced by Elizabeth DeLoughrey in *Allegories of the Anthropocene* (2019). Her point is that peripheral places such as small islands do not live the global climate situation as a crisis but as a consequence of a long history of natural, cultural, and geographical transformations (2019: 2). There is then in archipelagic regions especially of the Global South a certain sense of living with pending transmutations due to catastrophes. This suggests that natural catastrophe is lived as a continuum rather than as a *new* consequence of the Anthropocene. What is interesting in these poems is that this cyclic temporality is not configured in opposition to the conception of storms as rifts in the flow of time. Irma and Maria appear as exceptional hurricanes, breaking out a timeslot in the flow of time, yet they are part of a larger cyclic movement. They embody and cause repetition and difference.

On the one hand, there is the moment *in* the hurricane, captured in Sorhaindo's poetry notably. Here time is out of joint like the doors, the roofs, torn out of joints and nails by the strong wind. Resisting water, holding on, enduring, waiting for it to pass. It is as if her poetry seeks to relate to the hurricane while her lyrical subjects are entirely subjected to its force. People sing while courageously holding doors to resist the water that keeps pouring into the most sealed spaces. Their pushing and crying, sighing and singing cannot stop the flood, yet it gives sense and meaning to the desperate practice by means of relating to the water, communicating with it, making the forces of the hurricane respond in the midst of chaos. In Georges' poems the direct experience of the storm is that of turbulence blurring the frontiers between human and nature, liquid and solid. They seem to contradict the idea suggested by the title of the collection that natural catastrophe would lead to an epiphany, a revelation of a hidden truth: "No useful predictions. The prophets / are all mealy-mouthed

---

[3] Although it should be pointed out that with increasing global inequalities they do hit differently. In 2017, the damage caused by Maria was significantly lesser in Saint-Barthélemy saturated with luxury buildings for tourists, than in Dominica for instance.

and impotent. There is only this ball,//madly spiraling through space – and that is the most reassuring thing" (2019: 34). The revelation in Georges' lines, if there is indeed any, is that there is only continuity, history, culture, and nature intertwined. Rather than insisting on the hurricane as an exterminating force, he conceives in-between space. What lies in front of the people after the hurricane is "devastation not death," a liminal zone of destruction where life nonetheless endures.

On the other hand – and this is linked to the intensity of the hurricane passing – the poems convey a sense of an absolute and enclosed present after the hurricane. While international news spread about the storms, the local experience was that of being cut off from the rest of the world. Georges, Sekou, and Sorhaindo all suggest in different ways an uncanny silence. There was no power or internet, making it difficult to connect with loved ones at home and abroad. Sekou writes that he explicitly wanted to block out both international and local news because they politicize the event, wiping out the personal, intimate, and ultimately untranslatable experience of the storms that the poems seek to express. The world is smashed to pieces, both land- and soundscape: "we hear nighttime noises we don't recognize / we don't hear tree frogs we don't hear crickets we hear generators" (Sekou 2019: 25). The silence of nature seems frightening, as if it materializes the idea that people will now exist differently in the world. After the storm wires become "lifeless veins" (Sekou). There are houses with gaping roofs and windows (Georges). There is rubble everywhere and the earth is completely turned inside-out. Mangroves are mauled, trees wiped off their leaves, hillsides turned into wetlands. Birds, frogs, crickets are all gone and their noise replaced by the sounds of helicopters cutting through the sky, generators supplying electricity. In these ruins, the modern world and contemporary society are entangled with other types of memories, evoked by the poems' immersion in deep-time. In Sekou's hurricane protocol 11.8.17: "2017 *the daily herald* reports: looting in st. martin//1648 *the treaty of Concordia* records: looting of st. martin" (2019: 25). "Beneath every inch of this ground is blood" (2019: 23), Georges writes in the poem "Pathfinder," juxtaposing these traces of an older history to contemporary inscriptions of memory as in "graffiti histories" on "the leaning bricked facades, hollowed like tombs" (2019: 23). What the hurricane does is bring these hidden memories to the foreground where they coexist with modern ruins.

By placing the 2017 hurricanes in a longer history that also expands spatially, capturing Caribbean time and temporalities as layered, Georges, Sekou, and Sorhaindo clearly work within the Caribbean literary continuum in pursuing a major strand in Caribbean literature concerned with recuperating silenced pasts and memories beyond the written archive. This strand has, to a large extent, been focused on finding traces of memory in landscapes, articulating a geopoetics, as in Glissant's claim in *Poetic Intention* that the landscape "is a monument," that rocks and mud are drained with blood that is only visible to the observer who pays attention and listens to silent whispers (2009: 33). Citing Tobgonian poet Eric Roach and his explorations of island landscape and its ability to absorb the corporeal residues of history, DeLoughrey concludes that there is a "complex relationship between geography and history" (2007: 1) in the Caribbean. Nonetheless, there is a certain coherence in the ways in which geopoetics links time and landscape, which is unsettled when the poets directly face hurricanes. The ravaging forces of the storms expose the time-layers in one chaotic movement and create an acute interconnection between present, past, and future, which is the tourbillon. This is no longer a "poetics of the trace" (Glissant 1997), but of chaotic temporal juxtaposition and layering. In their attempt to respond directly to the hurricane, other temporalities emerge. It is on this point that their poetry can be said to also break with that Caribbean continuity of poetic tradition and introduce temporalities of the tourbillon.

The hurricane takes on a "material representation," to use Deckard's expression (2017: 42); words are like debris. In Sorhaindo's poem "Invoked" (2017: 14–15) the voice is given to the hurricane speaking and the words on the page mimic the storm's frenzy. The words fall on the page and in between them there are blanks, coming in like blows under heavy winds coming from the side. Between the debris and the blasts, the voice of the hurricane, personified, emerges:

```
            I am your              mother
       Of a hurricane so    look                    now,
Intimately into       the white   cosmic chaos of my    cyclops eye; listen
Intently    to the thundering     doom of my clack-clack   cloven hooves.
[. . .]
Pat your   broad back   for your safe     house --- I will   trap you for days
                Inside your mausoleum,    force you    to loath   loved ones
                Unburied bodies           on your bloody    marble kitchen table
```

The poem materializes the devastation caused by the storm, creating a sense of directness. Yet this immediacy is contrasted by the movement forward suggested by the assertive voice of the hurricane. It speaks in future tense, foreseeing the measures that will be taken by people to resist its powers and predicting the futility of these actions. The future tense is deployed in such ways that it relies on previous observations: we know what will happen because we have seen it before. In other words, time turns in a circle within the limited space of the island, as it moves forward, spiraling.

In Sekou's poems, a similar drama unfolds in language. He works with graphs, punctuation, and spacing on the page and expands time through sound within the poems, carving out zones where the whirlwind movement occurs through words merging and separating:

> iiiiiiiiiiiiiiiiiiir//malonglongsong//ahlingehlongahsong//ahsirensingsingahgolonglong//song (Hurricane Protocol 11.23.17).

Language condenses meaning, creating a poetic temporality that is actualized in the act of reading. The line unsettles the linearity of language, forces that linearity together so that it starts to whirl, spiraling, as its beginning and end merge into one. Words fuse into one another, repeat themselves and are separated yet connected by the lines on the page.

Generally, then, we note that the suspended time caused by the hurricanes does not transform into a narrative or story; it does not reinvent itself as linearity in these poems. Instead, the poets explore what people do. The last poem of *Guabancex* is entitled "Hurricane PraXis (Xorcising the Maria Xperience)." It presents a play with a serial and contrapunctual simultaneity: we are, feel, experience, and express all this at once. The poem forms lines in parallel, one image, statement or feeling appearing side to side with its opposite or its continuation. It carves out a catalogue or an impossible dictionary of praxis and feelings as in the following lines:

> we go in search of clean water we carry water we carry water carry water carry water
> we care for the injured the best we can   we bury our dead
> we cannot find our dead   our dead are already buried
> we try to stay positive   we laugh   we laugh hysterically
> we cannot imagine ever laughing again (Sorhaindo 2020: 24)

The anaphoric "we" gives an obsessive sense of continuity. Then the sentences break up, fall to pieces and are mended together again with the help of another sentence. This is repetition with endless variation and contradiction: a poetic materialization of facing the aftermaths of devastation with praxis. There is no time to narrate a story of the storm or think of symbols. Time is filled with action, there is no duration that needs fulfillment to be meaningful. The practices themselves are presented as fragments, separated with blank spaces, creating a chaotic sense of simultaneity. It is difficult to detect when one action starts and when another ends; they unfold in parallel as if Sorhaindo's effort here was to break the spell of writing's linearity. She works with parataxis so that alterities can be expressed side by side, conflicting perspectives can co-exist in one timespace. And this gathered heterogeneous time of fragmentation and over-laps is that of a community taking shape: "I have started learnin//Growin from the xperience" (2020: 32), Sorhaindo writes, signaling a process grounded in praxis that carves out new temporalities to come.

These poems coming out of the hurricanes deploy a fragmentation of time, where links between past and present are no longer causal or spatially articulated, but undulate their own non-linear, chaotic and expansive temporality that moves like a whirlwind. The poems work in the Caribbean literary continuum in deploying multidirectional and multilayered temporalities. Yet they also explore new dimensions, unsettling the "geopoetic model of history" (DeLoughrey 2007: 2) that has permeated Caribbean poetics. In responding to the hurricane, as opposed to representing or narrating it, the poets operate through a strategy of relation (*mise en relation*) to make sense of it, to understand how to exist with it and the devastation it causes rather than giving it a transcendental meaning. The sonic fabric of the poems, the graphic lay-out, the fragmentation of words which materializes the storm are means by which Georges, Sekou, and Sorhaindo release a poetic time-space allowing us to rethink the idea of the continuum in line with Glissant's tourbillon/troubouillon. They draw on the extremely localized time-space of the hurricane experience as something enclosed (*trou*), linked to island space, but that extends elsewhere, shifting and repeating (*tourbillon*) by its connection to the ocean. The poems thus carve out a site of uncertainty where writing the hurricane becomes an exploratory practice, which relates the outside world to the personal, unfolds layers of history and places, while sounding out the devastated insular landscape.

References

Anderson, Mark D. (2011): *Disaster Writing: The Cultural Politics of Catastrophe in Latin America*. Charlottesville: University of Virginia Press.
Bonilla, Yarimar/LeBrón, Marisol (eds.) (2019): *Aftershocks of Disaster: Puerto Rico Before and After the Storm*. Chicago: Haymarket Books.
Brathwaite, Kamau (1984): *History of the Voice: The Development of Nation Language in the Anglophone Caribbean*. London: New Beacon Books.
Campbell, Chris/Niblett, Michael (eds.) (2017): *The Caribbean: Aesthetics, World-Ecology, Politics*. Liverpool: Liverpool University Press.
Deckard, Sharae (2017): "The Political Ecology of Storms in Caribbean Literature." In: Campbell, Chris/Niblett, Michael (eds.) (2017): *The Caribbean: Aesthetics, World-Ecology, Politics*. Liverpool: Liverpool University Press, pp. 25–45.
DeLoughrey, Elizabeth (2018): "Revisiting Tidalectics: Irma/José/Maria." In: Hessler, Stefanie (ed.) (2018): *Tidalectics: Imagining an Oceanic Worldview through Art and Science*. Boston: MIT Press, pp. 93–101.
DeLoughrey, Elizabeth (2019): *Allegories of the Anthropocene*. Durham, NC: Duke University Press.
DeLoughrey, Elizabeth (2007): *Routes and Roots: Navigating Caribbean and Pacific Island Literatures*. Honolulu: University of Hawai'i Press.

Doumerc, Eris (2021): "Celia A Sorhaindo, *Guabancex*." In: *Miranda*, 22. https://doi.org/10.4000/miranda.38241.
Fonseca, Carlos (2021): *The Literature of Catastrophe: Nature, Disaster and Revolution in Latin America*. London: Bloomsbury.
Georges, Richard (2019): *Epiphaneia*. London: Outspoken Press.
Glissant, Édouard (1993): *Tout-monde*. Paris: Gallimard.
Glissant, Édouard (1997): *Poetics of Relation*, trans. B. Wings. Ann Arbor: University of Michigan.
Glissant, Édouard (2009): *Poetic Intention*, trans. N. Stephens. Callicoon: Nightboat Books.
Grove, Richard (1995): *Green Imperialism: Colonial Expansion, Tropical Island Edens and the Origins of Environmentalism, 1600–1860*. Cambridge: Cambridge University Press.
Kappeler, Florian (2018): "The Chronotope of Revolution: 'Volcanic' Narrations of the Haitian Revolution." In: *Karib: Nordic Journal for Caribbean Studies*, 4, 1, 6, pp. 1–10. https://doi.org/10.16993/karib.46.
Kullberg, Christina (2022): "Vernacular Soundings: Poetry from the Lesser Antilles in the Aftermaths of Hurricanes Irma and Maria." In: Kullberg, Christina/Watson, David (eds.) (2022): *Vernaculars in an Age of World Literatures*. London/New York: Bloomsbury, pp. 101–25.
Lestringant, Frank/Tarrête, Alexandre (eds.) (2017): *Îles et insulaires (XVIᵉ–XVIIIᵉ siècle)*. Paris: Presses de l'université Paris-Sorbonne.
Lestringant, Frank (2002): *Le Livre des îles: Atlas et récits insulaires de la Genèse à Jules Verne*. Geneva: Droz.
Mackey, Nathalie (1995): "An interview with Kamau Brathwaite." In: Brown, Stewart (ed.) (1995): *The Art of Kamau Brathwaite*. Wales: Seren, pp. 13–32.
Munro, Martin (2015): *Tropical Apocalypse: Haiti and Caribbean End Times*. Liverpool: Liverpool University Press.
Nixon, Rob (2013): *Slow Violence and the Environmentalism of the Poor*. Cambridge, MA: Harvard University Press.
Reckin, Anna (2003): "Tidalectic Lectures: Kamau Brathwaite's Prose/Poetry as Sound-Space." In: *Anthurium: A Caribbean Studies Journal*, 1 (1), 5. http://doi.org/10.33596/anth.4.
Rudwick, Martin (2005): *Bursting the Limits of Time: The Reconstruction of Geohistory in the Age of Revolution*. Chicago: University of Chicago Press.
Sekou, Lasana (2019): *Hurricane Protocol*. Philipsburg: House of Nehesi Publishers.
Sorhaindo, Celia (2020): *Guabancex*. London/Roseau: Papillote Press.
Watts, David (1987): *The West Indies: Patterns of Development, Culture and Environmental Change since 1492*. Cambridge: Cambridge University Press.

Other material

Joseph, Anthony (2021): "Language (Poem for Anthony McNeill)." In: *The Rich Are Only Defeated When Running for Their Lives*. London: Heavenly Sweetness.
"The Strength of Islands." In: <https://www.youtube.com/watch?v=lT6Q5Udg3Mg> (accessed 24/5/2021).

Sara Brandellero
Night-time Mobilities in Contemporary Brazilian Cinema: Spectralities in the 24-hour City and the Case of *Burning Night* (2019)

1 Introduction

This chapter focuses on the representation of night-time urban mobilities in the Brazilian fiction film *Burning Night* (*Breve miragem do sol*), directed by Eryk Rocha and released in 2019. The focus is on the significance of the chronotope of the urban night and on the aesthetic construction of the figure of a night worker's experience in the 24-hour city. *Burning Night* constitutes Rocha's second fiction feature and follows the transits through the city of Rio de Janeiro of middle-aged taxi driver Paulo (Fabrício Bolivaira), who, despite having a degree in journalism, is forced to take on work as a night-shift taxi driver after becoming unemployed. The film follows the anguish experienced by Paulo who, because of the fraught relationship with his former wife, has limited contact with his son, something he struggles with while also contending with a precarious housing and employment situation.

The film places an intense focus on the character's psychological drama, which we follow through his interactions with his passengers as well as with those who live and work in the night-time city. Within this context of everyday life, the question of race is significant. Indeed, Paulo's struggles with poor working conditions are aggravated by the structural racism he has to contend with as a black man living in Brazil. Thus, this chapter will discuss the film from an analytical perspective that considers issues of mobility and spatial practices interconnected with questions of class, gender and race, in their

---

Acknowledgements: This chapter is a revised version of an article originally published in Portuguese: Sara Brandellero (2021): "Mobilidade noturna no cinema brasileiro contemporâneo: espectralidades na cidade 24-horas." In: *Revista Visuais*, 7, 2, pp. 91–107. The author acknowledges funding from her Fellowship at the Hanse-Wissenschaftskolleg Institute of Advanced Studies in Germany (2021) (https://hanse-ias.de/) and the Humanities in the European Research Area (HERA) and EU Commission grant no. 2.060 (Heranet.info) that supported the writing and revision of this chapter.

Sara Brandellero, Leiden University

https://doi.org/10.1515/9783110762273-012

intersection with the category of time. It understands the night as a distinctive urban space-time that is shaped and, in turn, shapes the experiences and representations of urban mobility, including defining the limits of the "right to the city" (Lefebvre 1968; Harvey 2008).

The theme of displacement is central to the film. Rocha's affinity with the motif of travel was already evident in his acclaimed road documentary *Pachamama* (2008). A politically engaged film, *Pachamama* investigates the legacy of colonialism in Latin America and the relationship between Brazil and neighboring countries. It does so through an uncompromising reflection on the plight of indigenous people in the face of colonial violence and the unbridled plundering of the region's natural resources, with a focus on the border between Brazil, Bolivia and Peru. With his first fictional feature, *Transeunte* (*Walker*, 2011), Rocha began to explore urban space, again through the motif of displacement, this time through the character of Expedito (Fernando Bezerra), whom the camera follows in his solitary wanderings through the streets of Rio de Janeiro. Isolation and an experience of non-belonging are expressed in the character of Expedito as he navigates the city's geography. In his solitude, he displays some commonalities with the figure of the flâneur, an emblematic character of urban modernity and its "street" literature. As Matthew Beaumont points out, authors such as Virginia Woolf identified in the figure of the lonely pedestrian a social type that seemed increasingly out of place in mechanized society, given that "the pedestrian's experience is peculiarly symptomatic of certain social tensions" (Beaumont 2020: 15).

The solitary pensioner we meet in *Transeunte* might not share the economic affluence and upper-class status that define the traditional figure of the flâneur but, similarly to the flâneur, he does crystallize certain social tensions of everyday life in his wanderings through the streets of Rio. We can also draw parallels with the character of the driver Paulo in Rocha's *Burning Night*, given that the character can be seen as an iteration of the urban pedestrian, now in a context of deep social crisis and in his relationship with the city's night labor. The film's focus on what happens "after hours" provides a valuable insight into an often overlooked dimension of the urban cycle. In addressing this blind spot, this chapter, therefore, aims to analyze the filmic representations of life experiences and social practices after dark, in order to refocus the conversation onto the significance of the night-time city for a fuller understanding of urban life. Often associated with the leisure and entertainment industry, the urban night is increasingly recognized for its contribution to economic and social wellbeing, for example. Yet, often overlooked is the fact that, to function properly, it relies on an army of night-shift workers, often invisible and subjected to precarious work conditions and the lowest wages. It is these same workers who ensure the social life of others and the smooth transition from night-life to the daytime functioning of the city. By homing in on this reality through the urban transits of the taxi driver, Paulo, the film gives form to the spectral beings that inhabit everyday life (Blanco/Peeren 2013). In the context of the growing commoditization of the night, Rocha describes Paulo's condition in a city increasingly revolving around the gig economy as a "foreigner, a refugee in his own territory" (Rocha in Fonseca 2020).[1]

2 The Night, Labor and its Specters

Recently, the so-called "mobilities turn" (Sheller/Urry 2006) in the humanities and social sciences – with its emphasis on the construction of identities and experiences in a contemporary world of intensifying space-time compression and transnational processes, including the phenomenon of large-scale global migration and displacement, for example –, has provided an exciting and productive theoretical lens in different fields and transdisciplinary perspectives, film studies among them. Within this approach, it has also been necessary to highlight the need to avoid easy romanticization of mobility experiences, that of nomadic identity, for example, as noted by Freire-Medeiros/Piatti Lages (2020).

With this in mind, it seems productive to turn our attention to the representation of urban mobilities, while recovering the importance of the temporal dimension for the understanding of spatial practices, drawing on the emerging theoretical field of "night studies" (Kyba et al. 2020). In order to think about the temporal relations that the film problematizes, this chapter takes as its starting point the classic definition of night as "frontier," coined by Murray Melbin in his canonical article of 1978. In his text, Melbin presciently drew parallels between the increase in nocturnal activities, what we now call the 24-hour city, and forms of territorial colonization. Melbin comments on the "temporal ghetto" (Melbin 1978: 20) in which most night workers find themselves, marginalized and neglected by decision-making bodies who operate during the day. It is from this multifaceted liminal reality of nocturnal space-time that I propose to analyze the figure of the night worker through the lens of spectrality, following Peeren/Blanco when they underline the importance of both time and space of the spectral entity and the growing spectral dimension of everyday life (Peeren/Blanco 2010: xi, xiii). The authors

---

[1] My translation. All translations into English are mine unless otherwise stated.

draw attention to the specter's liminal, borderline condition, between visibility and invisibility, materiality and immateriality (Blanco/Peeren 2013: 2). The authors refer to De Certeau's thoughts on the urban space as being intrinsically haunted by its past (Peeren/Blanco 2010: xiii), which seem pertinent to this discussion. Indeed, *Burning Night* penetrates both the daily life of the night taxi driver and the layers of a history of social conflicts that this same daily life unveils.

Avery Gordon observes that to "study social life it is necessary to confront its spectral aspects [. . .] The ghost is not just a dead or missing person, but a social figure, and studying it can lead to that place where history and subjectivity produce social life" (Gordon 1997: 8). In *Burning Night*, the camera lens builds a view of the city that fluctuates between the kaleidoscopic, a vision that is saturated with blurred city lights, and the spectral. The lens removes any veneer of "commodified urbanism" (Sandhu 2006: 12) from the city view and rejects the glamour of the night in its utilitarian dimension of "night economy." Paulo's wanderings translate the double meaning implied in the verb "to haunt," which can mean both to "frequent a place" and to visit it as a specter.[2] In this way, the film takes us through the invisible side of the city and the lives, often unrecorded, of the so-called essential workers. The ghostly look that permeates the film, with its play of blurred lights and shadows, reflects the experiences in the labyrinthine streets of Rio de Janeiro that balance on the razor's edge between saturation and scarcity. This, we will argue below, is articulated through what we will call an aesthetic of evanescence.

3 Taxi/Night Drivers

The figure of the taxi driver in film has been understudied to a large extent, despite the fact it has provided some memorable characters and scenes in world cinema, in classics such as *Taxi Driver* (dir. Martin Scorsese, 1976), *The Taxi Driver* (*Il Tassinaro*, dir. Alberto Sordi 1983), *Night on Earth* (dir. Jim Jarmusch 1991), *Taste of Cherry* (dir. Abbas Kiarostami 1997), *Ten* (dir. Abbas Kiarostami, 2002), *Taxi* (dir. Jafar Panahi 2015). The centrality of the theme of displacement, even when restricted to the urban perimeter, the symbolic load projected onto the space of the vehicle, as well as the focus on personal dramas and social dynamics that unfold within this space, are all features that connect these films to the road film genre, in which, David Laderman observes, car travel "becomes not merely a means of

---

[2] On this point, I draw on the connection Sandhu (2006) and Beaumont (2015) make between nighttime mobility and haunting.

transportation to a destination; rather, the travelling itself becomes the narrative's primary focus" (Laderman 2002: 13).

Generally, the life of a taxi driver is deeply intertwined with the city's network of relationships: the driver is familiar with the city's official and unofficial cartography, discovers and creates shortcuts, and articulates, we might say, a motorized counterpart to the city's "writing" tactics managed by the figure of the pedestrian defined by De Certeau in his classic *The Practice of Everyday Life* (1980 [1984]). In a similar vein, recalling the figure of the pedestrian of De Certeau, who "writes" the city through spatial practices (tactics) that go against the official order (strategies), geographer Nigel Thrift draws parallels with the practice of motorized mobility, increasingly naturalized in our everyday life and which, thanks to technological advances, provides an increasingly "embodied contact with the road" (Thrift 2004: 51). Moreover, encounters that take place in taxis commonly cover a wide range of personal experiences and social relationships – from work, to leisure, medical emergencies, family arguments, love trysts etc. Indeed, the taxi driver often appears as "the eyes and ears of the city," from silently observing what happens in the back seat to chatting eagerly with the customers.

Some of the movies mentioned above focus on the figure of the night taxi driver. Jim Jarmusch, prolific director of road films, in his classic *Night on Earth* (1991), followed the adventures of different taxi drivers over the course of the same night in five cities – Los Angeles, New York, Rome, Paris and Helsinki. Jarmusch explained that the appeal to focus on the taxi ride stemmed from the fact that it facilitates the meeting and exchanges between people who (generally) do not know each other and who, therefore, have the freedom to say or share what they want. At the same time, Jarmusch commented on the fact that the taxi ride is often thought of as nothing more than an insignificant interval, a period of "wasted" time, between the point of departure and the desired destination, and that he had been inspired to reveal precisely this period of perceived suspended temporality (Jarmusch 2010). In this approach, Jarmusch seemed to have tuned into the cinematographic character of the night taxi itself, as pointed out by Jonathan Romney when he stated: "At night and in taxis, lives are temporarily suspended and stories are told, just as in cinema" (Romney 1992: 59).

The diverse stories woven into the five locations of *Night on Earth* connect through the common trope of the chance encounter, while in films such as *Taxi Driver*, for example, the emphasis is more evidently placed on the psychological drama of the figure of the driver, as it is triggered by encounters on the job. Laderman noted how this last theme appears particularly representative of the American road film of the 70s, which he sees as defined by an ironic perspective on the social and political crisis of the period through the "personalizing of social conflict" (Laderman 2002: 86). Such emphasis projected on the taxi driver's psychology leads to the dramatization of a complex unraveling of relationships with the world around, oscillating between that of the voyeur, as pointed out by Rausch (2010), and that of the self-appointed avenger (Conard 2007). With a focus on the personal alienation of the driver Paulo, *Burning Night* shares this greater psychological emphasis, and a specific concern for the subject's experience in relation with the urban night. To this end, *Burning Night* contextualizes the character's personal drama within the social reality of contemporary Brazil, creating a world in which social challenges take on an added dimension in the urban labyrinth immersed in darkness, as will be discussed below.

4 Paulo's Night-time Rio

In a recent interview about the film, director Eryk Rocha referred to the link between the character of Paulo and the national context in which his personal drama plays out: "I think that Paulo is the living expression of a country in deep crisis, in convulsion, aimless and without a clear vision, but which urgently and imaginatively needs to reinvent itself in search of a way forward, a project, a new horizon, a future or a brief mirage of sunshine" (in Fonseca 2020). In Rocha's film, the director's concern with the national crisis is evidently connected to his treatment of Paulo's drama right from the film's opening shots, in which the camera positioned inside the vehicle supports a closed cinematography that captures the figure of Paulo at the wheel in extreme close-ups, suggesting both a sense of entrapment and alignment with the plight of the character. For almost the entirety of the film, the camera maintains its position inside the vehicle in transit, taking on the role of inconspicuous witness to Paulo's encounters with his various passengers. Among these passengers is Karina (Barbara Colen), a hospital nurse who works night shifts and with whom Paulo ends up having a romantic relationship. Their exchanges provide glimpses into the back stories of these so-called essential workers and the financial and emotional difficulties they endure. Apart from these and other brief exchanges, the film is dominated by long takes with rare extradiegetic sound accompaniment that immerse the audience in a temporality that seems suspended, consumed by endless hours of Paulo's night shifts, often spent in silence and in his solitary drive through the city's semi-deserted streets.

Indeed, the narrative and aesthetic significance of the nocturnal temporality is established from the film's outset. Close-ups of Paulo's face, barely visible in the half light of the car, and the play of city lights and reflections that whip the interior of the moving vehicle, set the scene of night-time labor. From the opening moments of the film, in fact, we are exposed to a double sensory experience – that of a sense of scarcity and, at the same time, a sense of sensory overload from the evanescent lights that come from the space beyond the car. This phantasmagoria seems to suggest Paulo's complex position (and that of the space of the car) in relation to the city – a space that seems at once distant, violent, strange (Figure 1, Figure. 2).

Figure 1: Paulo at the wheel. 3:08 min. (Source: https://www.youtube.com/watch?v=rtA0SigxDAc).

Figure 2: Driving through the city. 8:16min. (Source: https://www.youtube.com/watch?v=rtA0SigxDAc).

A dizzying low angle shot of the city's towering buildings captured by the camera at street level, in the moving car, conveys the experience of urban architecture as hostile and daunting, conveying the driver's social invisibility and his conflict with the city, reflecting Rocha's view of urban space as his "antagonist" (in Fonseca 2020). In fact, there are no shots that capture the city night as a glittering spectacle of urban lighting or seductive nightlife venues where one can disconnect from the worries of work. Moreover, the camera gaze that observes the city from the car's windows avoids capturing the familiar postcard landscapes of Rio de Janeiro. On just one occasion, and for a brief shot, the camera takes us to one of the iconic places of Rio's geography, as it tracks the vehicle's route along the illuminated perimeter of the Copacabana promenade.

In these urban crossings, the film dovetails documentary footage of the city with the fictional narrative, drawing on what the director described in terms of the porosity of the real and fictional in the film (in Castro 2020). As Paulo drives around in search of possible passengers, the camera in the taxi captures glimpses of the city from Paulo's point of view – scenes of deserted streets alternating with tense images of night workers waiting for buses and navigating an urbanization hostile to the city's pedestrian users. Among the human figures documented by Paulo's gaze is also that of a mother, clearly from the poorer class, who carries a child in her arms while apprehensively trying to cross the street. These images of everyday life, after sunset, help to compose a vision of the night city disjointed from the mere experience of leisure or rest in the private spaces of the house. Indeed, the tension and subliminal violence that pervade the urban space culminate in one of the most emblematic sections of the film, which records football crowds leaving the iconic Maracanã stadium at the end of a game with the popular Flamengo team. Here the atmosphere quickly descends into violence, initially between fans and then by the police, as Paulo drives past in search of a passenger.

5 The Taxi

As it navigates the city streets, the taxi provides a space for chance encounters that unveil deep social divisions. In this sense, it is significant that the first passengers to get into Paulo's car are a group of upper-class young people who wish to continue their night out at one of the haunts frequented by the city's privileged classes. On board the taxi they debate whether to move on to the exclusive Jockey Club or one of the lively night spots in the neighborhood of Botafogo, in the affluent Zona Sul (South Zone) of the city. Paulo quickly becomes the target of mockery and taunting by the drunk young crowd, which leads Paulo to force them out of the vehicle before reaching destination, even having to fight to get them to pay at least part of the fare due. This encounter is captured by a subjective camera positioned in the back seat that behaves as an invisible observer, a spectral presence in the scene. The spectrality of the camera's gaze is emphasized at the beginning of the scene, when the three young men get into the back seat without triggering any camera movement to allow space for the joining passengers. In other words, the camera remains in position and unnoticed, *as if it were not there*. This narrative device contributes to the spectrality of the space of the taxi, supported by camera takes of blurred compositions, unusual angles, and numerous close-ups that do not allow us to have a real sense of the vehicle's physical environment. The camera also supports the characterization of Paulo as a presence that shifts between the physical and the spectral. This condition is also conveyed in the scenes in which Paulo's face (and the same applies to other taxi drivers) takes on a ghostly appearance, as is suggested by the blue light of his cell phone in the darkness of the taxi, pointing to the precarious and disposable nature of his existence in today's permanently connected, 24/7 "smart city."

Paulo's interaction with the young men enjoying their night out reveals his marginalized and exploited condition in the context of the city's "night life." A subsequent ride involving a businessman whom Paulo picks up at the Santos Dumont Airport emphasizes the driver's alienation in relation to the 24-hour world of business and his status vis-à-vis the reality of the night as a "frontier" (Melbin 1978). The social dynamics at play are established as soon as the businessman settles into the back seat and informs the driver of his desired destination by addressing him as *migão* (mate). This seemingly affectionate and informal form of address denounces the "cordiality" that masks the inequality of the social pecking order marked by relations of power, class and race, which at that moment have transferred from the everyday life in the city to the circumscribed space of the car.[3]

Paulo remains silent during this meeting, assuming a spectral presence in the twilight of the taxi's interior, thus incorporating the condition of subordination and invisibility that is conferred onto him. The camera positioned on the front passenger seat records the call that the businessman takes on his cell phone, and which revolves around transactions in real estate speculation and removal of former residents from areas to be "revitalized." This shows the brutal disjunction between those for whom "money never sleeps" and those who, like Paulo, do not sleep because they are key to the functioning of the city, but who never manage to escape financial hardship – as emphasized by the repeated scenes in which Paulo appears counting his meagre night earnings. As Jonathan Crary comments in his essay on the "useless" hours of sleep, seen as an affront by late capitalism: "Sleeplessness is a state in which producing, consuming, and discarding occur without pause, hastening the exhaustion of life and the depletion of resources" (Crary 2013: 17).

Stage of social dynamics marked by inequality in an almost incessant cycle of work, the vehicle does not become an intrinsic part of the film's iconography to glamourize life on the road or celebrate countercultural mobility, as takes place in *Night on Earth*, for example. As the night progresses, the space of the taxi reflects an experience not uncommon among cabbies, for whom it becomes "a pressure chamber, an emotional landfill" (Sandhu 2006: 77). Occasionally, shots from the windscreen capture futuristic images of the urban topography, as happens with the stylized environment of one of the tunnels in the South Zone of the city. In another striking windscreen travelling shot, the highway suddenly appears upside down, creating a hyper-reality science fiction scenario from a banal urban landscape, in which the experience of urban mobility seems to become contiguous to an extraterrestrial journey (Fig. 3).

As John Gold (2001: 337) reminds us, filmmakers have traditionally been drawn to the nocturnal urban landscape when deploying the science fiction genre to address social issues. In the case of *Burning Night*, these expressly futuristic intervals seem to coincide with moments in the narrative in which the taxi driver is lost in thought, in a kind of reverie of other, unreachable worlds

---

3 The concept of "cordiality" in relation to Brazilian social theory was introduced by historian and sociologist Sérgio Buarque de Holanda in his classic essay *Raízes do Brasil* (*Roots of Brazil*), of 1936. In his essay, Holanda argued that Brazil's colonial and patriarchal historic structure had led to the blurring of private and public domains that perpetuated and continued to sustain the privilege of the elites and social inequality in postcolonial Brazil.

Figure 3: Driving as extraterrestrial travel. 1:02:29 min. (Source: https://www.youtube.com/watch?v=rtA0SigxDAc).

that serve as a counterpoint to the urban images that are mostly glimpsed from the car in motion: of anonymous and bleak urban locations that are far removed from well-known, glitzy tourist landmarks. Indeed, the camera's critical gaze remains aligned with the plight of the night taxi driver, who navigates the city's labyrinthine cartography. These night-time transits become a metaphor for the transience and precariousness of the experience of the dispossessed worker, trapped in a relentless cycle of unrecognized and exploited labor, from which there seems to be no way out. Given this situation, the photo of his young son that Paulo glues to the dashboard of his hired car, the owner of which is never revealed, becomes the only material expression of his own individuality, in the grinding work routine spent within the claustrophobic confines of the taxi. Paulo's lack of prospects and social invisibility echo that of countless over-qualified workers stuck in unfulfilling low-paid jobs, for whom life as night cabbies seems the only alternative. As Sukhdev Sandhu comments on a common plight: "And so the cabs become floating coffins carrying the corpses of countless hopes and future-dreams" (Sandhu 2006: 72).

6 Breaks in Urban Transits

Laderman (2002) noted how, in road movies, breaks in the journey provide important intervals for reflection on the meaning of the journey and for providing a deeper insight into the relationships that are formed on the road. In *Burning Night*, three locations seem particularly relevant to understanding Paulo's experience when he is not behind the wheel of a taxi. The first is the taxi headquarters, where Paulo parks his car at the end of the day and gives over the firm's share of his night takings. The second is the apartment he's been living in since separating from his wife. And finally, the beach, where one of the meetings with Karina takes place.

The scenes set in the taxi headquarters emphasize Paulo's subaltern status as anonymous employee of the company. A traveling shot that captures rows upon rows of identical vehicles poignantly underscores the anonymity to which the workers are relegated. This is also evidenced during the moments when Paulo has to give an account of his earnings at the end of the shift, and we see him dealing with an invisible interlocutor sitting behind a screened counter, when the driver inevitably ends up out of pocket.

During some fleeting moments, the film homes in on the camaraderie among taxi drivers, but the main focus of Rocha's film remains on the protagonist's experience of isolation. Echoing the futuristic images of the city mentioned above, Rocha seems to make an ironic allusion to the iconography and atmosphere of the science fiction genre when he captures the arrival of Paulo's taxi in the headquarters' parking lot in slow motion, backlit and framed by a blue neon light. The scene also suggests a dialogue with the opening of *Taxi Driver*, playing with the audience's expectations while debunking a cinematographic tradition that has glamorized the car as a metaphor of modernity, and which does not resonate with the Brazilian reality that Rocha engages with.

Leaving this public space, Paulo is filmed in the private sphere of the small apartment where he lives. The scenario emphasizes the character's precarious financial situation, and the scenes in the apartment seem to be spent in a mostly frustrated attempt to catch up on sleep. The almost constant noise coming from the passing trains moving along the railway line that runs under Paulo's apartment window provides a sound commentary on the city as a hub of connectivity, and the marginalized position of the figure of the night worker, whose schedules are out of synch with the majority of the city's population.

In this way, Paulo's meetings with Karina, also a night worker, constitute important moments of human connection, although the film's outcome does not clarify what the future of their relationship will be. Indeed, Paulo's love life seems as unstable as his work life. In this sense, among the encounters with Karina, one that takes place on the beach at night seems especially revealing. Temporarily unconcerned with their own personal safety in this isolated night-time setting on the edge of the city, Paulo and Karina reflect on their lives, on the difficulties of maintaining effective personal relationships and the violence they increasingly witness in the workplace.

During this exchange, Paulo draws an explicit connection between his experiences and the situation of the country as a whole. It is significant that the national dimension projected onto their personal experiences takes place in a moment of communion on the margins of the urban space, in a visualization of the characters' liminal condition. At the same time, Rocha constructs the scene by inserting a montage of waves breaking onto the sand – a landscape immersed in a starless darkness, where the boundaries between sea, sky and land are blurred. This aesthetic of evanescence, replicated throughout the film, contributes to the subversion of the postcard image of the city of Rio de Janeiro and, consequently, of the stereotypical association of Brazil with the image of a tropical paradise. Moreover, Rocha's exploration of the symbolic potentialities of darkness emphasizes the fact that his focus rests on the fragile and often ignored life experiences that exist on the other side of the 24-hour city.

7 Conclusion

Burning Night closes with Paulo's dreaming of a longed-for reunion with his son at a night-time fairground. Conveying a mix of memory of past evenings spent together and dreams of future encounters, the final moments of the film are a sequence of night-time shots of a fairground setting, ranging overexposed images of artificial lighting, interspersed with a dark cinematography of diffused and out-of-focus lights and contours. In this dreamlike denouement, the film eludes the mirage of the sun to which its title alludes. Implied in that image is the possibility of freeing himself from the grinding routine of night shift work, from which Paulo seems to have no means of escape. Thus, an aesthetic of evanescence translates a reality immersed in the shadows, of spectral lives played out in the invisible side of the 24-hour smart city. One could argue that this same aesthetic, with its subversion of clear boundaries, contributes to questioning the very notion of night as a frontier to be conquered, a chronotope of new opportunities.

The film's construction of Paulo's romantic relationships falls into a questionable, one-sided characterization of Paulo's ex-wife, who never appears on screen and whose voice we only hear in audio messages left for Paulo and relating to the custody and care of his son, Mateus. Paulo appears simplistically as a victim of the ex-wife's lack of recognition of the difficulties he faces, and the film invites the audience to sympathize with the male character, leaving the female stance open to criticism, through a characterization that could have been more nuanced. That said, Rocha's feature offers an important look at the often-forgotten drama of the night workers who, like Paulo, in our increasingly connected, non-stop productivity world, ensure services are offered and comfort provided at any time of day or of the night.

Bibliography

Beaumont, Matthew (2015): *Nightwalking: A Nocturnal History of London*. London: Verso.
Beaumont, Matthew (2020): *The Walker: on Finding and Losing Yourself in the Modern City*. London/New York: Verso.

Blanco, María del Pilar/Peeren, Esther (eds.) (2013): *The Spectralities Reader: Ghosts and Haunting in Contemporary Cultural Theory.* New York: Bloomsbury Academic.
Castro, Malu de (2021): "Debate with Eryk Rocha." 16/10/2020. https://www.youtube.com/watch?v=NNHhGOJJa4w (accessed: 12/7/2021).
Conard, Mark T. (2007): *The Philosophy of Martin Scorsese.* Lexington: The University Press of Kentucky.
Crary, Jonathan (2013): *24/7: Late Capitalism and the Ends of Sleep.* London: Verso.
De Certeau, Michel (1984): *The Practice of Everyday Life.* Trans. Steven Rendall. Berkeley/Los Angeles/London: University of California Press.
Fonseca, Rodrigo (2020): "Breve Miragem de Sol: Eryk Rocha e os dilemas sociais do Brasil." 2/8/2020. https://c7nema.net/entrevistas/item/51829-breve-miragem-de-sol-eryk-rocha-leva-os-dilemas-sociais-do-brasil.html (accessed: 7/7/2021).
Freire-Medeiros, Bianca/Lages, Mauricio Piatti (2020): "A virada das mobilidades: fluxos, fixos e fricções." In: *Revista Crítica de Ciências Sociais*, 123, pp. 121–142. https://doi.org/10.4000/rccs.11193.
Gold, John R. (2001): "Under Darkened Skies: The City in Science-Fiction Film." In: *Geography*, 86, 4, pp. 337–345. www.jstor.org/stable/40573613 (accessed: 21/7/2021).
Gordon, Avery (1997): *Ghostly Matters: Haunting and the Sociological Imagination.* Minneapolis/London: University of Minnesota Press.
Harvey, David (2008): "The Right to the City." In: *New Left Review*, 53, pp. 23–40.
Holanda, Sérgio Buarque de (1936): *Raízes do Brasil.* Rio de Janeiro: José Olympio.
Jarmusch, Jim (2020): "Interview on *Night on Earth*." 1/7/2010. https://www.youtube.com/watch?v=CEqMxgLHql4 (accessed: 16/7/2021).
Kyba, Christopher, et al. (2020): "Night Matters – Why the Interdisciplinary Field of 'Night Studies' is Needed." In: *Multidisciplinary Scientific Journal*, 3, 1, pp. 1–6.
Laderman, David (2002): *Driving Visions: Exploring the Road Movie.* Austin: University of Texas Press.
Lefebvre, Henri (1968): *Le droit à la ville.* Paris: Anthropos.
Marreira, Michele (2020): "Relembre quem são os simpáticos taxistas da ficção." In: *O fuxico.* 6/5/2020. https://www.ofuxico.com.br/noticias/relembre-quem-sao-os-simpaticos-taxistas-da-ficcao/ (accessed: 29/7/2021).
Melbin, Murray (1978): "Night as Frontier." In: *American Sociological Review*, 43, pp. 3–22.
Peeren, Esther/Blanco, Maria del Pilar (eds.) (2010): *Popular Ghosts: The Haunted Spaces of Everyday Culture.* New York: Continuum.
Rausch, Andrew J. (2010): *The Films of Martin Scorsese and Robert De Niro.* Lanham: Scarecrow Press.
Rocha, Eryk (dir.) (2019): *Breve miragem de sol.*
Romney, Jonathan (1992): "Night on Earth." In: *Sight and Sound*, 2, 4, p. 59.
Sandhu, Sukdev (2006): *Night Haunts: a Journey Through the London Night.* London/New York: Verso.
Sheller, Mimi/Urry, John (2006): "The new mobilities paradigm." In: *Environment and Planning*, 38, pp. 207–226.
Stone, Oliver (dir.) (2010): *Wall Street: Money Never Sleeps.*
Thrift, Nigel (2004): "Driving in the City." In: *Theory, Culture & Society*, 21, 4–5, pp. 41–59.

www.ingramcontent.com/pod-product-compliance
Lightning Source LLC
Chambersburg PA
CBHW050525170426
43201CB00013B/2090